Marketing Led, Sales Driven

The Marketing Series is one of the most comprehensive collections of books in marketing and sales available from the UK today.

Published by Butterworth-Heinemann on behalf of The Chartered Institute of Marketing, the series is divided into three distinct groups: *Student* (fulfilling the needs of those taking the Institute's certificate and diploma qualifications; *Professional Development* (for those on formal or self-study vocational training programmes); and *Practitioner* (presented in a more informal, motivating and highly practical manner for the busy marketer).

Formed in 1911, The Chartered Institute of Marketing is now the largest professional marketing management body in Europe with over 24,000 members and 28,000 students located worldwide. Its primary objectives are focused on the development of awareness and understanding of marketing throughout UK industry and commerce and in the raising of standards of professionalism in the education, training and practice of this key business discipline.

Books in the series

Marketing Led, Sales Driven

Keith Steward BA(Hons), FInst.SMM, MCIM

Published on behalf of
The Chartered Institute
of Marketing

Butterworth-Heinemann Ltd
Linacre House, Jordan Hill, Oxford OX2 8DP

 A member of the Reed Elsevier plc group

OXFORD   LONDON   BOSTON
MUNICH   NEW DELHI   SINGAPORE   SYDNEY
TOKYO   TORONTO   WELLINGTON

First published 1993
Reprinted 1995

British Library Cataloguing in Publication Data
Steward, Keith
   Marketing Led, Sales Driven
   I. Title
   658.8

ISBN 0 7506 0148 5

Composition by Genesis Typesetting, Laser Quay, Rocheseter, Kent
Printed and bound in Great Britain by Clays Ltd, St Ives plc

Contents

Part Five   Selling Communication

Preface

The objective of this book is to try to fill part of the divide that exists between texts written by teachers with limited practical experience of selling and the almost intirely anecdotal books written by middle-aged sales managers. The latter, at least, are usually a good read.

The contents has been used many times in lecturers and in training courses so consequently the text has been prepared both for working executives and those seeking professional qualifications before obtaining these highly sought after positions in selling and marketing. The material has been specifically targeted at the Chartered Institute of Marketing's Certificate subject: 'The Principles and Practice of Selling'. The material also covers much of the syllabus for the London Chamber of Commerce Level 3 paper on Marketing.

Throughout the book, there is considerable emphasis on the importance of the practical application of the teaching material. The author would like to acknowledge his debt to all those people who have given the benefit of their experience in an attempt to make this text more complete, accurate and hopefully instructive in an interesting way.

In Chapter 2 the rather difficult topic of explaining how the large number of women working in senior management positions has influence the sales environment is addressed. The author would like to express gratitude to the City Women's Network and, in particular, to Christine Birtles. Without their guidance, the prospect of post-publication correspondence on this topic would be daunting.

Chapter 4, Consumer behaviour, could not have been written easily without reference to Henry Assael's book *'Consumer Behaviour and Marketing Action'* (3rd edition), published by PWS-Kent Publishing Corporation of Boston Massachusetts. Dr Assael expresses very clearly and lucidly with supporting research how consumers respond to sales and marketing stimuli and reach purchase decisions.

Chapter 5 benefitted from material included in a survey on 'Customer Satisfaction' by Industrial Market Research Ltd. David Jamieson, Managing Director of the Company and author of the report, kindly gave his permission for extracts to be included in this chapter.

In Chapter 15, permission was granted by Pitman Publishing to use a detailed example of a time series analysis from the work of Paul and

Geoffrey Whitehead, published as *Statistics for Business*. I would recommend this book to anyone interested in the subject for the clear explanations of mathematical techniques for non-mathematicians.

In Chapter 19, 'Telephone selling and marketing', it was necessary to explain the restrictions imposed by the Data Protection act 1984. The Market Research Society very kindly provided a paper on this subject written by Anthony Cowling, Chairman of Taylor Nelson Research Ltd. Not only was this document most informative, but Mr Cowling also found the time to read and comment on the draft of the chapter.

The sales promotion chapter was written with the enthusiastic support of Lesley Tadgell-Foster who runs Shelfline Promotional Consultancy Ltd. Her wide experience of the subject both as a consultant and lecturer was invaluable.

Exhibitions, conferences and seminars (Chapter 21) was written with help from Alan Baker, Managing Editor of *Which Exhibition*, published by Conference and Travel Publications Ltd.

The section on corporate identity in Chapter 22 was produced with reference to Wally Olins' book on this subject.

Throughout the period of writing, this book has benefited from the well-researched and authoritative articles that are a regular feature in *Marketing*. Being able to refer to up-to-date surveys and topical material was of invaluable assistance. Alan Mitchell, the Editor, was kind enough to give permission for some of this material to be used.

Finally, my thanks go to Caroline Ashton who not only wordprocessed much of the manuscript, but commented freely about the inclusion of some of the examples supporting the text.

Keith Steward

Part One   Selling and Marketing

1
Professional selling in a marketing environment

1.1 The development of the concept

Sales and marketing activity can be analysed in terms of various relatively well-known business philosophies. It is possible to identify five different philosophies, examination of which should help to establish clearly the role of professional selling in a caring marketing environment.

The production concept
The production concept is based on the philosophy that customers prefer readily available low-cost products. The management in such companies generally concentrate on production efficiency and blanket distribution. The concept is not capable of universal application with any chance of commercial success except in certain situations and for certain types of product.

One such situation is that of relative scarcity, where the consumer is more interested in obtaining the generic product than paying attention to its brand identity. Good examples of this might be petrol, milk, sugar, salt or potatoes, particularly if the purchase occasion is at night when many outlets are closed. There is not a lot of actual selling involved at the point-of-sale.

The product concept
This philosophy is based on the notion that consumers prefer quality products or those offering high performance or novel features. Product managers working for companies espousing this doctrine need to keep in focus the tangible benefits to the customer of these features by applying the 'so what' test. Market research should be used to measure the size of the various market segments for these speciality features. These small connoisseur markets need careful budgeting and planning so that where the selling is done, 'real benefits' can be offered to justify

the price. Otherwise the consumer's wants can be misunderstood or misinterpreted, leaving the product unsold. The marketing department needs to maintain close contact with the people at the point of sale in these companies.

The selling concept

The selling concept is largely responsible for the buying public's negative attitude to the sales profession. It is crudely based on the idea that consumers do not know what they want or how much of it, and that the supplier has a duty to encourage them to make their purchases. This encouragement can be quite aggressive in extreme cases. It is always offensive and frequently results in great unhappiness on the part of the purchaser. Fortunately some steps have now been taken to protect the consumer. The Financial Services Act 1986 provides for a fourteen-day cooling-off period for purchasers of insurance policies. There has also been an initiative towards better customer relations by certain retailers: Curry Motors, a chain of garages selling Peugeot and Ford cars, voluntarily offers customers a fourteen-day part-exchange deal on used cars for a car of the same or higher value.

These are much-needed advances for the protection of the consumer. It is a great pity that people are allowed to be employed to sell without being suitably qualified. The engineering, accountancy and medical professions distinguish clearly between those who are qualified and those who are *not* qualified. Similar standards should exist for people entering the selling profession. Without a certificate in practical salesmanship, a certificate showing relevant product training and at least associate membership of a relevant professional institute, sales activity should be restricted to a supporting role.

Other businesses widely practising this heavy selling include sellers of the proverbial encyclopaedias, suppliers of kitchen units, and indeed some colleges trying to fill up their classes. The latter use exclusion as the pressure point on the basis that if you do not sign and pay now, the class may be full later on. This heavy selling is used because the various essential marketing functions have not been employed to support the sales activity.

Marketing professionals should have completed the essential pre-selling work of needs assessment, market research and product development, and have performed pricing strategies and selected appropriate sales channels before any serious attempt is made to sell the product or service.

The marketing concept

This business philosophy emerged to challenge the other approaches in the mid 1950s. It focuses on determining the needs and wants of target market segments and delivering the desired satisfactions more effectively than competitors.

The marketing concept expresses the company's commitment to the concept of customer sovereignty. Much of the company's activity is geared to producing an integrated approach to satisfying the customer's needs. Because of the very low priority accorded to the role of selling, this concept is usually only successful in the retail marketplace, of which Marks and Spencer, the House of Fraser, Dixons and Boots are the glittering UK examples. Even in these successful stores the would-be purchaser has to work quite hard to find a sales person. The normal procedure is to allow the shopper to select, lift and carry the purchase to a cash and wrap area.

It is probably fair to say that most companies have yet to grasp fully the essentials of the marketing philosophy. There are marketing vice presidents, brand managers and even small customer service centres, but the vast majority of staff who have contact with the consumer have been denied any effective training in this area. Boredom with a repetitive job leads many to merely tolerating the customers until it is time to clock off. This is not to say that all customers are much maligned, courteous patrons. They are frequently a nuisance, but if the philosophy of the business is to make them happy, then the staff who deal with them must be trained to deal effectively even with the short-temperered, arrogant clowns. Otherwise they will not be happy, and consequently will spend their money somewhere else.

The societal marketing concept

In 1989 Prime Minister Margaret Thatcher and a large percentage of the ABC1 socio-economic groups underwent a substantial change in attitude in about three months. They became environmentally concerned. What had for some twenty years been the preoccupation of a few liberal do-gooders became a doctrine of national importance. The environment and what industrialized western society and the developing countries are doing to destroy it became a topic of great concern.

There are strong and rising feelings against the use of fast food containers and drinks bottles and cans that are not biodegradable. Many people would support a 1992 or 1993 deadline for the prohibition of vehicles not converted to lead-free petrol. Industrial pollution of streams and rivers could be made an offence, attracting heavy fines and a custodial term for the senior executive of the business involved.

The societal marketing concept states that an organization's task is to determine the needs, wants and interests of target markets; then to deliver the desired satisfactions more effectively and efficiently than the competition in a manner which preserves and enhances the well-being of society and the natural environment. Marketeers are called on to consider and balance consumer wants, society, and environmental interests against corporate profits when preparing marketing plans.

Professional selling in a marketing environment
Professional selling cannot easily stand alone without the disciplines of marketing (hence this book's title). Successful selling is where the consumer wants to buy from the seller again and indeed again. However, to achieve this on a large scale requires effective communication and co-operation between the sales and marketing functions. The skills of both professions are required, working closely together to offer the old truism 'the right product at the right price', now extended to include 'to the right people in a manner which is viewed as socially acceptable'. There is a role for selling and a role for marketing in making a successful sale. Over the past twenty-five years the level of skill required to succeed in both professions has increased substantially because the consumer has grown more sophisticated, and is better informed. Also, society has produced 'watchdogs' who comment on the less acceptable aspects of business and who are widely reported in the media. In certain specific areas there is legislation on the statute book which can impose strict penalties on those individuals found selling and marketing in ways no longer considered acceptable.

1.2 Selling as an element of the marketing mix

The major difficulty when attempting to discuss the relationship of selling to the marketing mix is that most textbooks relegate selling to part of promotion. Students in their first marketing lecture are fed 'the four Ps'. Unfortunately, the four Ps, while having the virtue of being easy to remember, are also rather misleading and are actually misinformation. How this has happened is probably due to the fact that many marketing lecturers and theorists have little direct experience of professional selling. The average consumer rarely experiences timely professional selling because the value of most consumer products is too low to justify the cost of a qualified salesman. The most expensive purchase made by most people is their house or flat. This experience is usually one fraught with anguish rather than one providing an image of professional selling. Buying a new car or an insurance policy is probably the best example most consumers get in seeing a professional salesman at work.

The main area for professional selling is in selling to other businesses and governments. High value complex products or high volume basic products require a high level of expertise and experience to win contracts in the face of competition. Unfortunately only the people who work in this business environment can appreciate the essential role of selling. Consequently, the author draws the conclusion that most models of the marketing mix (including the four P's) are relevant to consumer products. Industrial and government markets require a model with a different emphasis; the suggested mix is shown below.

To omit selling may be likened to having a football team without a striker, designing a gun without a firing pin, a chemical formula without a catalyst or an organism without the means of reproduction. The item may be absolutely perfect in design, targeted at segments of the consumer population who crave it, promoted with great flair and prices structured to meet every possible combination of purchase occasion. However, if no professional selling effort is involved, the product is likely to remain on the pallets in the warehouse. Selling is about making things happen. Related professions are described by different adjectives, such as creative, ingenious, novel, stylish, technically competent. These skills and talents are absolutely essential for successful selling, but similarly, successful selling provides the proof that everybody has done their job right too!

Hence the industrial marketing mix may be redefined more realistically as:

Market research
- Identification of new needs.
- New markets, existing products (sales research).
- Testing concepts.
- Test marketing new products.

(New) product development
- Developing new product concepts.
- Extension to an existing line of products.
- Features/modifications to existing products.
- Branding.
- Pack sizes.

Communications
- Promotions.
- Advertising.
- Packaging design.
- Public relations.
- Character merchandising.
- Sponsorship.
- Customer care.

Pricing policy
- Discount structure.
- Warranty.
- Credit terms.

Selling policy
- Direct sales force.
- Dealer/distributor.
- Franchise.
- Direct response marketing (TV, telephone, direct mail, catalogue, off the page advertising).
- Overseas manufacture.
- Exhibitions.

1.3 Additional sales force tasks

A company's sales force provides a unique link between the company and its customers. Relatively few of the other professionals who are engaged in the overall marketing function have as much contact with the people and organizations who actually purchase the company's products. Consequently, serious thought should be given to the design of the sales force and the job specification of the sales executive to enable them to undertake these extremely important tasks.

Gathering market intelligence or sales research
Clearly, selling a budgeted quota of products and/or services should feature very high on the sales executive's list of tasks. However, that is by no means all of it. Management requires information for planning and control of sales areas and territories. Obtaining this from the sales executive is generally thought to be functional and compatible with his/her interest. Managers require up-to-date, accurate and objective information about the markets for their products.

This information can be the size in terms of number of customers, the potential sales value of an individual organization and the mix of products required by different groups. Managers need to allocate resources in the optimal way that fulfils the corporate objectives of market share, return on investment or indeed maximum profit. Without this information they are forced to make decisions based on guesses.

Other items of interest of course relate to the activity of competitors:

- Detailed specification of major competitive products.
- Comparisons feature by feature with home company products.

- Names of major competitor accounts, their volume of business, suggested reasons why customers buy a competitor product, names of key decision-makers.
- Names of organizations and the dates of their purchase cycle.

Prospecting
The business environment is dynamic in nature: new companies enter a market and others leave. New technology means that a company's products can be used for previously unforeseen purposes. However, these changes are for the most part not highly publicized. The task of the sales executive is to dig out these new opportunities and establish contact. It is a great mistake for a territory sales executive to be so preoccupied with selling to existing customers that no time is left to track down new prospects.

Communication
Sales executives have an important communication role. This is telling customers and prospects about new product developments, improvements to existing products, informing them, it is to be hoped well in advance, of price changes, and other developments in company policy.

Consultancy
Sales executives, by virtue of their product knowledge and appreciation of their customers' business environment, are often in a position to offer advice and guidance. This may be of a technical nature, financial or just good after-sales service expediting something that should have happened in another part of the organization.

1.4 Different types of selling job

There is an enormous variety of jobs that involves some negotiating with a prospective customer for the sale of a product or service. Indeed there are so many that categorization to avoid a long list of titles is quite difficult. After considerable deliberation it has been decided to classify the different types into the following groups: almost certainly qualified in another profession as well as selling (accountant, engineer, marketing specialist, physicist etc); those unlikely to be qualified in anything but selling and the driver/delivery sales person.

Graduate/selling jobs with other professional qualifications
The overriding reason why these jobs require highly qualified people to do the selling is that the products are either technically complicated,

conceptually difficult to understand or very expensive. Another reason perhaps is that this type of purchase decision is usually made by someone senior in the buying organization. Using a semi-skilled or junior person to do the selling would clearly place the selling organization at a competitive disadvantage.

The first type of job to fall into this category might be classified as the 'capital goods' sales executive. These capital items could be engineering plant, communications equipment, computers, cranes, vehicles, ships, aircraft, military equipment or industrial buildings. Specialist product knowledge is required for each of these jobs plus a complete understanding of how the would-be purchaser can benefit from their use. Furthermore, an appreciation of the politics of the industry is also required plus highly developed negotiating skills.

Typical job titles might be sales engineer, technical sales executive, account manager, project manager, systems engineer or similar titles but with director as the status level. The volume of sales expected with this type of job is generally high and targets of £500,000 to several million pounds are usual. The salaries are also high, though a major part of this is paid as commission.

Also included in this classification of selling job would be the 'political fixer': someone who is able to set up contracts as a result of knowing the right people. After the initial introduction this person tends to assume more of a public relations or consultative role. Examples of people with this type of role are to be found in the setting up of large government contracts or complete plant procurements.

Selling jobs without other professional qualifications
The level of selling skill required to succeed in these jobs is frequently identical to that of the previous category. It is the volume of product knowledge that is generally smaller, because the product or service is less complicated. Other distinctions are that there are likely to be consumer products that are sold to the general public rather than an organization and the selling price is unlikely to be more than £20,000.

Examples of this type of job are the selling of cars, life assurance, central heating, planned kitchens and bathrooms, carpets and pleasure boats. Retail selling also falls into this category, as sellers of small desktop computers and household goods are unlikely to be either graduates or members of the British Computer Society. The consumer goods sales executive (selling to the retail outlets) is also in this category, as are manufacturers' agents and 'multiples' sales executives. The latter usually work for a large wholesaler or builder's merchant, carrying a very large number of different products for sale.

Specialists such as the merchansider, the sales promoter and telephone sales person also fall into this category. Merchandising is the highly specialized art of product display that requires a good understanding of the character of the store, its spatial concepts, display techniques and the philosophy of the store's management. Good examples are the displays in Harrods and the Laura Ashley chain of shops.

Telephone selling requires a good sales vocabulary, a pleasant voice and considerable empathy for dealing with customers. Telephone sales people are used in a wide variety of commercial organizations, both in generating new business leads and in topping up stocks of fast-moving consumer goods.

The sales promoter is used to compliment the everyday territory sales force but tasked with achieving specific short-term objectives. This may typically be increasing the number of distribution outlets for a consumer product, increasing the level of sales for an existing product by a free extra-value offer 'or assisting with the launch of a new product'.

The driver/delivery sales person

Examples of this type of selling job include the milkman, the bread salesman and suppliers of food products to independent retailers. The job involves a regular round of calling on customers either daily or twice weekly, taking an order to build up the retailer's stock, unloading the vehicle, calculating the cost of the products ordered, and collecting payment. These jobs can be something of an endurance test with the early start to load the vehicle, the large number of sales calls, busy traffic in city routes, double parking and banking money collected. However the good salesman can make sales in excess of £250,000 per year.

1.5 Environmental forces that can affect selling

It is easy for a company's sales force to be so heavily focused on selling their products to an identified group of customers that they fail to notice major events happening in the world outside. This can be a great mistake for events in the 'outside world' can have a major impact on that company's sales. A company that fails to monitor these events and assess their likely impact on their business can find themselves severely disadvantaged. Global economic recessions, sudden dramatic increases in the price of oil, armed aggression and massive changes in public opinion can thoroughly devastate a company's business plans. It is possible to group these major forces under six headings when considering their impact on selling.

Demographic influences

There are a number of trends that are of interest to those selling in the western industrialized countries by which the most important are:

- slow down in the birth rate,
- an ageing population,
- increase in number of non-family households,
- a better educated population,
- changes in the ethnic population, and
- increasing demand for specialist products.

The effect of these changes is to both dramatically and subtly alter the level and type of demand for many companies' products and indeed the way in which these products are bought.

Economic influences

A market is not just dependent on the resident population – it is their purchasing power that determines the volume of products sold. This purchasing power is itself a factor of income, credit, savings and the level of prices. This individual purchasing power is profoundly affected in most cases by the economic climate of the town or place where the person lives, the region or country and indeed the continent. It is only the 'super rich' who continue with their preferred pattern of purchases irrespective of economic trends.

The high interest rates experienced in the UK (mortgages at effectively 15 per cent for the whole of 1990) and industrial borrowing rates closer to 20 per cent in the Government's attempt to curb inflation have led many consumers to search for opportunities to reduce expenditure. This has obviously meant buying the less expensive brands and indeed omitting many luxury products.

Companies whose business is particularly sensitive to the prevailing economic climate, should be well advised to obtain some expert advice forecasting the future trends. This way they can make preparations for any predictable recession or downturn.

The influence of the physical environment

The task facing individual companies is to assess the impact of these environmental issues on their businesses and take steps to minimize any negative influences. Sources of concern might be:

- The cost of modifying certain manufacturing processes to reduce pollution levels in the atmosphere.
- Devising methods of testing new products that avoid animals.
- Developing ways to use energy more efficiently.
- Developing methods of pollution control and the re-cycling of waste products.
- Strategies for limiting their business to conservation programmes and developing ecologically superior products.

Technological influences

The strongest force impacting on the sales environment is the rate of technological change. Each new development creates new markets and closes down existing business sectors. The development of computers spawned the direct mail business but cancelled the need for many clerical jobs with mechanical adding machines. The contraceptive pill emancipated women which increased the labour force which increased family incomes which led to an increased demand for holidays and quality consumer durables (washing machines, microwave ovens, TVs, hi-fi equipment).

Scientists continue to work on new ranges of technologies that will revolutionize life-styles and consumption patterns in areas such as biotechnology, and solid-state electronics. These developments in turn will change consumer and industrial demand and consequently the way existing and new products are sold.

While much of the technological progress is unreservedly beneficial, there are those that decry the movement away from traditional life-styles and familiar technologies. Examples include nuclear power, chemical fertilizers, motorway expansion and the reduction of the natural environment. Sales and marketing executives need to thoroughly understand these technological developments and work closely with scientists to encourage more human-orientated developments.

Political and legal influences

Legislation, government agencies and consumer pressure groups exert a powerful influence on companies and the way they are permitted to undertake their business. The development of company law over the past 150 years has been a continuous attempt to create an environment where business can develop with a reasonable amount of risk to the entrepreneurs, yet afford the wider public some protection against unscrupulous individuals abusing the status of 'limited liability'.

Extensive consumer protection legislation has been a particular feature of the past thirty years in western and industrialized societies (see chapter 2). The traditional concept of *caveat emptor* (buyer beware) has now been substantially replaced by a requirement for producers to only sell and market products that are suitable for the purposes on which basis they are presented to consumers. Sales and marketing executives need to have an appreciation of where this legislation impacts on their working environment otherwise they can unwittingly find themselves the defendant in a suit for litigation.

The development of the European Economic Community and the movement towards 'one market' is going to have a certain impact on business. Similarly the breakdown of the strictly controlled 'Eastern block' economies will open up new opportunities for the entrepreneurial adventurous.

Sociological influences

The society in which people grow up and live shapes basic beliefs and values that in adult life are expressed by attitudes and behaviour patterns. Sales and marketing executives need to be able to understand these values and anticipate any changes in these cultural norms in case opportunities for profitable business arise. Alternatively the impact of these changes could be adverse and this would also require a planned reaction to avoid a loss of revenue.

Attitudes to work and physical fitness have undergone major changes in the 1970s and 1980s. A safe job and a steady income is regarded as less attractive by many than an exciting job with some risk. Professional people in predominantly sedentary work have expressed a major new interest in sport and exercise. This has meant significant changes in the demand for many products: food, drink, clothing, sports equipment and indeed preferred type of holiday or recreational pursuit.

2
Changes in the past twenty-five years

Twenty-five years ago most manufacturing companies had a hierarchical structure of employment. A national sales director or manager divided the country into sales areas, each under a manager. Each area sales manager was responsible for a number of territory salesmen. The number was generally between five and twelve for each area though there are some examples where area sales managers had twenty salesmen reporting to them. The word 'salesman' is used here in place of the term 'sales executive' that is used throughout the rest of the book, because at this time they were indeed, with very few exceptions, men. Companies like Playtex were still employing men in the UK as territory salesmen in 1977.

In those days before the Mark 1 Ford Cortina, the most popular car with salesmen was a Hillman Minx, and complete with trilby hat the salesman combed his territory on a four or five week journey cycle. Retailers' stocks were counted, new orders taken and point of sale material arranged for display (that of the competition being carefully moved to one side or in extreme cases put in the bin). However, vast changes were just over the horizon.

2.1 Specialization in selling

The first change that can be readily identified in selling over the past twenty-five years is that selling itself has become more specialized. The status of the person doing the selling has in many industries been enhanced and the potential for a substantial income now exists where commission is paid without limits. The effect of this has been that companies use other staff to do some of the preparatory work which does not involve making the sale or taking the order. An example of this is merchandising, where specialists in this area organize the point-of-sale material. These displays are now larger and more extravagant (cigar cabinets, racks for greetings cards and cassettes, display refrigerators and sun awnings in the company livery etc).

Sales promotion has also developed into a highly specialized part of the business of marketing and selling products. Once restricted to an extremely attractive young woman encouraging consumer sampling of the product she was promoting, it now has a separate institute. Sales promotion includes the work of creating and designing campaigns with coupons, free offers, competitions, event sponsorship, reduced price packs and tailor-made campaigns for individual retailers.

Franchise operations now exist in many industries (fast food, home improvements, parcel delivery, retail clothing, hotels, retail health and beauty products, vehicle services and maintenance, printing and even accountancy services). Yet in 1965 there were only the Wimpy hamburger bars, Dyno Rod plc and Kentucky Fried Chicken (GB) Ltd. All the other well-known household names came in the next few years: Holiday Inns (UK) Ltd. (1969), Budget Rent a Car (UK) Ltd (1968), Prontaprint Ltd. etc. Indeed the British Franchise Association was not formed until 1977 and then it had only eight members. In 1990 there are now some ninety full members and thirty associate members of franchisors with more than 20,000 outlets. Sales are estimated to be between five and six billion pounds annually.

Direct mail has also grown into a specialist activity, initially helped by the invention of Xerography but given a major boost with the introduction of wordprocessing in the late 1970s. When every letter had to be individually typed, there were clearly restrictions on the number that could conveniently be produced. However, once the body of the text only needed to be typed once and a sort-merge routine with an address file could produce thousands of letters each individually addressed, this limitation was removed.

Now, when a company decides to enter a new industrial market segment, part of the campaign may involve writing a sales letter to thousands of prospects. Frequently these personal names and job titles, company names and addresses are rented from a list broker who has compiled and maintained these details as a database. Consequently within a few days a saturation campaign can launch a new product to the targeted prospects. In the late 1960s the only course of action was to buy a business directory, identify those businesses in the targeted segment, telephone to establish the name of the prospect, retype the sales letter and then type the envelope.

The modern trend in exhibitions, conferences and seminars is for more of these to be held, but on more specialized topics, each targeting a particular market sector. For example, the major broad-based exhibition for the computer industry, 'Which Computer', is complemented by many specialist shows such as 'Unix user', 'PC user', the Computers in Manufacturing show, CADCAM exhibitions (computer-aided design and computer-assisted manufacturing) and indeed those focusing on a particular industry sector such as 'Health Computing'.

The growth of telephone selling and marketing over the past twenty-five years is directly attributable to major companies using their territory sales force to pursue only qualified leads. Other staff, frequently employed by agencies, are used to generate these initial leads. This method is cost-effective because the telephone sales people are quickly trained and earn much less per hour than sales executives. Also, they are generally only employed for the specific period of the contract.

Corporate identity, on the other hand, has been widely established as important for over 100 years. The symbolism that was originally used to distinguish between soldiers from different regiments and armies has been applied to businesses. Over the past twenty-five years it has been taken further in terms of the items included in the identification programme. What was once just company ties has now extended to uniforms, and motor vehicles are sprayed in the company livery as never before.

The public relations industry has grown in parallel with the expansion of the media, of which television is the most important. This is owing to the speed with which images and sound can be relayed around the world by satellite. Twenty-five years ago a fractured tanker spilling oil over a natural beauty spot in the third world would have attracted little interest. It could have happened several days before a report was received by a news editor, and it would take two days to get a camera and sound crew with a reporter on location, then two days to get the film back to the newsroom. Today, there is more concern for the environment and the tanker captain, knowing that the spill must be detected and attributable, would probably radio for help. The offending company would then mount a massive public relations campaign to publicize their immediate contribution of, say, ten million dollars towards the clean-up. Operation damage limitation would publicize the fact that a full enquiry was being organized. The film crew would be on the spot within twenty-four hours and the report shown on public broadcast television a few hours later.

Sponsorship in twenty-five years has grown from a vehicle used by the tobacco companies to obtain publicity for their brands where direct advertising was restricted, to a multi-billion pound industry. Tennis players' shirts and Formula One cars are festooned with company logos, and all major cricket test matches are sponsored by the clearing banks, major insurance companies or brewers.

2.2 Consumer power

The second major development in the selling arena in the past twenty-five years has been the enormous growth in the power and influence of the consumer. The *Moloney Report on Consumer Protection* (1961) stated that 'the business of marketing and selling is highly organized, often in large units, and calls to its aid at every stop complex and highly expert skills. The business of buying [is frequently] conducted by the smallest unit, the individual consumer, relying on the guidance afforded by experience, if he possesses it, and if not on instinct but it is not always a rational thought processes'.

The Consumers' Association (CA) was formed in March 1957 to help redress this imbalance of power between the buyer and the seller. The CA has done this by providing independent technically based guidance to the consumer on a wide variety of goods and services. The results of regular investigation and testing of a range of broadly comparable branded products are published in the monthly magazine *Which*. These reports are comparative and comment on the performance, quality and value of the brands tested.

The fact that the annual subscriptions to *Which* now exceed 1,000,000 is testimony to the fact that many people (including the author) do not purchase a piece of domestic equipment without consulting *Which*.

In 1962 the CA collaborated with the BBC to produce a consumer TV programme series called *Choice* based on *Which* test results. This has subsequently led to a number of very popular consumer affairs programmes that regularly report on investigations into manufacturers' dubious practices and products that have been the subject of public complaint.

The year 1970 saw the CA's sponsorship of an Institute of Consumer Ergonomics at Loughborough University to work on fundamental design studies of consumer products. In 1972 following two years of pressure from the CA, Britain appointed its first Minister for Consumer Affairs, Geoffrey Howe.

2.3 Legal regulation of selling

Parallel with the work of the Consumers' Association has been the work of successive governments to strengthen the laws regulating the activities of businesses. This is borne out by looking at the dates of some of the principal reforming statutes:

- Hire Purchase Act 1964
- Misrepresentation Act 1967
- Trade Descriptions Act 1968
- Unsolicited Goods & Services Act 1971
- Trade Descriptions Act 1972
- Fair Trading Act 1973
- Supply of Goods (Implied Terms) Act 1973
- Consumer Credit Act 1974
- Unfair Contract Terms Act 1977
- Consumer Safety Act 1978
- Supply of Goods & Services Act 1982
- Data Protection Act 1984
- Consumer Protection Act 1987

The reasons for these changes are the result of changes in social attitudes to the old concept of *caveat emptor* (buyer beware) and a response to new direct methods of selling (mail, telephone, TV) and products of increasing complexity (computers, pensions). It is widely recognized that the consumer should no longer be required to rely on his own judgement without additional protection when buying goods and services.

2.4 Technology and communications

The fourth clearly identifiable change in the sales environment over the past twenty-five years is in the area of technology and communications. Communications in their broadest form have expanded tremendously in the period, as indeed has the use made of the facilities. Since the M1 was started in 1959, 1,863 miles of motorway have been constructed, reducing considerably the journey times to the major towns and conurbations (at certain times of the day – not Sunday evenings and the rush hour) – of course, car performance has also increased and now many production cars will cruise for hours at speeds over ninety miles per hour. However, the fact remains that driving from London to Bristol is quite possible in one hour forty-five minutes, and London to Manchester in two hours forty-five minutes. Twenty-five years ago the journey times were some 50 per cent longer.

Similar reductions in journey time have been made by British Rail Intercity services. The Kings Cross to Doncaster non-stop service is now scheduled at one hour thirty-nine minutes (two hours nineteen minutes in 1968). Paddington to Plymouth is now two hours fifty-nine minutes (four hours fifteen minutes in 1966).

Other major developments in communications include the use of air travel for business, and the Heathrow to Manchester, Glasgow and Edinburgh shuttle service is a great advance on the mid-1960s alternative, which was a British Rail overnight sleeper. The other aspects of communications that are microchip technology based are described in some detail in Chapter 3.

2.5 Women in business

Another major change over the past two or three decades has been a substantial increase in the number of women working as executives. Once more or less restricted to secretarial or personnel work or careers in nursing and teaching, women are now found working in all departments and at all levels in business. Young salesmen may find that their manager is a woman, that many of their colleagues in selling are women, that marketing managers are women, and indeed that the people they sell to are women. This fact has necessitated a fundamental change in the attitudes held by many men.

Other changes have also taken place at work, where sexual harassment is now an offence and punishable in the Courts and discrimination on the basis of gender is illegal (Equal Opportunities Act 1975). This has led to more and greater opportunities for women. Many women now start their own businesses and manage them with great success. This fact is borne out by statistics, which show that more new businesses started by women succeed than those started by men. This means that women have been selling and managing their businesses in this sector of the market to higher standards than their male counterparts.

The increase in the disposable income of this new wave of women executives has resulted in a substantial increase in demand for products and services. Once obliged to rent furnished apartments with several friends, these high income earners now buy their own property. This increase in single adult households has increased the demand for houses and flats, furniture and white goods (refrigerators, washing machines, cookers, microwave ovens, freezers and washing-up machines). Demand for foreign holidays has also increased as has the growth in demand for convenience food.

Service industries are rapidly expanding to do the work that these career women no longer have the time for (home shoppers, cleaners, gardeners, cooks for dinner parties, decorators, daycare staff and now even dog walkers). Other growth industries that are associated with the increasing earning power of women, if not directly attributable to the fact, are the health, fitness and beauty sectors.

Before women entered business and the professions at senior levels, there were a few clearly defined groups who were paid for their good looks. These were workers in the 'display professions' – fashion mannequins, actresses and dancers. Today the 'Professional Beauty Qualification' (PBQ) has been widely instutitionalized in television journalism, advertising, merchandising, design, and estate agencies, auction houses and the recording and film industries. This, coupled with the modern idea of healthy living, has made millions for those marketing fitness, of which Jane Fonda, Maria Callan and Anita Roddick are perhaps the most famous. This trend led to a massive increase in demand for sportswear of all kinds which then attracted top designers as the market grew in size and value. This in turn created more jobs, many of them for women in businesses run by women.

3
The influence of information and communications technology on selling

---

In the past twenty years there have been two major developments in computer and communications technology that have had a great influence on selling in the business environment. They are the invention of the silicon chip and the ability to transmit data (as well as speech) along a telephone line from one computer to another. To put these developments in perspective, if the advances in aircraft technology had been similar, we would now be able to fly from Europe to America in one hour for £1 in an aircraft carrying 3,000 passengers and which used only a gallon or two of fuel for the entire journey.

In the late 1960s, many of the largest companies in the UK were installing their first computer. Frequently the initial application was the payroll, followed by customer orders and records for invoicing purposes. All letters and reports were produced on a mixture of electric and manual typewriters, and as Rank Xerox photocopying machines were a relatively new feature in offices, all correspondence and reports were typed and retyped and retyped.

3.1 Wordprocessing letters and reports

In twenty years the production of business correspondence and reports in many sales offices has progressed from individually typed and retyped 'top copies' and their carbons to wordprocessed letters incorporating a standard text with an individual salutation. This has been achieved by the development of a larger silicon chip memory and the large capacity, though physically compact, storage disks.

The body of a letter is stored in a file and the names and addresses of those to whom the letter is to be sent are placed in another file. The salutation for each has already been determined: 'Dear Mr Smith' or 'Dear Bill'. An individually addressed letter for each person is produced by merging the letter file with the name and address file and directing the output file to an electronic printer. Where the printer has a sheet-feeder attachment capable of storing letter-headed paper, letters can be printed without further human intervention.

The significance of this development is not readily apparent until one considers the only alternatives available with the previous levels of technology:

Alternative A

500 wordprocessed leters – time taken to key in names and addresses and salutation at the rate of 40 per hour	12½ hours
Time to key in text of letter	½ hour
Total	13 hours

(The printing can be left unattended or done as a 'background' task while the secretary continues with other work.)

Alternative B

Individually type 500 letters (and probably the inconvenience of recruiting another secretary)	250 hours

Alternative C

Print letter text by offset lithography and later add the individual name, address and salutation. Estimate 50 per cent longer than free typing due to difficulties of positioning and wastage due to errors. Of course the finished item would be that of a mass-produced letter rather than an individual one, thereby detracting from the effect of the exercise.	19¼ hours

(Including ½ hour to type the text of the letter.)

When it comes to report writing, the time savings are even more dramatic: consider for example a ten-page 3,000-word report.

By typewriter

(i) Original typing by typewriter	2 hours
(ii) Retyping	2 hours
(iii) Final retyping	2 hours
Total	6 hours

Using a wordprocessor

(i) Original typing	2 hours
(ii) Retyping (alterations only)	⅓ hour
(iii) Final typing	⅓ hour
Total	2⅔ hours

Time saved 3⅓ hours or 56.67 per cent.

There is one more important factor and that is the saving of the sales executive's time reading the three versions of the report. Using the typewriter, it is likely that 'unforced' errors will occur, hence careful reading of the entire text is required. When a document is word-processed, only the alterations need to be checked, thus making a substantial saving in the salesperson's time. This is the real contribution of the technology to the capital goods salesperson and the retail national account manager. Their selling is done substantially through the preparation of detailed and informative proposals and reports. Without the benefits of this new technology, they would not be able to carry such high sales quotas due to being desk-bound editing complex documents. Errors in these instances, be they technical, commercial or legal, not only look unprofessional, but if held to be contractually binding might cost the selling company thousands of pounds.

3.2 Desktop publishing

Desktop publishing is technically and commercially a logical extension of wordprocessing. It is effectively bringing black on white artwork, lettering and graphics into the normal sales office that already has a desktop computer. The additions are a typesetting software package and a laser printer.

The benefits are improved document quality for proposals, reports and tenders, giving a really professional image. A wider choice of lettering in both style and size (fonts ranging from 4 to 127 points are available) than if using wordprocessing software alone. Furthermore, there is the ability to do extensive graphics (lines, boxes, circles, pie charts, histograms and other shapes, including half-tones), which the user can define using the 'paint brush' or 'spray gun' facilities.

Effectively, the system as specified (appropriate software and laser printer) offers setting without the ability to reproduce good quality artwork and colour. A consultation from a graphic designer can provide both the fine tuning on layout and the bromide transparencies for original artwork with the recommended pantone colours. This brings brochure layout and design as well as customer history profiles within the sales office, saving time and effort. Desktop publishing greatly reduces cost, if you are prepared to forgo colour and artwork. At about £10,000 there is a device called an 'image setter' that can reproduce artwork in-house, but unless security is of concern or vast quantities of work are being produced, it is commercially expedient to leave this to the graphics designer and printers.

3.3 Direct mail and mailing list broking

Have you ever wondered how you receive so many unsolicited letters and where the people who sent them obtained your name and address? The answer is from a mailing list broker or from a company's own customer/contact database. Among the developments in computer and communications technology, one of the most significant has been in data storage. Since 1988 one, two, four and eight gigabyte disks have been available that can respectively store one, two, four and eight hundred million bytes of information. A byte is a character which can be a letter, a number or a piece of punctuation. Thus, very large lists can be compactly stored in an object the size of a suitcase mounted on a disk drive no bigger than a domestic oven.

Many people are members or have their name and address kept by ten or twenty different organizations (Access, Visa, the Chartered Institute of Marketing, the electoral roll, the electricity and gas boards, department store charge or account cards, motoring organizations, the National Film Theatre, the Ski Club of Great Britain, hotel business club cards, the Chamber of Commerce, their old school, university or college, the company that they booked their holiday with, magazines and newspapers that are received on a subscription or complimentary basis, or indeed a list compiled of everybody who visited a certain exhibition). Every coupon clipped from the press and sent off may result in your name being added to a list which is then rented to organizations who have a commercial interest in writing to you.

A whole industry has grown up in the past twenty-five years that is represented by three professional bodies, the Direct Mail Producers' Association (formed in 1963), the British Direct Marketing Association and the British List Brokers' Association. The methodology of direct mail is to segment a market accurately and then target precise groups of specially selected prospective customers according to previously calculated purchasing requirements.

The Business Data Base, for example, marketed by Yellow Pages Business Data, a division of British Telecom, has the contents of seventy-four yellow pages and business pages directories on disk, representing some one and a half million business locations. There is a three-tier structure which is progressively specific. In the first tier there are five groups:

	Sectors	Categories
Retail and consumer	13	240
Services	22	472
Agriculture and materials	29	621
Transport and construction	17	369
Manufacturing (general)	35	978
Total	116	2,680

Within the retail and consumer group and comprising the second hierarchical tier are thirteen sectors:

Code		Categories	Businesses
AA	Books, stationery and office supplies	11	31,767
AB	Clothing	28	52,285
AC	Clubs, hotels and catering	30	155,758
AD	Consumer goods – repairs	20	11,532
AE	Consumer goods – wholesale	28	7,639
AF	Foods	18	101,528
AG	Furnishings	9	26,466
AH	Hobbies and gardening	21	25,993
AI	Household	21	21,722
AJ	Medical and photographic	9	21,275
AK	Multi-retailers	10	10,027
AL	Road vehicle services	25	67,012
AM	Vehicles	10	22,921
Total		240	559,925

Within the sectors there are categories which comprise the third tier, for examples within sector AA Books, stationery and office supplies, there are:

Category code		Quantity
0256	Books – rare and second-hand	654
0266	Booksellers	3,172
4479	Greetings card shops	1,554
8225	Newsagents and news vendors	22,368
6624	Office equipment and supplies retailers	2,036
3380	Photocopiers	231
8651	Reprographic equipment suppliers	92
8199	Stamp wholesalers	15
8266	Stationery retailers	1,213
8249	Typewriter dealers	387
6296	Wordprocessor dealers	45

Across the vertical market classifications, it is possible to segment again but geographically using the following classifications:

Postcode area – RG (Reading) or AB (Aberdeen)
Postcode district – RG1; AB3.
County (or region in Scotland)
Yellow pages book area
ITV region (ISBA or BARB particularly useful for consumer goods test marketing)

The manipulation, selection and storage of such vast quantities of data is only possible using large mainframe computers with powerful memory capabilities and mammoth on-line disk storage facilities. The importance of on-line disk storage is that files running to hundreds of thousands of names can be searched in seconds. Outdated tape technology would have required a small team of dedicated computer staff to load and continuously unload 2,400-foot long magnetic tapes on to and from their drives, making the task one of hours rather than seconds. The effect of this additional labour cost meant that the economics of this form of selling were much less attractive, the AA and *Readers Digest* probably being the best known exponents.

The unsuspecting but carefully selected prospective purchasers of the company's goods and/or services then receive a letter through the post. The letter should be personalized using a wordprocessing package, with the christian and surname of the individual concerned and with the correct address. Frequently included with the letter is a brochure and special offer as a stimulus to a positive response.

The response to this method of selling is almost invariably in single figure percentages and generally well below 5 per cent, however certain types of products it is still cost-effective. This is because the capability of the computer is such that the names and addresses of hundreds of thousands of people can be stored easily and cheaply, and specially selected sub-groups can be extracted from the database. The selection can be printed onto labels, envelopes and/or continuation paper and rented to third parties for between £60 and £80 per thousand on a commercial basis.

Thus, a direct mailing to 10,000 people might cost:

	(£)
Rent of names and addresses	700
Postage (2nd class, standard weight)	1,800
Production of letter and/or brochure	500
Assembly of mailing (i.e. folding, inserting and franking)	500
	3,500

1 per cent response produces 100 suspects
2 per cent response produces 200 suspects
3 per cent response produces 300 suspects

This has been achieved for a fraction of the cost of employing a salesman.

3.4 Information databases and market research

Faster, cheaper and more reliable computers coupled with the developments in communications technology mean that computers can now be connected together almost irrespective of geographical distance. By means of an 'intelligent' retrieval system, the user can search and retrieve data held in a computer system hundreds or thousands of miles away. This facility is not usually provided as a public service, so consequently a subscription charge and/or usage charges are payable. However, many people and organizations find this is the quickest and most convenient, and ultimately 'the cheapest way, to obtain information.

Responding to public demand, a number of organizations have become information producers. These are usually commercial, but there are also a few academic and trade organizations who collect data and store it for access by their subscribers.

The *Financial Times* Business Reports Database, for example, comprises four main sections: 'Fintech' concentrates on the business aspects of new technology. It provides news, comment and evaluation of six areas: telecom markets, the electronic office, personal computer markets, the automated factory, software markets and updates on new computer products. The information is stored in 'full text', i.e. not abbreviated, and contains over 10,000 articles published since February 1984. Other sections include the 'Media', which focuses on developments in the world's technical markets and new media; the 'Finance and business' section which provides what it says, and the 'Energy' section providing full-text reports of energy news.

Other *Financial Times* database services include:

- *Financial Times* Full-Text Database.
- *Financial Times* Company Information Database.
- *Financial Times* Currency and Share Index Database.
- McCarthy On-Line information service on companies.
- Finstat offering details of share, gilts and securities prices.

- International Finance Alert, highlights trends in the foreign exchange and commodity markets.

Dunn & Bradstreet, Reuters, ICC, Extel and Mead Data Central offer a similar but slightly different range of services. Lexis is a very large legal database service marketed by Butterworths Telepublishing with details of tens of thousands of law reports.

To access on-line information services, it is necessary to invest in some computer equipment, documentation and training. The computer equipment can either be just a terminal, or a complete desktop system (terminal with its own memory, disk drive(s) and printer), and is connected to the host (database system) by either a dedicated telephone line or by a 'dial-up' service plus a modem where a telephone number is called to make the connection.

Once the connection is made, the user uses the computer equivalent of a number of directories to find the specific subject area of interest. Once located, it can be read on the remote terminal screen or, where the user has a computer (rather than just a terminal), printed out as hard copy or downloaded for further manipulation.

Obviously, the uses of any type of information are as varied as the users. But in a sales context, on-line databases are often used:

- To gather background information on markets and consumers. *MAID* (which covers advertising and marketing strategy), ICC's *Key Note Reports* and the pan-European *Euromonitor* reports can be scanned in a matter of minutes for relevant paragraphs.
- To create prospect lists to a sales executive's own criteria. Using similar methods to those outlined in 3.3, a company can set its own parameters and produce tailor-made mailing or call lists. The advantage of this do-it-yourself method is particularly relevant to small companies. Lists can be as specific as you need: just so names in one very closely-defined sector can be downloaded, without the expense of paying brokers' minimum charges. ICC, Jordans and Infocheck all produce comprehensive companies' databases.
- Credit-checking. Many small businesses get into considerable cash-flow problems by extending credit to defaulting companies. On-line databases can give, in a matter of minutes (while the client is on the telephone), an indication of credit-worthiness or a 'credit rating', minimizing risk. Infolink and ICC are predominant here.

The above are just a few potential uses: as computer ownership increases, the on-line database industry will grow with it, to produce increasingly sophisticated and 'user friendly' information sources.

3.5 Portable computers and hand-held devices

The portable computer has allowed the territory salesperson to rapidly transfer sales order data back to his office without having physically to call in. At each call the salesperson keys into a hand-held micro-computer the customer's order requirements in terms of quantity and price. Once that has been completed, the hand-held device is plugged into a small printer in the car or van which produces the customer's copy of the order (which may be already in the format of a proforma invoice).

At the end of the day the salesperson plugs the hand-held computer into a modem attached to the domestic telephone line. By dialling an appropriate number, the day's orders are transferred quickly and accurately to the office computer for production of the appropriate stock requisitions, despatch notes, customer invoices and to update the salesperson's commission record.

Other products include briefcase printers rather than the car- or van-mounted variety. In addition to the printer facility, each briefcase includes a battery power supply. The rechargeable battery supplies the printer with sufficient power for a day's calls. The briefcase also houses the connector for data communication to the office computer, and if the hand-held computer is left in the briefcase, the data can be communicated at the same time as the hand-held computer is being recharged.

Other varieties of portable (light enough to be carried easily) and transportable (less easily because they weigh 15–30 lbs) computers are designed to provide the salesperson or manager with computer power on the train, during a conference or at home.

3.6 Computerized prospect recording and evaluation systems

These prospect prioritization systems come in two different forms, both microcomputer based. The most common approach is a computerized sales prospect and time management recording with an automated forward facility. Updating the prospect database provides sales management with an accurate and effective central mechanism that can automatically print monthly statements recording actual sales against budget by territory, a forward projection status report, and clearly flagged priority contacts. This can be of great help to sales management and salespeople as an aid to focusing on priorities.

The other approach, which is being developed by Dr Andrew Wayne and the author, involves the use of what is called an expert system. These are computer systems that employ artificial intelligence (AI) reasoning techniques in order to solve problems posed by their users. The expert system makes use of knowledge that has been gathered from a human expert about how to solve a particular kind of problem.

The essential features of such systems are the ability to understand natural language (that is, instructions that are constructed using spoken English statements) and the ability to reason. Just as in human conversation, a natural language system is able to understand a request in the context of requests that preceded it. For instance, one might ask: 'What is the value of potential business in France?' The system might respond with a total value or, according to how the system has been designed, ask the enquirer to specify:

- public or private sector,
- year 1992, 1993, 1994, 1995
- by industry or vertical market,
- by project type.

Table 3.1

Year 1992	a) Project value to company figs. in millions £	b) Opportunity rating %	Est. money value (a × b) figs. in millions £
1) Power stations			
Rouen	15.0	80%	12.0
Lyons	20.0	55%	11.0
Bordeaux	12.0	80%	7.2
2) Oil refining depots			
Marseilles	20.0	60%	12.0
Brest	12.0	40%	4.8
3) Water treatment			
Tours	10.0	55%	5.5
Nantes	10.0	45%	4.5
Lille	8.0	40%	3.2
4) Hydro-electric			
Chamonix	20.0	60%	12.0

If the user responded:
- public sector,
- power stations, oil refining depots, water treatment plant and hydro-electric project,
- 1992, 1993,

the system would respond with a table showing the value of potential business for the four types of project in the two years specified.

If the user then decides that the information is required in descending order according to value and weighted according to estimated percentage probability of obtaining the business, the display might look like Table 3.1.

The reasoning strategies from which the opportunity rating factor is calculated are based on such factors as can be seen in Table 3.2.

Table 3.2

Project success	(A) Relative weight	(B) Company advantage factors	(A×B)
		0,.1,.2,.3,.4,.5,.6,.7,.8,.9	
1 *Project factors* Country Potential value to company Work/type Client			
2 *Competition* National Political Technical Price			
3 *Company factors* Timescale (resources) Company gross profit Likelihood of payment 'Spin-off'			

Notes

1.0 Opportunity rating =
Opportunity rating scale   0.00–0.40 poor
                                       0.41–0.75 fair/good
                                       0.76–1.00 very good
Present minimum acceptance 0.60

To assist in the construction of these expert systems, several software tools are now on the market. Dr Wayne and the author are using 'Guru' sold by MDBS Inc. They offer a major step forward in managing the forward potential business schedule and will have a big impact on decision making and the management of sales.

3.7 Telex and facsimile

Telex has been used for decades to send messages internationally where businesses are separated by several time zones such that the telephone is impractical, and the post involves an unacceptable delay. Facsimile on the other hand offered electronic document transfer from one subscriber to another, but the quality was generally appalling.

Recent technological developments have resulted in wider use of both services. Telexes can now be sent from a desktop computer (with the appropriate software) to offices with telex-receiving equipment. It is used as a substitute for memos and is a fast and convenient way of issuing instructions and confirming arrangements.

Facsimile is now much improved in quality and also reduced in cost, proving attractive to businesses of all sizes. The quality is still only really acceptable for internal use, and sending a floppy disk or cassette first class to somebody with compatible hardware and software will long remain a cost-, quality- and time-efficient method.

3.8 Teleshopping

In the 1970s the first tentative steps were made towards the introduction of teleshopping in Britain. It offered groceries which were neither particularly fresh nor very competitively priced and a very restricted range of goods and services. However, the technology has been improved and retailing had an unprecedented boom in the late 1980s, with the result that trading space for some years was difficult to obtain at anything approaching conventional prices, and the social services are beginning to appreciate the potential of the medium in social terms.

A few local councils have combined with supermarket chains in a pilot scheme to offer elderly and disabled people teleshopping as a social service. In Gateshead (Newcastle) there is a waiting list for terminals linked into the local Tesco supermarket. Another scheme has been set up in Tower Hamlets (London) with the local Asda supermarket. However, there is a very long way to go before the medium has anything like the acceptance of the North American market, although there is a steady increase in the use of 0800 numbers in television advertising, where viewers can 'phone for information packs usually for information on financial services.

A new teleshopping project called 'Keyline' has been invented by Chris Curry (co-founder of Acorn computers). It comprises a lightweight computer terminal that plugs into a telephone socket and understands 'natural language commands' such as 'I want to buy a kettle.' The screen then displays a list of retailers, models that are available and prices from which the users can choose.

The services offered range from banking and betting to ordering groceries and booking travel tickets. Many of the big retail chains are participating: Sainsbury's, Gateway, Asda, Tesco, Kays, Littlewoods and Freeman. Banks and financial institutions are also participating (National Westminster, Bank of Scotland, Sun Alliance and Commercial Union). Many industry experts view this development as the natural heir to the mail order business, now estimated to be worth some £4 billion a year.

3.9 Cable TV and video

This is essentially a method of reaching the US market using a video and cable TV. It represents a new concept for UK companies wishing to reach the large US consumer public by screening their own video on a cable TV channel. The video can be an individual tape, or a group of businesses can co-operate to produce a 'corporate' tape, thereby sharing the production cost. The concept is called 'Showcase'. It offers companies access to the US market as part of a programmed schedule that is published in advance in just the same way as details of programmes are publicized in the UK.

World Access Television, for example, offers the following schedule on a Thursday:

11.00am EST* 10.00am ECT 9.00am MST 9.00am PST	Corporate finance and communications (companies, products, money matters, image videos and services)
11.30am EST 10.30am ECT 9.30am MST 8.30am PST	International art, antiques and photography (artists, photographers, galleries, antiques and auctions)

6.00pm EST	Fashion, design and cuisine (collections, fashion
5.00pm ECT	shows, cuisine and interior design and services)
4.00pm MST	
3.00pm PST	

6.30pm EST	World class autos, yachts and real estate
5.30pm ECT	
4.30pm MST	
3.30pm PST	

*EST = Eastern Standard Time (New York City)
 CST = Central Standard Time (Chicago)
 MST = Mountain Standard Time (Denver)
 PST = Pacific Standard Time (Los Angeles)

The 'Showcase' on international antiques, art and photography includes:

- Work from artists all over the world.
- Gallery owners exhibiting their latest finds.
- Auction previews and details of prices realized at previous auctions.
- Photography.
- News and details of other objects that are collected ranging from coins and stamps to Japanese ceramics.

A video production scheduled for the summer of 1988 by Dox Limited was called 'Your Guide to Antique Shopping in Britain'. This production was directed at members of the Kensington and Chelsea Chamber of Commerce, particularly those members in Kensington Church Street, the Kings Road, the Brompton Road, the Fulham Road, Westbourne Grove and Portobello Road.

The scheme worked like this. A one-hour quality video including editing costs about £80,000. Dox Limited were looking for a sponsor (for the full amount) or co-sponsors (for between £10,000 and £30,000 each). Up to one-third of this production cost can be funded by a grant from the British Tourist Authority, subject to the approval of their sponsorship committee. Shops and galleries were included in the production entirely on the basis of their interest and uniqueness of their wares, and the attitude and willingness of the owner to participate in the production. The galleries and antique shops are not charged for the production of the video.

The video featured visits to certain shops and galleries focusing on collectable items of particular interest and/or uniqueness. There were interviews with the proprietors and various theme specialists, advice on repairs and restoration, and 'fake-spotting'. Also, there was be a guide to the parts of London where the 'important' outlets tend to be located, plus details on shipping and insurance. It was also proposed that the video would be screened on UK hotels' video information channels as well as incoming intercontinental flights and certain point-of-sale areas such as car hire reception areas.

World Access Television also offers the facility for merchandising using a free-phone US 800 number with credit card charging for such things as:

- travel programmes,
- antique shop directories,
- British Rail passes,
- London and Provincial Antique Dealers' Association customized shopping guide.

Other marketing facilities that were offered included: direct mail to hundreds of thousands of visitors to Britain each year to annual meetings of their trade or professional association. These visitors were identified and mailed in advance with an offer to buy a copy of the video. Also, there were seminars for Eastbound transatlantic voyagers on the *QEII*, and publicity in video mail order catalogues.

The size of the audience that can be reached in this way is vast. April 1988 'Tempo TV' subscription figures for certain US states are as follows:

California	596,640
New Jersey	260,097
New York	621,822
Ohio	585,850
Michigan	419,834
Texas	735,451

'Teleworld' was launched on 1 May 1988 on Tempo TV and is the first globally accessible television service that provides both individuals and corporations with a medium to promote and 'showcase' themselves. This new concept is at the lowest cost ever offered by a broadcasting or cable service. A twenty-five minute programme would cost approximately £8,750 (subject to exchange rates); spread between fifteen clients; this would be less than £600 each.

Part Two The Customer Focus

4

Consumer behaviour

The relevance of consumer behaviour to a book designed to help people sell more effectively is quite simply this: the volume of sales has a great impact on profit, and collective consumer purchase decisions determine sales. The recognition that marketing and selling strategies must be based on defined consumer needs has become known as the 'marketing concept'. Acceptance of this fact has focused attention on consumer behaviour.

During the depression of the 1930s, the Second World War, its aftermath and the Korean war of 1951–53, there was a shortage of consumer products. Consequently people were happy to buy what was available. However, this changed in the mid 1950s and for the first time in many years, supply exceeded demand. For economists this was familiar territory; in the short term an increase in supply causes the curve to shift to the right from S to S1, the price falls from P to P1 and the quantity demanded increases from Q to Q1 (see Figure 4.1). Unfortunately in the longer term this change in the market situation resulting from the lower price P1 will cause consumers to re-evaluate their purchase decisions.

This means that some 'old sellers' in the market found their sales falling as 'new sellers' offered more attractive product options. In this

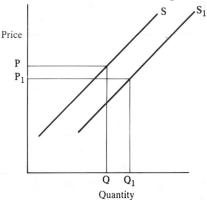

Figure 4.1 An increase in supply

situation selling harder or reducing the price of the old products may not have achieved the required result. Subsequently some enlightened sellers turned their attention toward consumer needs.

4.1 A model of consumer behaviour

The simple model in Figure 4.2 shows the interaction between the marketer and the consumer. The central component is consumer decision-making. This is how alternative product choices are perceived

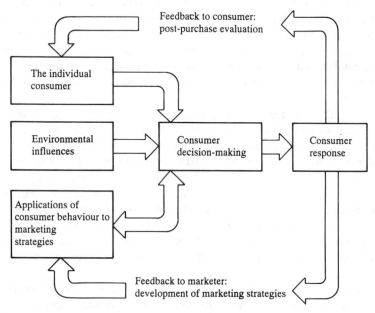

Figure 4.2   A simple model of consumer behaviour
Source   Assaell, Henry (1987) *Consumer Behaviour and Marketing Action*, Kent Publishing Company, . . .

and evaluated before a decision to purchase a particular product is made because it best meets the consumer's particular needs.

Environmental influences and the marketing strategies of the seller organization also influence consumer decision-making. The environmental factors include culture, regional or ethnic sub-cultures, social class, face-to-face groups (friends, family and reference groups) and the circumstances or situation in which the product is purchased.

Marketing strategy represents variables within the control of the marketing and sales functions that are used to inform and influence the consumer – product features, pricing policy, the advertising plan and sales distribution channels. The current thinking is that marketing professionals should undertake consumer and product research prior to developing strategies. The model also demonstrates that the consumer has a learning curve and subsequent post-purchase evaluation takes place which may affect subsequent purchase decisions.

4.1.1 Consumer decision-making

The model in Figure 4.2 was simplified in order to introduce the concept: most sales and marketing people can acknowledge that there is a difference in the purchase decision between a consumer durable – perhaps a car costing £15,000 and a tube of toothpaste costing £1. In Figure 4.3 the difference is made between decision making and habit.

Figure 4.3 distinguishes between 'high involvement purchasers' and 'low involvement purchasers'. High involvement items involve a degree of risk to the consumer: financial risk (expensive items); social risk, (where peer group approval is important; and psychological risk (where the wrong decision might cause stress). In these instances the consumer will take time and effort over the decision. By contrast, low involvement purchases will be made with much less thought. However, different varieties of behaviour are observed: variety seeking which may involve switching brands out of boredom as opposed to buying the usual brand out of 'inertia' (because it is just not important enough to give it any thought).

This area of complex decision-making is particularly important to marketing people since it involves many of the key behavioural concepts that are relevant to a marketing strategy. However, this will not occur in all cases of high involvement; where the choice is repetitive, past experience regarding the most satisfactory product produces brand

	High-involvement purchase decision	Low-involvement purchase decision
Decision making (information search, consideration of brand alternatives)	Complex decision-making (autos, major appliances)	Variety seeking (cereals)
Habit (little or no information search, consideration of only one brand)	Brand loyalty (cigarettes, perfume)	Inertia (canned vegetables, paper towels)

Figure 4.3 Consumer decision-making
Source Assaell, Henry (1987) *Consumer Behaviour and Marketing Action*, Kent Publishing Company . . .

loyalty. Products thought to fit into this category are perfume, cigarettes, beer, soap, magazines and newspapers.

Figure 4.3 shows two types of purchase occasion where the consumer is not closely involved with the product. When the involvement or interest is low, brand switching is likely to take place just as a result of the low level of satisfaction. In these instances, the brand decision is not considered important enough to warrant pre-planning and will often take place within the shop. This means that point-of-sale displays, packaging and price are the key determinants for making the sale. This type of consumer decision has been called 'variety seeking'.

A slightly different type of low-involvement behaviour has been labelled 'inertia'. This is where the consumer buys the same brand because it is not worth the time and effort necessary to consider an alternative; brand loyalty is consequently tenuous.

4.1.2 The individual consumer

Products that sell well do so because their target market (consumers) perceive the product as satisfying their needs. This process is assisted by competent marketing stimuli – advertising, promotion, merchandising and face-to-face selling (see Figure 4.4).

Frequently consumers practise what behaviourists call 'selective perception' – they screen out information seen as irrelevant to their needs. Conversely they also select information which conforms to their beliefs and predispositions about brands and products and companies.

Consumer thought variables are the cognitive processes involved in deciding in favour of one product and not another. There are three types of thought variable: the consumer's perceptions of a brand characteristic, the consumer's attitudes toward the brand and the consumer's needs.

Attitudes are a consumer's predisposition toward specific products resulting in a favourable or unfavourable response to the purchase decision. Needs are specific goals held by a consumer. Generally sales and marketing executives think in terms of satisfying these needs with their products. A popular model of needs proposed by Maslow describes a five-layer hierarchy where the basic needs are attended to as a priority, then safety and the need for recognition. People only concern themselves with self-fulfilment when their other needs are satisfied.

1 Basic psychological needs (food, sleep, comfortable temperature).
2 Safety needs (protection from danger).
3 The need for recognition (love, belonging).
4 Ego needs (self-esteem, respect from others).
5 Self-fulfilment.

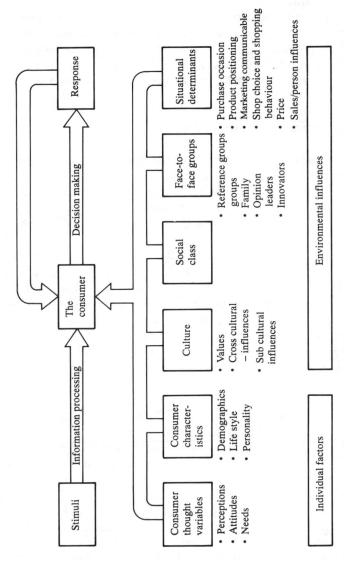

Figure 4.4 Individual factors and environmental influences on the purchase decision

Source Assaell, Henry (1987) *Consumer Behaviour and Marketing Action*, Kent Publishing Company, ...

Consumer characteristics comprise such variables as demographics, life-styles and personality traits. The marketing manager's job is to determine whether or not these characteristics are related to patterns of behaviour and influence this behaviour through appropriate stimuli to increase product sales.

The third influence on consumer choice is to do with the response; while frequently this results in the selection of a particular brand there are other permutations – a product category (French wine) or a particular shop (to buy curtain material) or of a particular stimulus (the decision to read a particular magazine or to listen to the salesperson).

4.1.3 Environmental influences

The most influential environmental fact is culture. These influences are the norms, beliefs and customs that are learned from society and result in common behaviour patterns between people from the same cultural background. Examples of this are attitudes to weight and dieting, sports and keeping fit, eating certain types of food and not others and indeed smoking cigarettes.

In the 1980s cultural values underwent some major changes and individuals became concerned with what has been called the 'me-orientation'. This has been described as a rather selfish, self-indulgent approach to life, keen on enjoyment and somewhat less interested in chores and social responsibility – hence people marrying later and choosing 'alternative careers'. This has meant that sales and marketing professionals have needed to concentrate on product quality, service and indeed the range and variety of products offered to appeal to these more individual tastes.

The greater emphasis on self-fulfilment has meant an increased interest in entertainment, hobbies, books and magazines to fill these demands. The desire for greater knowledge and culture has been translated into the consumption of the sources of this information. Similarly the focus on health and keeping fit has led to a greater demand for sports clothes, equipment and fitness and leisure centres.

Another trend is towards 'voluntary simplicity'. This is an anti-materialistic culture requiring a generally less stressful life. In sales and marketing terms, this has meant a demand for smaller, simpler and more functional products. Indeed many disciples of this life-style are committed to 'do-it-yourself' furniture, bread, vegetables and clothes. Indeed consumer durables are regularly bought second hand by these groups.

A fourth trend reinforcing the preference for voluntary simplicity has been a greater scepticism toward business and political institutions.

Consumers are now more questioning and some show greater willingness to search for obscure brands and different products although many remain loyal to the major brands. The reason for this is clearly to save time and avoid the risk of the unknown. However, the general scepticism has meant that marketeers have needed to be very convincing about product quality and the legitimacy of advertising claims.

Cross-cultural values are also very important to companies selling and marketing on an international scale. Different countries have very different attitudes and subsequently different behavioural purchase patterns. Consumer attitudes towards what might generally be regarded as the cultural fundamentals such as the frequency of cleaning the home, the importance of children relative to other priorities, and attitudes towards personal hygiene differ greatly between nations. These cultural values are translated into purchase behaviour in the shops, supermarkets and in the choice of leisure activity.

Social class also exerts a big influence on consumer behaviour, it refers to the position of an individual or family on a social scale and is based on such criteria as occupation, education, and income. Members of the same class may not meet but they are likely to share similar values, attitudes and behaviour patterns. The interest to sales and marketing executives is that each social class has different purchasing, shopping, media and communications habits. These differences need to be understood and reflected in the sales and marketing efforts directed at influencing each product/class segment if there is to be any serious expectation of selling the product in any quantity.

Another important source of information and influence on consumer behaviour is called 'face-to-face' groups, some of these are reference groups, because they serve as a point of reference in the formation of an individual's beliefs, attitudes and behaviour. These reference groups are very important to those involved in selling and marketing consumer products. Products are frequently advertised on television with the family round the table eating a meal, or a well-known personality is seen endorsing a brand (Daley Thompson and Lucozade was perhaps one of the better known during recent years in the UK).

Various types of reference groups have been identified by sociologists, behaviourists and psychologists:

	Informal	Formal
Primary	Family	School group
	Peer group	Business group
Secondary	Shopping groups	Alumni groups
	Sports groups	Tenant organizations

Reference groups have a number of functions, they provide norms of conduct, assign roles within the group to individuals and act as a medium for influencing consumption. This power over consumption is exercised by information (called expertise), comparison (referent influence) and normative influence (reward).

The influence of the information depends on the credibility of the information source, while the comparative influence depends on the degree of similarity between influencer and consumer. Normative influence is based on an acceptance or rejection of the goods purchased by the group. Acceptance can take the form of praise, rejection can sometimes result in ridicule.

4.2 Shop choice and shopping behaviour

Consumer buying behaviour is not just about choices between products and brands, there is also a choice involved about where the purchase is made. This is called shop choice. This distinction means that sales and marketing people should consider the difference between buying behaviour and shopping behaviour. It is important to try and understand how the two types of behaviour interact, the motives for shopping for example may be quite different from the reasons for buying a particular product or brand. This means that the marketing communications strategy may require alteration from an out-of-store emphasis (TV and press advertising for example) to an in-store focus, where merchandising and indeed an active selling involvement by the staff is important. This will be particularly the case where a number of competing brands from different companies are retailed in the same outlet. Consequently a sales promotion strategy will be required as well as a level of staff training. Where this is difficult, promotions will have to be considred that involve a merchandiser–sales promoter being located in the store for the duration of the promotion. This will of course add to the cost of selling and marketing the product.

4.2.1 Shopping behaviour

Shopping behaviour is a specific form of consumer behaviour. Consider the following example: two people may visit the same shop because it is close to their home or office, and the sales staff may be especially courteous and well trained. However, one shopper may find shopping a chore while the other may regard it as something of an occasion whether it is the satisfaction of consuming, the thrill of buying a bargain or just an afternoon out of the house.

There have been a number of studies by researchers to categorize consumers by shopping behaviour patterns. One study[1] distinguished between shopper types by the amount of information search and analysis done by the consumers.

- Constructive shoppers – they spend a lot of time searching for information by visiting retail outlets.
- Surrogate shoppers – leave the shopping to other members of the household.
- Preparatory shoppers are more likely to do in-depth secondary research. A good example of this would be those who avidly study the product comparisons produced in *Which* each month.
- Routinized shoppers – know in advance what they want and spend relatively little time specifically gathering information.

Marketing managers can use the results of the study as input to their communication strategies; the surrogate shopper is likely to be responsive to TV advertising for example whereas in-store brochures and information sheets will only be sought by constructive shoppers.

Another study by George P. Moschis related shopping types to purchase behaviour and identified six distinct types of people who purchase cosmetics:[2]

- Special-sales shopper.
- Brand-loyal customers.
- Shop-loyal customers.
- Problem solvers.
- Socializer (who buy brands used by friends).
- Name-conscious shoppers (who judge cosmetics by the prestige of the shop selling them).

The message for marketing managers is that clearly the in-magazine free sample will have most impact on the special-sales shoppers who will also require price information and details of the product size or weight. The brand-loyal and name-conscious shoppers will respond to advertising in prestige fashion magazines and will also need to know the shops stocking these products. The Falke advertisement in GQ lists the London stockists.

4.3 The influence of price

Price has an important influence on consumer behaviour both in terms of brand selection and store choice. Consumers make a conscious link

Exhibit 4.1

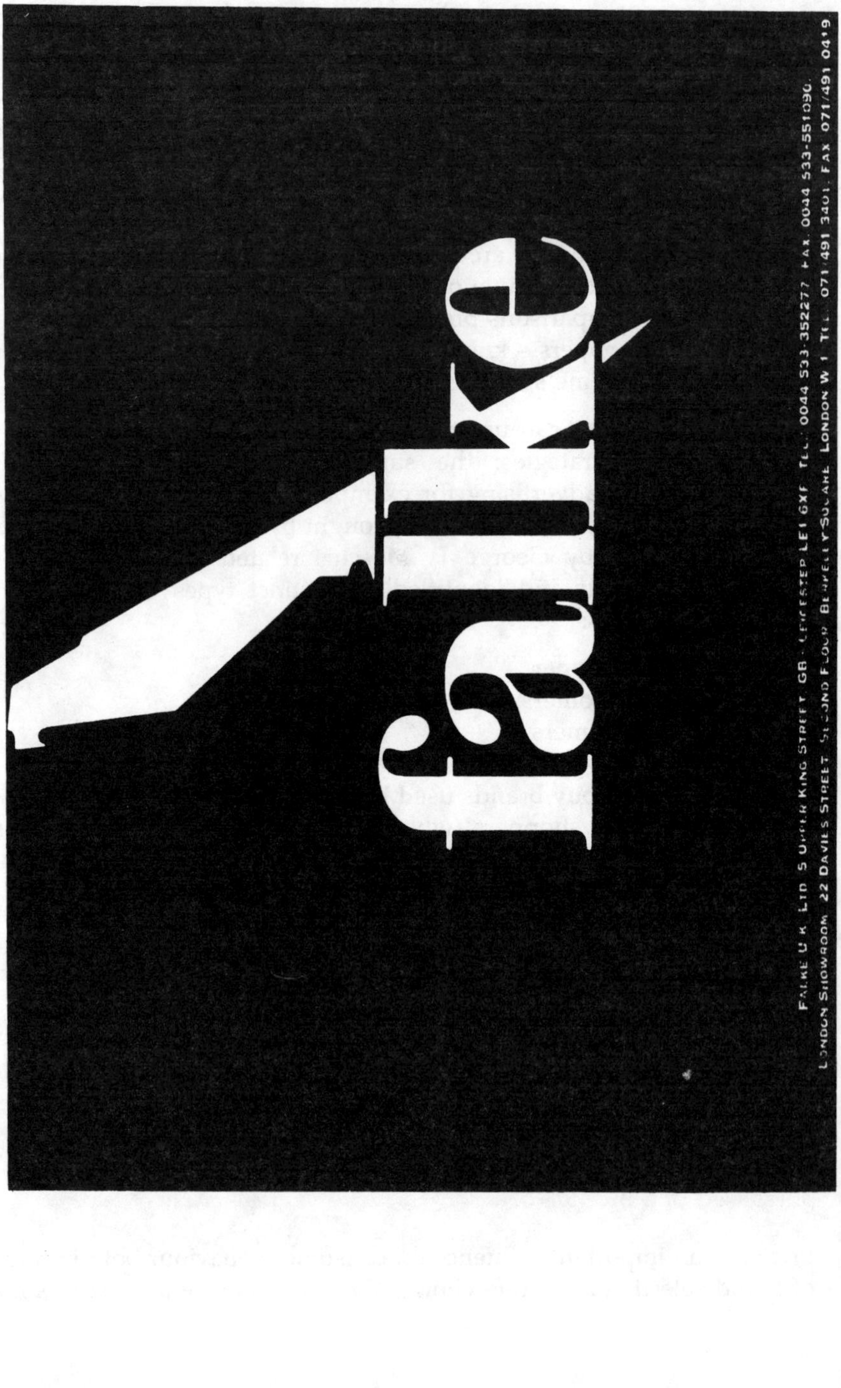
falke
FALKE U K LTD 5 UPPER KING STREET GB - LEICESTER LE1 6XF TEL. 0044 533-352277 FAX. 0044 533-551090.
LONDON SHOWROOM 22 DAVIES STREET SECOND FLOOR BERKELEY SQUARE LONDON W 1 TEL. 071/491 3401. FAX 071/491 0419

Source: GQ British Edition, August 1991

between price and quality that has an impact on both the particular product that is chosen and where the purchase is made.

Economic theory has quite a lot to say about the effect of price on demand. However, the absence of a simple explanation that is applicable to a wide range of products by a wide range of consumers means that a consumer's price perceptions, price sensitivity and price awareness should be studied on a product-by-product basis. These behaviour patterns should then relate to the characteristics of particular groups of consumers identified as the target market for each of these products.

4.3.1 Price perceptions

Price–quality relationship
The most important inference from price is one of quality, particularly where there is an absence of additional information about the product. Different studies have shown that this price effect is, however, reduced where for example housewives have specific brand experience.[3] This experience overcame price as the dominant factor when choosing a particular brand. The fact that consumers seemed to see price as a quality indicator in some instances and not others prompted further research. These studies showed that price became an important indicator where consumers held strong beliefs that quality differences did exist between products but they had insufficient information or product knowledge on which to make a decision. Price was then used as the only available criteria.[4]

Psychological pricing
Consumers also appear to be sensitive to certain price points. 'Odd–even pricing' is used by retailers in the belief that £2.99 is seen by the consumer as less expensive than a product price at £3.00. Further justification for this approach to pricing has been provided by research[5] showing that increasing odd prices is less noticeable to consumers than increasing even prices.

4.3.2 Price sensitivity

Another factor that has an impact on retailer and manufacturer pricing strategies is the reaction of consumers to changes in price. The price elasticity of demand expresses the percentage change in the quantity purchased of a product compared to a percentage change in price.

$$\frac{\% \text{ Change is quantity demanded}}{\% \text{ change in price}}$$

If price changed by 15 per cent and the quantity demanded by 10 per cent, this would be 15/10 = a price elasticity demand of 1.5. Demand is said to be price elastic where the percentage decrease in the quantity demanded is greater than the percentage increase in price. Where the percentage decrease is less than the percentage increase in price, demand is relatively inelastic.

Price elasticity

Clearly an important approach in segmenting markets is to classify consumers by their relative price elasticity. Where price sensitive consumers have particular demographic or geographical characteristics then sale promotions offering '10 per cent free' or '20 per cent off' or 'three for the price of two' might be very successful at attracting new consumers and 'brand nomads' (consumers without any strong brand loyalty).

A major reason for marketing managers developing strong brands is that not only will consumers become loyal to the product and buy it regularly in preference to others, but that they will continue to do so despite increases in price. This provides the opportunity for the company to make above average profits.

Curiously, little research seems to have been done in this area, although one study by Monroe[6] made the distinction between upside elasticity (sensitivity to price increases) and downside elasticity (sensitivity to price decreases). In the study of three products, it was shown that consumers were more likely to increase consumption with a decrease in price than to decrease consumption with an increase in price.

Another study[7] found that consumer price elasticity declined when the consumer is accompanied by a friend. Clearly many consumers are reluctant to be thought mean by friends and peers.

Price expectations

Consumers develop a standard price for many products – this is one regarded as fair in terms of the satisfaction derived from these products. This is then used as a norm for judging other prices. Prices outside this range can produce brand switching. A study by Gabor and Granger[8] established the existence 'of an upper limit above which the article would be judged too expensive and a lower limit below which the quality of the item would be suspect'.

The price-sensitive consumer

A study by Yankelovich, Shelly and White showed that the most price-sensitive consumers are likely to be senior citizens, single, less educated, lower income, or blue-collar workers.[9] However, being price sensitive did not always mean taking advantage of the lower prices.

4.4 Sales person influences

Consumers are frequently brought into contact with sales people when shopping. Although most personal selling takes place in the industrial, government and technical markets it is also important for consumer goods.

Direct influence by a sales executive can have major impact on consumer behaviour. This is particularly the case where the sales person has received adequate training in the areas of product knowledge and selling techniques.

4.4.1 Referent power

The sales executive's influence on consumer behaviour comes initially from what is called referent power. This is based on a sense of personal identification or shared identity on the part of the consumer with the sales executive. The personalized shopper in need of a little social interaction from the retail sales staff may be most subject to this type of influence.

Research studies have demonstrated the importance of referent power by showing that where the customer sees the sales executive as being similar to themselves, a sale is more likely to be made.[10] F. B. Evans in a study found this to be true for insurance sales people.

4.4.2 Expert power

Secondly the sales executive may be considered to be particularly knowledgeable about the product and therefore valuable as a source of information. Various studies have attempted to rank the importance of the referent power and the expert power. Woodside and Davenport produced the following results from their work:[11]

Customer exposed to	% of customers making a purchase
1 Expert sales persons seen as similar	80
2 Expert sales persons seen as dissimilar	53
3 Non-expert sales persons seen as similar	30
4 Non-expert sales persons seen as dissimilar	13

These results emphasize that both role/skill areas are important – for successful selling. The importance of skill acquisition through training is widely acknowledged though infrequently undertaken or so it seems in retail selling. However, companies still make the most fundamental mistakes of expecting non-Yorkshiremen to sell in Yorkshire, public schoolboys to sell in D and E socio-economic environments and unqualified engineers to sell to qualified engineers.

Other studies have found that the influence of expertise (insurance) was more important than a referent power. Where the product is less complicated it seems that the referent power is the more important.

Notes

1 Furse, D. H., Punj, G. N. and Stewart, D. W. (1982) Individual search strategies in new automobile purchase. In *Advances in Consumer Research* (ed. Andrew Mitchell), **9**, Association of Consumer Research, Ann Arbor, Michigan: 379–384.
2 Shopping orientations and consumer uses of information (1976) *Journal of Retailing*, **52**, (Summer), 61–70.
3 Monroe, K. B. (1976) The influence of price differences and brand familiarity on brand preference. *Journal of Consumer Research*, **3** (June), 42–49.
4 Obermuller C. and Wheatley, J. J. (1984) Beliefs in quality differences and brands choice. *Advance in Consumer Research*, **12**, (eds Hirshman, E. C. and Holbrook, M. C.) Association for Consumer Research, Utah.
5 Schindler, R. M. (1984) Consumer recognition of increases in odd and even prices. *Advances in Consumer Research II* (ed. Kinnear, Thomas C.) Association for Consumer Research, Utah, pp. 459–462.
6 Monroe, op. cit., p. 47.
7 Woodwise, A. G. and Sims, J. Taylor (1976) Retail sale transactions and customer 'purchase pal' effects on buying behaviour. *Journal of Retailing*, **Autumn**, 57–64.
8 Gabor, A. and Granger, C. W. S. (1978) Prices as an indicator of quality. *Economics*, **46**, (February), 43–70.
9 Supermarket Shoppers, p. 31.
10 Evans, F. B. (1963) Selling as a dynamic relationship – a new approach. *American Behavioural Scientist*, **6**, (May), 76–79.
11 Woodsize, A. G. and Davenport, W. (1974) The effect of salesman similarity and expertise on consumer purchasing behaviour. *Journal of Marketing Research*, **II**, (May), 198–202.

5
Customer satisfaction

Customer satisfaction is what makes a consumer repeat the purchases of certain products and services. It is based on the ability of the selling organization in meeting customer needs precisely. The absence of complaints is not a sufficient indicator that this is being achieved. The time and effort involved in complaining is a deterrent to making these views known.

A recent report[1] states that:

- It costs five times more to obtain a new customer than to retain an existing customer.
- The average business never hears from 96 per cent of its dissatisfied customers.
- The average customer who has a problem with an organization tells nine or ten people about it.
- Companies whose product quality, in the eyes of customers, was judged to be high, showed six times higher profitability compared with those of low quality.

5.1 The importance of customer care

Customer care is an important part of successful selling, because keeping an existing customer contented is generally much easier, takes less time and involves less expense than finding new buyers. The reasons for this are that it takes time to find new prospective customers, and having found them the sales person needs to establish credibility before making a sale. With existing customers this has already been accomplished. Even though this idea is readily accepted by many businessmen and women, it is still remarkable how many companies gain a reputation for bad service.

A recent survey produced the results shown in Table 5.1 suggesting that customer service is ignored at the company's peril.

It is startling to note that the product itself counts for only 30 per cent or less of the customer's decision to stay with the current supplier.

Table 5.1   *Which do you belive is the factor which most influences customer loyalty?*

	Country (%)							
	Sweden	Finland	Norway	Denmark	UK	Benelux	France	Italy
Sales person	31	38	30	29	30	22	20	18
Product	24	14	27	30	30	22	22	15
Service	42	45	30	32	39	44	52	65
Price	4	1	11	8	0	6	4	2
Other	0	1	0	2	0	5	2	0

Source   Survey by Mercuri International, Sweden.

Service, however, counts for between 30 per cent and 65 per cent, and the sales person's contribution varies from 18 per cent to 38 per cent. While national characteristics differ, the key role of customer service cannot be ignored. The sales executive's influence on keeping customers is also clearly of major importance. Among the reasons given by survey respondents for the importance of service was the increasing similarity of many competing products.

A classic story about an organization's reputation for customer care concerns British Rail when Sir Peter Parker was chairman. BR was going through the process of choosing a new advertising agency and evaluating the creative presentations of the short-listed contenders. One agency, rather than take their presentation to BR's offices, specifically requested that the BR panel visit them.

A meeting was arranged for 9 am one particular morning and at the appointed time Sir Peter and his team arrived at the agency's offices. The receptionist was busy talking on the telephone and smoking a cigarette. After a few minutes, one of Sir Peter's colleagues interrupted the girl's conversation and explained who they were and that they had a meeting five minutes ago with a particular account director. With a pained expression, the receptionist said 'goodbye' to the friend and 'phoned through to the account director. She then asked Sir Peter to take a seat in reception. After a few more minutes' inactivity (apart from the receptionist who was filing her nails) the aide again reminded her who they were and what their business was. Again she called the office and replied that the director in question 'was tied up' but should be free shortly. She then offered coffee. This she brought a few minutes later (by this time smoking another cigarette) in plastic containers on an old metal tray. 'I got two with sugar and two without', she said hopefully. The coffee had quite clearly come from a vending machine and apart from being wet and hot very little else could be said about it with any certainty.

At twenty-five minutes past nine the party rose to their feet and with a good deal of impatience moved towards the exit. At this moment the account director appeared. All of the guests immediately started to voice their opinion as to their treatment and the time that had been wasted. The director listened to them in silence. When they had stopped speaking, he said, 'I wanted you to see our presentation having experienced something of what it feels like to be a customer of British Rail!' It is not recorded whether the agency won the account. Unfortunately, the traveller using British Rail is still exposed to dirt, delay and overcrowding much of the time. However, the former discourtesy is now replaced frequently by an admirable stoicism and a pleasantly helpful attitude.

The critical feature is that customers must perceive that they are getting good service. Companies can only know if they are succeeding by auditing their consumers' responses. The starting point is to identify precisely the consumers' requirements, then to attempt to measure how effectively these requirements are being satisfied. Work then needs to be undertaken to improve the degree of satisfaction. By far the best way of approaching this task is to implement a consumer satisfaction programme.

5.2 The objectives of a customer satisfaction programme

To meet the requirements of customers successfully, there are a number of fundamental objectives to be achieved:

1 To determine precisely your customers' product and service requirements.
2 To measure how the customer perceives your performance against their key requirements compared with that of your competitors.
3 To measure whether there are any significant differences in levels of customer satisfaction between different types of customer or within different divisions of the company.
4 To evaluate what your organization perceives to be the key attributes of service quality and to determine what problems and tasks are involved in providing high quality service.
5 To identify whether discrepancies exist between your customers' and your own perceptions of what constitutes the ideal level of service.
6 To determine the extent to which your distribution channels are maintaining the end-customer service quality desired by your organization.
7 To make the necessary product, service or organizational changes to achieve the ideal level of service.
8 To maintain an on-going monitoring service to measure changes in customer requirements and the degree to which your performance changes to meet these changing requirements.

The marketing function is best placed to establish customer requirements, by reviewing the needs of the market; it should also be responsible for identifying the key characteristics which determine the quality of the product or service in the eyes of the customer. Clearly, it is essential that the marketing function feeds this information back to other departments in the organization (see Figure 5.1).

It is important for an organization to realize that all departments have a part to play in establishing this quality factor.

	Company function	Quality factor (examples)
Physical product quality	R & D	■ ergonomics ■ features ■ repair time
	Manufacturing	■ product defects ■ reliability ■ product life
Services quality	Sales	■ enquiry handling ■ product knowledge ■ courtesy
	Marketing	■ brochure details ■ mailing frequency ■ enquiry response time
	Distribution	■ order-delivery time ■ order completeness ■ damaged arrivals
	After sales	■ problem response time ■ time to resolve ■ courtesy
	Accounts	■ accuracy ■ problem response ■ courtesy

Figure 5.1 The quality chain
Source Jamieson, David (1989) *Customer Satisfaction*, Market Research Ltd., . . .

5.3 The big secret of dealing with people

The desire to feel important is a fundamental human craving. It is this desire that motivates the children of low earning parents to become millionaires. Most people accept the fact that they are not very important and get on with living their lives quietly – until, that is, they buy something, a product or a service, that is sub-standard. Then, all of a sudden, they feel that they have the right to be taken seriously. In short, they have purchased the right to be treated as important dissatisfied customers. The company that fails to acknowledge this strong feeling could be heading for a lot of trouble.

Consequently, some companies channel all customer complaints to the chairman, who deals with them personally. A compassionate approach to the complaint with generous compensation for the inconvenience involved and a letter from the company chairman is a very efficient way of demonstrating how seriously the company responds to customers who have had the misfortune to be badly served by its products.

Other companies have customer service departments that are instructed to replace any faulty product reported or sent in. Among those with this responsible approach of which the author has had first-hand experience are W. D. & H. O. Wills, Givenchy, Austin Reed, Dunhill, Heinz and Sainsbury's. These companies are household names, and they are successful because 99.9 per cent of the time their products are superb, and when they are not for some reason, without any fuss they replace the product and reimburse the customer for any expense incurred. Consequently, people buy from them again and again. A good example of this occurred recently when the author had some difficulty obtaining a small replacement part for a Philips gas hob. Following a couple of telephone calls to the customer service department and a letter bringing the matter to their attention the letter shown in Exhibit 5.1 was received.

On the other hand, there are companies from which the author would never again purchase goods or services. These include restaurants which have given inferior service or whose staff have been impertinent and travel tour operators who clearly have not visited the hotel in the brochure for some years. However, the greatest no-go company is a certain supplier of fitted kitchens, from whom the author had the misfortune to purchase some units. They took over four months to deliver the units ordered, nine days to commence fitting after delivery (in the meantime some ten cubic metres of units were stored in the author's flat) and five months to complete the installation. Letters to the director of customer services remained unanswered until solicitors were involved. Finally this supplier made an out-of-court settlement of £500 which was accepted as compensation for the enormous amount of inconvenience incurred. However little was done to convince the customer that this was a 'one-off' problem and that any future custom would be managed with greater finesse.

Exhibit 5.1   An example showing a company that cares about its customers

---

Whirlpool (UK) Limited

Philips and Whirlpool Major Domestic Appliances

PO Box 45   209 Purley Way   Croydon CR9 4RY   Telephone: 801-649 5000   Fax: 081-649 5060

REF: RH/CEF

7 October 1991

Mr K Steward
26 Sinclair Road
West Kensington
LONDON
W14 0NH

Dear Mr Steward,

It has been brought to my attention by my secretary, Mrs Chris Frenchum, of the many problems that you have encountered with regard to the ordering of your spare part.

Please accept my sincere apologies for the obvious inconvenience that this matter has caused. With regard to the charges raised for our Spare Parts, the handling charge is a charge made for postage and packing, however I have noted your comments and I will bring this matter to the attention of our Spares Warehouse Manager.

Please rest assured that the comments with regard to our Customer Care Manager will also be raised at our next meeting. I understand from Mrs Franchum that she has raised a cheque requisition for the sum of £30.00 which I hope in someway compensates you for the inconvenience and out of pocket expenses.

Thank you for bringing this matter to my attention. If you should require any further assistance in the future please do not hesitate to contact myself or Mrs Frenchum.

Yours sincerely

R Hodgetts

R. Hodgetts
<u>Service Director</u>

5.4 Handling customer complaints

The first thing to appreciate is that every business from time to time has dissatisfied customers who complain. The reason may be a misunderstanding, an accident or the customer's expectations not being fulfilled. This is not to make light of the situation, but an attempt to explain something that is part of everyday business. As such it needs to be anticipated, procedures must be established, and staff trained in the principles and techniques of damage limitation. If customer complaints are not dealt with quickly, efficiently and with finesse the business has problems and so does the sales force.

Deal with the complaint immediately
Postponing any action is adding insult to injury. While no sales person likes to be on the receiving end of a complaint, frequently the problem can be easily resolved if it is dealt with promptly, efficiently and courteously. The more efficiently the complaint is received and resolved, the more difficult it is for the customer to escalate the problem into a major controversy. Also, and very importantly, goodwill may result from the prompt and efficient response.

Admit mistakes when they arise
The sales person should not be afraid to admit that a mistake has occurred, apologize appropriately and take steps to rectify the problem. It is an interesting facet of human nature that when the offender, or his representative, admits the fault, apologizes and offers to put the matter right, it is very difficult for the injured party to continue to feel aggrieved. Of course, the action taken must either be visible to the aggrieved party, or he must be kept informed of the progress. Progress there must be, otherwise insult will be added to injury.

Listen to complaints
Let the customer 'get it off his chest' and listen patiently with an open mind until the customer has finished his criticism. When the anger has passed, encourage him to express his views as to what has gone wrong. This will be seen as a positive step towards putting matters right. Whatever you do in this situation, do not interrupt, do not make jokes or be flippant. A customer with a complaint expects to be treated very seriously indeed.

You cannot win an argument
When a dissastisfied customer is telling you about the grievance, under no circumstances should you attempt to argue or dispute the matter.

Even if he is wrong this is not the time or the place. If you win the argument you may lose the customer; if you do not even attempt to argue you may well keep the customer (provided that you then resolve the problem). Nine times out of ten an argument ends with each of the disputants antagonistic towards the other person and more firmly convinced than ever that he is right. The only way to get the best of an argument is to avoid it.

Offer to investigate the complaint

When a customer has taken the trouble to complain, the very least that the sales person can do is to offer to look into the matter. Do this quickly and efficiently and report back to the customer with a proposal to rectify the complaint. Do this with a good grace and make the customer aware how important their business is to you.

Do not try to duck the responsibility

Where there has been a mistake, admit responsibility for it and take the criticism that follows. If the sales person is happy to take the credit for getting a sale, he should be prepared to face the music when things go wrong. There was an international construction company, one of whose senior managers said on one occasion, 'When we win a large contract, forty-seven people claim to have been instrumental in the negotiations; when we lose a contract it is difficult to find anyone who will admit to having been associated with the job.'

5.5 The customer's point of view

Sales people may sometimes suspect their customers of using fault-finding as a way of obtaining price concessions. Others they may label as petty-minded for making a fuss about very little. Indeed, an independent arbitrator might agree with the sales person; but who places the orders? It is of course the customer, and consequently the pragmatic sales executive should try to see matters from the customer's point of view.

The customer may experience a vast amount of trouble and inconvenience as a consequence of a faulty product. It can halt an assembly line for half a day; a batch of products may have to be recalled or thrown away. All this is expensive in terms of time and money. When the production line is closed for half a day, 100 people may be paid for three hours for doing nothing. This could be £9 per hour $\times$ 3 $\times$ 100 = £2,700. If recovery of overheads were to be included in the calculations at (say) 300 per cent, the figure becomes 3 $\times$ £2,700 = £8,100. Do not trivialize the customer's complaint, resolve the problem.

To handle a customer complaint skilfully, the sales executive must try to view the matter as the customer sees it. This will help him reach an understanding of the significance that the customer attaches to the problem. Frequently, a major reason for the customer's annoyance is the feeling that if he doesn't shout nobody will pay any attention. Angry customers inevitably calm down once they feel that their problem is receiving honest and considerate attention.

It is in this area that customer service desks or the customer relations department can be useful. They should be staffed by helpful, courteous people professionally trained to deal with dissatisfied customers. Their role is to take the heat out of a complaint, trace the source of the problem, liaise with the sales executive or account manager and assemble a response to placate the irate customer.

Other sources of dissatisfaction are highlighted below in comments made to researchers investigating levels of customer satisfaction:

- They appear to be complacent, having had the account for twenty years, maybe assuming we wouldn't look elsewhere. I wouldn't have thought to look elsewhere but I have had problems with price, quality and delivery and the competitors appear to offer the same quality at a lower price.

- They have a high quality product, but we have had problems with order-to-order consistency. They react slowly to complaints, sometimes there is an internal communication problem.

- I guess their sales representatives still have to learn to sell, but one-sided declarations of intent aren't sufficient. The customer has to agree too!

Another complication is that a company might produce a product precisely to their customer's specifications and deliver on time, but the overall level of satisfaction may be coloured adversely by the aggressive invoicing policy adopted by their supplier's accounts department. Conversely, although a company might have a similar price for its product to that of a major competitor, it might receive a lower level of customer appreciation because although list prices were the same, the discount policy was fundamentally different and difficult to comprehend.

5.6 Service contracts

In certain industries the technical performance of the product is so fundamental to the level of user satisfaction that the sellers offer their customers a contract to cover engineering maintenance. This type of approach is common where the product is based on electrical and mechanical technology. Parts wear out and need to be adjusted or replaced; a contract for their repair or replacement provides the customer with a fixed price insurance against this eventuality. This practice is commonly adopted by suppliers of kitchen appliances (refrigerators, cookers and washing machines), music equipment, televisions, computers and some makes of new car.

In the computer industry there is an added level of sophistication. Separate service contracts are offered for technical support (advice and guidance to the users of the product) and engineering maintenance (the adjustment and repair of the electro-mechanical components). Response times for the latter are priced for an engineer being on-site within one hour and four hours from receiving a call for assistance.

5.7 Measuring customer satisfaction

Customer satisfaction surveys should play a crucial role in enabling an organization to change and develop with its customers. Only by conducting systematic market research will a company be able to evaluate how it is perceived by its customers and lapsed customers and what changes are required to meet these requirements more effectively. Clearly, the information required differs fundamentally between different customer groups. The customers (or clients) of a firm of solicitors may have very different levels of expectation from those of a supplier of board products or a supplier of photocopier machines.

In some markets, the nature of the 'customer' is very complex and it may be appropriate to consider subsidiaries, distribution channels and consultants as 'customers' for some aspects of the product/service offering, because of their influence over the end-customer's views.

Another very important factor to bear in mind regarding customer satisfaction surveys is that they must be conducted on a regular basis, for a number of key reasons:

- customers' requirements change,
- improvements in your service must be measured over time, and
- new competitors enter the marketplace.

The key initial task, therefore, is to devise a research-based programme which will result in the company delivering consistent levels of service meeting customer expectations.

The results shown in Table 5.2 emerged after an exhaustive screening

Table 5.2   *Key decision forming factors in choice of suppliers among customers of the following organisations (ranked in order of importance)*

Solicitors	Photocopiers	Board products
1. Specialist expertise	Reliability of equipment	Product quality
2. Competitive fees	Product quality	Reliability of delivery
3. Competence	Reliability of delivery	Board performance
4. Fast response	Ease of operation	Speed of delivery
5. Personal contact with partners	Operational life	Value for money

Source   IMR survey on customer satisfaction by David Jamieson (1989).

of factors mentioned spontaneously by respondents and also those factors prompted during the interview programme.

Table 5.3 shows the results of a customer satisfaction survey. By comparing the company to an 'ideal' rating it is possible to identify areas requiring attention to redress a less than acceptable performance.

In any customer satisfaction study, it is important to target the correct respondent. 'I know my customers' is the common cry, but in many supplier–customer relationships, the day-to-day contact person is not the key decision-maker or the individual in the organization who looks further than the use of a particular product or service, towards the strategic implications for the company. In fact it is a multi-dimensional problem and often several respondents in a customer's organization need to be contacted.

A number of examples taken from recent IMR customer satisfaction surveys demonstrate this point. A computer hardware manufacturer found its 'traditional customer', the data processing manager, to be happy with the range of support services provided. However, when the survey was widened to include the financial director, he was dissatisfied because he was seeking an overall reduction in costs for externally commissioned services.

A firm of solicitors traditionally 'sold' to company secretaries and their legal departments and although high levels of customer/client satisfaction manifested themselves from these sources, the key decision-makers were found to be the leading directors of client companies, whose requirements were fundamentally different and more commercial than those of their more legally oriented colleagues.

Table 5.3 *Overall performance and ideal ratings*

Ranking	Factor	Ideal rating	Company rating
1	Speed of response to emergency call-out	4.8	4.2
2	Reliability of equipment	4.8	4.3
3	Overall quality of repair and maintenance services	4.8	4.3
4	Product quality	4.7	4.4
5	Reliability of delivery	4.5	4.1
6	Technical knowledge of sales force	4.3	4.2
7	Ease of using	4.3	4.4
8	Standard of technical advisory services	4.3	4.3
9	Ease of making telephone enquiries	4.2	4.1
10	Understanding of customers' business	4.2	4.0
11	Training on use of products	4.1	3.9
12	Ease of ordering by telephone	4.0	4.3
13	Speed of delivery	3.9	4.1
14	Quantity discounts	3.8	3.5
15	Quality of sales and technical literature	3.8	4.0
16	Listed purchase price	3.6	3.6
17	Quality of sales presentation	3.6	4.0
18	Payment terms and credit facilities	3.6	3.9
19	Product range	3.5	4.1
20	Access to top management	3.4	3.7
21	Frequency of sales visits	3.1	3.6
22	Availability of rental/leasing packages	2.7	4.3

☐ Underperformance ○ Overperformance

Source Industrial Market Research Limited report by David Jamieson, 'Customer Satisfaction', 1989.

5.8 The Institute of Customer Care (IOCC)

Started in 1977, the IOCC[2] was formed to satisfy a growing demand from both the public and private sectors for a source of impartial expertise on caring for customers. The IOCC provides practical assistance for organizations designing, implementing or refining their customer care strategy. In return for an annual membership fee the IOCC will provide members with free informal consultancy, network contacts for advice on specific issues, will run workshops to help develop strategies and will offer participation in a certificate and award scheme.

Notes

1 Jamieson, D. (1989) *Customer Satisfaction.* Industrial Market Research Limited,
2 The IOCC is at St. John's House, Chapel Lane, Westcott, Surrey RH4 3PJ. Telephone (0306) 76210.

6

The personal characteristics needed for success in selling

6.1 Why good sales people are like gold dust

Selling advanced technology to large business corporations and government departments may not be universally regarded as a prestige profession, but it is certainly a step up from selling second-hand office furniture. It is also much better paid. There is the feeling that the technology should be quite capable of attracting a steady stream of purchasers because of its detailed product specification.

These sales people and account managers are absolutely essential to their employers because frequently the people buying their technology product are not experts. The purchasers require the benefits to be explained to them in the traditional way by someone who speaks the language of their business. To do this job properly requires a combination of communication skills, inter-personal skills, experience of a particular vertical market and a solid background in computers and technology. People possessing this particular combination of skills are rare, generally highly paid and rather selective as for which company they will work. Companies are usually pleased to have these sales people on their staff because the next best alternatives cause problems: the 'good front man' with a superficial knowledge of the key 'buzz words' frequently sells the customer something somewhat different from their requirements. The other alternative, the technician lured or pushed into the sales area, frequently gets bogged down in technical detail and fails to appreciate things from the customer's point of view, consequently failing to make a sale.

6.2 What the employers are looking for

One computer hardware company produced the document shown in Exhibit 6.1.

Exhibit 6.1   Salesperson profile required characteristics – Company 1

People required: Account Managers and Senior Account Managers

The level of sophistication of our product range and the stature of its marketplace dictates that the people we seek must possess a dimension of personality and level of intellect which can cope with complex, high value negotiations. It follows, therefore, that maturity is considered to be an essential ingredient of the Account Manager – maturity which can be equally well reflected by attitude and presence, as by age.

A successful record in sales is imperative, together with a very sound appreciation of the data processing environment from both a user's and a manufacturer's point of view. Therefore the most easily recognizable candidate will already have a successful track record in selling computer systems to medium-large organizations. However, very great consideration will be given to applicants' personal qualities – and a real achiever whose previous experience relates to, say, the computer services industry could well be acceptable. Irrespective of specific background, the executives required will be people who clearly 'make things happen' – as opposed to 'have things happen to them'.

Similarly, an outstanding applicant who can demonstrate personal qualities which compensate for a less than ideal level of experience in minicomputer or computer service sales could be very relevant – although the actual sales record to date will be a strong indication of suitability.

Our company provides an exciting and stimulating environment which would not necessarily suit people of limited imagination. The use of entrepreneurial qualities is positively encouraged by giving great freedom in decision-making to the Account Managers. The right people will therefore thrive in an environment of change and welcome significant responsibility – essentially, people who see challenge as an opportunity.

We seek executives who are already, or who can rapidly become, among the most competent computer sales executives in the industry. We will provide the training – if you can provide the personal qualities, background experience, and determination to 'be the best'.

Personal Qualities

1 Nature and personality which will allow harmonious integration into a highly professional, yet friendly, environment.

2 Self-motivation in terms of both thought and action. Ability to instigate the development of relevant skills and learning in parallel with formal training – essentially a self-developer.

3 Sufficient intellect to be able to absorb rapidly the product capability relative to competitive offerings and marketplace requirements.

4 Personality, presence and communicating skills consistent with carrying out effective demonstrations to significant clients.

5 A level of sales awareness which will enable detection of business opportunity in a medium-large company environment.

6 A level of sales and business maturity consistent with assessing the real level of opportunity which exists without any particular negotiation.

7 The necessary combination of innovation and lucidity which will result in the construction of well written, influential and informative proposals.

8 Sound organizational qualities. Essentially the ability both to 'keep several balls in the air' without losing control and sensibly to organize others who may be required to contribute to a structured sales negotiation.

9 A strong personality without being overbearing or outwardly aggressive. The kind of personality which commands the respect of others and which can withstand significant competitive 'thrust' during critical stages of any negotiation. A courageous individual.

10 Speed and clarity of thought consistent with skilfully handling face-to-face negotiations with significant clients. A level of confidence which 'demands' the business.

11 Overall, the presence, maturity and sales skills to represent the company in a manner which further enhances both its considerable reputation and its business within the marketplace.

Three other technology employers have produced requirements for sales executives shown in Exhibits 6.2, 6.3 and 6.4.

Exhibit 6.2 Sales person profile required characteristics – Company 2

Age group: 28–35 (maximum 40).

Industry Background: A minimum of 5 years' progressive career with an industry-recognized computer manufacturer.

Track record: A clear proven track record in minis, mainframes or bureaux.

Education: Good education with good achievement, though not necessarily with a degree.

Ambition: It is important to establish that the individual has ambition and development potential.

Marital status: The individual will ideally be married with children and financial responsibilities and commitments.

Financial aspects: Commitments as above; where the applicant's partner is working, the influence of this must be examined.

Personal characteristics: The applicant will be well dressed, clean, and with a bearing which inspires confidence and shows maturity and authority. The team feels that the individual should be able to demonstrate good conversational ability, be widely read, articulate, and convey maturity. A key quality is the ability to demonstrate self-reliance and have initiative. Finally, the ability to work in a team will be examined.

Outside interests: In connection with the point mentioned above concerning an applicant's partner working, the group would want to assess the impact of this on the individual. Other points in this area are involvement in sport, community affairs, local politics etc.

Exhibit 6.3　Sales person profile required characteristics – Company 3

1 Computer sales experience.
2 Age 28–35.
3 Minimum of 3 years' progressive career in a large company with a clear proven track record of success.
4 Good education – Degree, ACA, ACCA; business experience in manufacturing, banking, commercial fields, government or health care.
5 Outside interests through school, college and business life. Must have leadership qualities.
6 Features to look out for: appearance, manner, voice, self-expression, conversation, maturity, enthusiasm, courage, cheerfulness, temperament, persuasion and ambition.
7 Dominance: sociability, drive, compliance?
8 Marital status: family, financial responsibility?

Exhibit 6.4　Sales person profile required characteristics – Company 4 account manager – briefing for interviewer

Factors to be considered	Essential	Desirable
1 *Physical*		
Age	Maturity	28–35
Health	No physical disability	
Appearance	Businesslike; formal in dress; articulate in speech	Confident but pleasant
2 *Achievements*		
Education	Minimum 2 A levels or equivalent	Degree standard – perhaps science-based
Professional qualifications/ Training		Has dealt with large companies/government departments; membership of appropriate professional institute; Has had some formal training in selling skills
3 *General intelligence*	Ability to apply logical thought to technical and commercial problems	Has broad range of intelligence to be able to communicate with senior management

4 *Special aptitudes*	Able to compile detailed technical reports	Some experience in using computers
5 *Interests* • Work-related • Sport • Social	Should have a special interest that can be discussed	Ideally a competent sports player of some sort
6 *Disposition* Stability	Not more than two jobs in past five years	
Reliability		Self-reliant. Able to make decisions
Industry		Shows evidence of willingness to work
Perseverance	Can obtain new business regularly	Evidence of finishing tasks that have been started
Motivation factors: money status, financial security, competitiveness, recognition, promotion		
7 *Circumstances* Home		Married
Area; mobility	Willing to relocate	Lives in area; will accept long and irregular hours
Driving licence		Clean

6.3 The essential characteristics for success

There are a number of reasons why the essential characteristics required for success in selling are somewhat different from what employers are looking for. Remember the people recruiting were probably selling earlier in their careers, but have moved into management. They will have made this move for a number of reasons: either they (or their partner) became status-conscious, or they preferred the security of a higher basic salary, or they took promotion to earn more because there is a ceiling on the total earnings of sales executives, or quite simply they became 'burnt out'.

The four company specifications for a sales executive detailed above are remarkably consistent and indeed could equally apply to a description for a sales director of a medium-sized company or the managing director of a small company – particularly where the candidate has seven to ten years' successful experience. The question arises as to why these highly qualified and experienced people are prepared to work at the level of sales executive or account manager when clearly they could aspire to line management. The answer is that they believe that they can earn more. Consequently the number one characteristic for success in selling is perception.

6.3.1 Perception

Perception is the key characteristic for successful selling because it determines the choice of sales environment. The sales executive's perception of the business potential in a product market will have a major influence on which manufacturer's product he decides to sell and to which targeted group of customers. Make no mistake, the best sales people neither stay thirty years with one company nor change employer on a whim. They change employer according to their reading of the marketplace, where the potential lies and which products can best meet the requirements of the identified niche. The best sales people are also marketing experts in their specialist area. If they are successful their total earnings can be 300–400 per cent above the basic salary – the sales professional does not leave situations like that to chance.

One long-term friend, former colleague and now a client started in the computer industry twenty years ago selling printers and display units for mainframes. Recognizing the potential of powerful minicomputers he then moved to a company dealing in these. Over ten years he sold in succession three different companies' minicomputers. With the advent of the powerful thirty-two bit workstation, and seeing the potential of this new product, he moved to the company responsible for the innovation. That was nearly ten years ago. Since then he has changed employer twice more, each time moving to the company with the best product for the market where he wanted to sell. In twenty years he nearly always exceeded sales target, always sold to the same vertical market and rose from sales executive to regional general manager. The reason for this success was not luck or closing skills: it was a particularly lucid perception of the product market where he chose to sell.

6.3.2 Perseverance

Most selling jobs where income is directly related to achievements involve long working days, great self-discipline and considerable job-related pressure. Selling is certainly not regular hours, because appointments with some customers need to be scheduled early in the morning at 100 or more miles away from the sales person's home. Activities like writing reports, preparing quotations and tender documents, conferences and some training sessions take place during the evening and weekends.

Most sales executives cannot be closely supervised on a continuous basis because they are away from the office calling on customers and prospects. Consequently considerable self-discipline is required by the sales executive to maintain momentum and continuously to apply the skills and effort necessary to obtain the sales. Selling is a lot about keeping going when you are tired and disillusioned.

Selling jobs involve pressure, particularly where income is directly related to the value of orders obtained. Survival in a company depends on the ability to manage this consistently. Those that do acquire a 'celebrity status' because there is always that element of personal flair which cannot be taught in the best of sales training courses. The ability to handle this pressure is a key element of the perseverance required to sell successfully.

6.3.3 An effective communicator

Selling success is affected by the degree of skill used by the sales executive both in transmitting his own message and listening to the customer. Selling is a two-way process and listening to the customer will provide the sales person with information essential for bringing the meeting to a sales-oriented close. When sales executives listen, they hear the customer telling them either what they do or do not want. The latter is extremely useful because it helps to formulate successful proposals.

Although one generally thinks of a sales executive having a discussion with or making a short presentation to a business prospect, there are other methods of communication which must be mastered if the sales person is to be consistently successful. The most important of these is written communication. Generally the more complex and expensive the product, the greater the importance attached to written communication. Therefore people selling in this area need to learn the skills of report writing and document preparation.

In the computer industry, when a government department or an experienced private sector company wants to buy processing capability, it produces a requirement document. Sales executives in companies interested in the business are required to produce a proposal detailing how their company would approach the task of meeting the requirements. The document needs to offer a technical response in terms of computer power and data storage facilities offered, and a detailed explanation about how the computer will do the job in question (how the essential features of the proposed software relate to the client's problem). Here the sales executive needs to understand the other person's business and communicate that understanding in terms of the applications software proposed. The sales person also needs to be able to calculate the correct standard price of the equipment offered and then decide if this is appropriate in competitive terms and whether a special discount should be proffered. In the latter case a written justification will need to be prepared for approval by senior management before being included in the business proposal. Finally, the proposal must be checked for accuracy, ease of comprehension and whether it is a complete and thorough response to the prospective customer's stated requirement.

6.3.4 Social sensitivity

Sales executives need to be capable of sensitivity towards their prospects and yet where necessary possess a 'thick skin' in the face of criticism. Although this criticism is usually directed at the product or another part of the organization, the sales person is usually the receiver of the message and must be able to deal with it in an impersonal manner.

Social sensitivity has a number of aspects which include sympathy to a client's business difficulties, and empathy, which means an ability to view the situation from the customer's point of view. Furthermore, he or she must play a positive role in resolving any problem. Further extensions of this quality include what has been called 'first-person sensitivity', where the sales executive has developed the ability to perceive what the other person thinks about him or her with some degree of accuracy. Key indicators for this understanding are to be found in body language and comfortable eye contact. Leaning forward and obvious relaxation are positive indicators. The prospect leaning backwards with arms tightly folded and with a marked reluctance to hold a gaze should be negatively interpreted.

'Second person sensitivity' refers to the ability of a sales executive to understand what another person feels about a particular situation or problem. Taking this into account when making a statement or voicing an opinion can make an enormous difference to success in selling. Most people are more comfortable with others who share similar opinions: they are able to relax because they feel a mutual understanding. Positive decisions including the one to buy are more easily made in a relaxed environment. Those who aspire to a successful career in selling should focus on sensitivity and develop the intrinsic characteristics most people have in this area to a fine art.

7
Training

7.1 The importance of training

It is vital that companies train their sales staff because selling is a competitive business. Those sales executives with the greatest skills have the better chance of winning the sale. This means that the company obtains revenue from the goods and services produced by the other employees. 'No sale' means no revenue to cover the costs incurred by production, marketing, finance and personnel departments.

Employees in other departments can make mistakes which pass unnoticed or may be corrected later. When a sales executive makes a mistake, it may be crucial and the sale lost. In first class sport it is visible all the time. A skilled and experienced player makes one mistake and the match or event is lost. This is the context in which to view the training of sales staff. Unless they are highly skilled, well prepared and superbly supported by non-sales functions, the company is effectively puting in a B-team to represent them in the (first class) commercial marketplace.

7.1.1 Objectives

Effective training programmes require specific objectives which are then used to formulate the content of the course. The skills taught on the training programme should be tested during the course. The level of skill achieved should also be capable of precise measurement to provide feedback on the success of the training received. Therefore, where the objective is an increased level of sales per sales executive or higher rate of sales achieved per sales call, then these comparisons should be made. If this is not done, training budgets will be eaten into by pressure to redirect scarce resources elsewhere.

Other training objectives might include:

- Improved product knowledge.
- Improved applications knowledge of the products.

- Tutoring on pricing and discounting rules.
- Presentation skills.
- Territory and time management.
- Report and letter writing skills.
- Negotiating skills.
- Knowledge of competitors' products.

7.1.2 What training can achieve

Regular and effective training in key areas can help the sales force perform efficiently in the competitive marketplace of modern business. It can also attract a better class of sales executive to the firm who is keen to be more effective at selling and earn a higher level of sales commission. It can also have as a motivating influence and reduce the requirement for continuous close supervision of the sales staff for the area or district manager.

However, no amount of training will make a silk purse out of a sow's ear. Generally speaking a potential sales person should possess certain qualities before they are even remotely considered for a selling job. While these will vary according to the particular sales job under consideration, they should include:

- enthusiasm
- pleasant outgoing personality
- basic or above average educational skills
- some eloquence
- self-motivation
- interest in achieving success
- interest in an above average income
- confidence
- capacity for hard work
- discipline.

In short, effective training can realize the full potential of the sales force given there are no compensating demotivators such as over-authoritative sales management, shoddy products or other effective restrictions imposed on the sales morale.

7.1.3 Who should be trained

Switchboard operators
The first people to be trained and indeed some of the most important should be telephone switchboard operators. A prompt response, and

efficient routing and indeed re-routing or switching to a message reception service make a very good impression. Waiting for the 'phone to ring twenty times before being answered by an unhelpful person who puts you through to an unmanned extension is commercial suicide. In the re-privatized BT, electricity companies, gas companies, and the public sector, the caller can generally expect to waste several minutes before obtaining the appropriate extension. Insult is then added to injury by simultaneously blasting bad recordings of Scott Joplin down your ear. Switchboard operators should be well educated in how the company functions, be well paid and given management support for up-to-date information, and modern equipment. If a 'phone is not answered after five rings it should be routed immediately to a message handling facility.

Anyone potentially in customer contact
Secretaries (full-time and temporary), accounts clerks, programmers, engineers, personnel staff, warehouse staff, security staff, in fact anybody who might remotely answer a call from a customer should be trained. The required basic skills should include:

- Always have a pen and paper ready.
- Pick up the handset promptly (less than six rings).
- Be friendly and helpful to the caller.
- Sound positive.
- Tell those around you to be quiet while you speak.
- Present an acceptable office accent.
- Follow up the enquiry promptly.
- Offer to call the enquirer back if you cannot resolve the problem.

All people involved in selling should attend courses (including managers and directors) on company products, company procedures, presentation skills, markets for company products and indeed negotiation and selling skills.

7.1.4 Cost and time spent on training

Good effective training from experienced professional sales executives (as opposed to full-time instructors) is expensive and also involves the company sales force being 'off-territory' for the period of training. This involves an 'out-of-pocket' cost for the training, accommodation and subsistence of perhaps £1,000 per week plus the opportunity cost of a few lost sales. There is, however, no feasible alternative for the professional sales operation.

The following is a useful rule of thumb for the number of weeks a sales executive effectively has on territory:

Number of weeks in the year		52
Bank holidays	2	
Company holidays	4	
Training courses	2	
Conferences/leave	1	9
		———
Effective selling time		43 weeks

7.2 Types of training required

The syllabus for formal training should cover five main subject areas:

- Product knowledge.
- Applications for the product by target market.
- Selling skills.
- Presentation skills.
- Company policy and administrative procedures.

Furthermore, the training should be divided into three stages: new sales executive programme, continuous training up-dates and sales management training for managers and potential managers.

Product knowledge
The key to successful selling is detailed product knowledge. Answering a prospect's genuine questions in a clear and enthusiastic manner alleviates any need to stoop to 'high pressure' techniques of persuasion. A responsive attitude plus detailed knowledge is impressive and puts the sales person in a good light.

Basic product training for a computer sales executive might include for example:

1 Hardware description
- processors
- disks
- printers
- screens

2 Communications devices
- modems
- local area networks

- wide area networks
- satellite communications

3 Software
- operating systems
- utilities – wordprocessing
    - database management
    - links to other manufacturers' systems
    - conversion from old/competitors' computer program-
      ming languages

4 Systems configurations
- technical factors
- pricing factors

The course would include both classroom lectures and indeed
'hands-on' instruction in using the company's products.

Applications knowledge
This relates to the use of the company's products and services by specific
industries. A computer manufacturer might offer hardware and
software to its customers. The software could be specifically designed to
meet the needs of major users of computers. These would generally
include:

- banks and building societies
- market-making businesses
- manufacturing industry
- defence
- health service
- retail multiples

In order to achieve a measure of success the computer sales person will
need to know how a computer system can be used to increase efficiency
or save money in the specific market sector where they work. Someone
selling to the National Health Service would need to have an
understanding of how the following systems work and interconnect:

1 *Medical systems*
  Cytology
  Radiology
  Microbiology
  Histology
2 *Medical support systems*
  Supplies information systems
  Pharmacy
  Dispensary

3 *Community health, patient care and administration*
   Family Practitioner Committee
   Master patient index
   In-patient administration
   Out patients
   Waiting lists
   Attendance analysis
   Bed statistics
   Primary care
   Child care
   Community health index
   Blood transfusion
   Patients' private monies
4 *Transport and paramedical support*
   Ambulance scheduling
   Vehicle fleet maintenance
5 *Personnel, training and pay*
   Personnel records
   Direct input of pay
   Travel expenses
   Union returns
   Nurses' training
6 *General administration*
   Audit planning and controls
   Creditor payments
   Budgetary controls
   Capital projects monitoring
   Endowment ledger
   Office automation
   • wordprocessing
   • spreadsheets
   • financial modelling
   • data entry and validation
   • electronic mail
   • calculator
   • diary

Market knowledge
This relates to the customer in the marketplace, their profile or structure, who they buy from, what they buy, product and service combinations, any buyer cartels, key influencers on purchasing, buying cycles, any political or legal influences, economic influences (European Community) specific requirements and tendering policy.

For example the National Health Service in England comprises 192 authorities organized into fourteen regional health authorities. Three large companies sold computers to the medical market in the early and mid-1980s: ICL, DEC and McDonnell Douglas. Various regional authorities had their preferences for computer suppliers.

Selling skills
These are the essential skills for selling:

- understanding the planned selling process,
- negotiation and closing skills,
- territory management,
- prospect identification,
- report writing,
- product and service pricing,
- letter and proposal writing, and
- forecasting territory sales accurately.

Presentation skills
A selling presentation is where a sales executive stands in front of a group of prospective customers and professionally explains the available product or service. This may involve the use of slides, video, overheads etc., and at the end there will usually be a question and answer session.

The presentation will require organization in terms of choosing and equipping a venue, inviting the audience and preparing an interesting and informative programme.

The sales executive will need training on delivery skills such as language, humour, speed of delivery, use of jargon, use of quotations, anecdotes, question handling, coping with interruptions, maintaining interest and technical skills for handling the equipment, planning the length of the presentation and deciding whether a stenographer is required to produce a record of the key issues which can then be formulated in a report.

Administrative knowledge
This is an important area for the sales executive because comprehension reduces the amount of time spent on administration which is only a supporting activity to effective selling.

There are a number of aspects which should be included in the training programme, the first is an explanation of the structure of the company. This might include details of the manufacturing divisions, where they are and which makes certain company products. The names and job titles of key individuals is also important because those are people that the sales executive might need to contact in the course of selling. These will include:

- Name and location of sales managers and their responsibility by territory, product or customer.
- The various product marketing managers.
- Industry marketing managers.
- Staff managers for market research sales promotions, advertising, event sponsorship, exhibitions.
- Accountants.
- Customer service people.
- Engineers in delivery, installation and maintenance.

The second part of administrative training concerns form filling and the procedures involved in recording sales. In a computerized business this will involve completing a data entry form so that details of the sale may be conveniently logged into the system for transmission to the factory or warehouse, engineers, recording against the individual's area sales budget, creating a customer file and also the part of the accounts department that calculates sales commission.

7.3 Training for different selling skills

The emphasis in this book has been on major accounts and industrial selling where the sales executive has responsibility for a territory or customer base with a sales budget of £500,000 to perhaps £2 million pounds. There are, however, other types of selling job that require different skills and approach. Frequently people who succeed at these jobs move on to major accounts and a higher earning potential.

Telephone selling
The first aspect of 'tele-sales' training is diction or elocution – if the individual cannot speak in an acceptable business manner sales will be lost. 'You know', 'somefink' and calling strangers by their christian name are taboo. Simulated job training (preferably video-taped) is required to teach the professional approach.

Second, tele-sales people need training in product knowledge for the items that they are involved in selling. You cannot expect to sell without detailed knowledge of the product, what it can do, advantages over competing products and the price/discount and delivery terms.

Third, tele-sales people need to be able to construct a dialogue plan in much the same way as other sales executives anticipate objections and mark counter points on their call plan. This has the advantage of providing a ready response to a negative reply rather than having to struggle and invent a good reply 'on the spot'.

Retail selling

The essential difference between retail selling and other types is that some customers in their area need no selling, they know exactly what they want, in fact they come to buy. However, this still leaves plenty of opportunity for selling 'added value' benefits. For example, where someone particularly asks for a cheap product, the retail sales executive can politely suggest the customer might like to try a better product. Another example might be selling shoe polish, spare laces or shoe trees to go with a new pair of shoes, or a tie for a new shirt.

The unique skills associated with retail selling (particularly where there is no shop counter) lie in making the approach to the customer. Saying 'Can I help you?' frequently invites the immediately response of 'No!' and drives the browser out of the shop. Similarly ignoring the customer completely is not to be recommended. The skill required is to keep an unobtrusive eye on the customer until such a moment as it looks as though they would like to talk to a sales assistant. Then a polite approach may be made. At this time the person selling is 'weighing-up' the customer trying to calculate if they are a serious prospect for the product that they have been studying in some detail. Perhaps they should be looking to purchase a different product?

The third skill area is dealing with complaints and products that are returned. The stores should have a policy (hopefully in line with modern thinking about consumer rights). It is then a matter for the sales person to interpret this policy in terms of the current situation. Clearly, regular customers need to be accommodated where possible if they have a valid complaint. On the other hand the 'tricksters' need to be politely but firmly discouraged.

Export selling

Those sales executives engaged in exporting will require additional skills, in particular handling the documentation and payment procedures.

Payment procedures. The essential difficulty with export business lies in the fact that the customer is a resident of another sovereign state. If a problem arises, enforcing payment is consequently very difficult because the law in the country of destination may be rather different to UK law.

Similarly, exporters who have in the past obtained payment in advance have not always supplied a good product. Consequently sophisticated procedures have been developed to protect the interest of both exporter and importer. The most popular method is a 'confirmed irrevocable letter of credit' sent by the importer through his bank to the British bank who for a charge confirm that they will make payment to the exporter should the importer or importer's bank default on payment.

Export terms and conditions of sale. There is a whole series of terms dealing with export trade which the sales executive will need to learn. Table 7.1 explains those in common usage.

Table 7.1   *Export terms and conditions of sale*

Terms	Charges paid by the seller	Delivery takes place (at/on)	Property and risk pass (on)
Loco	Nil	'Where they are'	When contract is made
Ex works	Packing (unless the contract otherwise provides) and preparation for despatch	Seller's premises or other notified warehouse	Notification that goods are at buyer's disposal
FOR}C/F	Loading onto rail/truck[1]	Rail siding or depot	Delivery to carrier
FOT}C/P	Freight to port of shipment[2]	Factory gates	
FAS	Charges to and at port of shipment to 'alongside'	Under the ship's hooks	When vessel able and ready to load
FOB	Dock and port expenses and outward customs formalities[3]	When safely loaded	Over the ship's rail
C & F	Shipping expenses, documentation and ocean freight	On tender of B/L to buyer	Over the ship's rail
CIF (seller selects ship	Marine insurance	On tender of B/L to buyer	Over the ship's rail

Table 7.1 *(Continued)*

Terms	Charges paid by the seller	Delivery takes place (at/on)	Property and risk pass (on)
Ex ship	Inward port dues[4]	On discharge from ship	When vessel able and willing to discharge
Landed or Franco Quay	Cost of discharge, lighters to shore, and quay charges	On landing	Landing
Franco Warehouse	Dock handling charges and transport to warehouse[5]	At warehouse	Delivery to Warehouse
Franco Domicile	Duty, clearance and delivery to buyer's premises[6]	Buyer's premises	Delivery to buyer's premises

Notes
1 In the USA, this is called FOB point of origin.
2 In the USA, this is called FOB port of shipment. They do not include railhead to dock haulage or port or shipment costs.
3 This must not be confused with the US expression. Continental use of Fob includes all costs of loading, shipping and documentation leaving the buyer to pay only the freight and insurance charges, the seller taking out and paying for a 'freight forward' bill of loading. In the UK, loading costs are paid by the ship and are recovered in the freight paid by the buyer; but this is not the case in a tramp ship loading under a charter party. In such cases the seller must pay the cost of loading. There is considerable disagreement in the UK over the liability for port rates, dock dues and customs specification charges. The practice on this varies from port to port and trade to trade.
4 In the USA, this is called FOB port of destination.
5 This may or may not include customs duty and clearance charges. This should be made clear – e.g. Franco Warehouse duty paid.
6 If the right of disposal has been reserved, the property and (normally), the risks pass only when the seller's conditions have been fulfilled. Thus on C & F or CAD (cash against documents) the seller could be both at risk and uninsured.

Table 7.2 shows how the retail price might be constructed for a product once it has reached the country of destination.

Invoicing in foreign currency and foreign exchange procedures. In the past a large part of world trade was conducted in sterling and there was no need for British traders to operate in any other currency than sterling. The very fact that one party, whether buyer or seller, was operating in sterling, meant that the other party had to operate in what was for them

Table 7.2   *Calculating the extra costs*

Standard home market		£640
Modification to Danish standards	£80	
Development amortization	£10	
Costs of obtaining translations and		
Danish acceptance board approval	£10	£100
Overhead allocations		
Marketing	£10	
Administration/documentation	£30	
Advertising/promotion	£30	£70
Ex works		£810

	Packing for export	£50
FOT		£860
	Loading	£5
		£865
	Transport to docks	£10
	Insurance cover to docks	£5
FOR		£880
	Wharfage and porterage	£25
FOB		£905
	Port rates	£10
	Sea freight to Copenhagen	£35
	Landing charges in Copenhagen	£20
C & F		£970
	Marine insurance	£15
CIF		£985
	Unloading, handling and insurance	
	cover to warehouse	£15
Franco Domicile		£1,000

Source   A financial handbook for sales and marketing managers.

foreign currency. As a consequence those countries which are now Britain's keen competitors have always been accustomed to dealing in other currencies.

Sterling no longer enjoys the same predominance, and the British firm trading overseas should now be prepared to consider conducting

Table 7.3   *Building up to the retail price*

Total invoice value (Franco Copenhagen)	£1,000
plus VAT at 17½%	£175
	£1175
Price paid by Danish wholesaler	£1175
less VAT	£175
	£1,000
plus 20% mark-up	£200
	£1,200
plus 17½% VAT	£210
	£1410
Price paid by Danish Retailer	£1410
less VAT included	£210
	£1,200
plus 20% mark-up	£240
	£1,440
plus 17½% VAT	£252
	£1692
Price paid by final purchaser	£1692

Source   A financial handbook for sales and marketing managers.

business in foreign currency. A company which is prepared to quote prices and invoice in the buyer's currency can gain some advantage. In the first place it has a marketing attraction because it simplifies the whole transaction for the buyer, telling them immediately what is the true cost. Second, because most sales are made on credit terms there is a possible extra profit available by selling the expected currency receipts on the forward exchange market. Most of the principal currencies (US dollar, German mark, Japanese yen) are at a premium for future delivery which means that when sold forward those currencies realize more sterling. Operations in foreign currency present few problems, because the banks are fully equipped to provide all the information and facilities required. Indeed, the London foreign exchange market is the most efficient and comprehensive in the world. Any foreign currency received in payment of exports can be readily sold through the exporter's bank.

The forward market

When goods have been sold at a price expressed in a foreign currency and the credit terms have been agreed, payment will not be received until some future date. The prudent exporter will cover the risk of changes in the exchange rate by selling the expected currency forward. The exporter has only to inform the bank that a certain sum in a foreign currency will be received on such a date and establish with the bank a 'forward' contract. The bank will now quote a rate at which it will buy the currency on the date when the currency is received. The exporter thus knows exactly how much sterling will be received when the payment is made.

Example of a forward rate calculation:

Here an exporter has sold to Germany on 1 February goods on ninety day terms and asks the bank to arrange forward currency cover. The rate quoted by the bank will be calculated as follows. If on 1 February the bank's spot rate for Deutschmarks is 3.10 1/2 – 3.11 1/2, and one month forward is at a 3-2 Pf. premium and three months forward is 9-8 Pf premium, the exporter will be selling Deutschmarks to the bank, therefore the bank will apply its buying rate based on spot 3.1 1/2. (3.10 1/2 is the selling rate which is lower.)

The Deutschmark payment is expected in three months' time, so the bank will calculate on the basis of the three months forward rate 9-8 Pf. premium. The forward rate is at a premium, i.e. dearer in the future, so the rate will be lower and the premium deducted from the spot rate. But the bank is buying, so will wish to keep the rate as high as possible (i.e. wanting more Deutschmarks for the amount of sterling it provides) and will therefore deduct the smaller premium, i.e. 8 Pf. The forward rate would therefore be 3.11 1/2 less 0.08 = 3.03 1/2. If on the other hand the exporter is expecting payment sometime during March and wishes to cover forward, he/she will cover one month fixed, with an option for one further month. The one month fixed takes them to 1 March, to receive the benefit of the one month premium, but as payment may be received any time between the 1–31 March, benefit of any extra premium cannot be received for the second month, and so the rate will be: 3.03 1/2 less 0.02 = 3.01 1/2. This means that the bank will give the exporter one pound for every 3.01 1/2 Deutschmarks.

7.4 Training methods

Training methods may be conveniently divided between formal training which takes place in a classroom situation and 'on-the-job' or field training which is of an inherently practical nature.

7.4.1 Formal training

An important aspect of training often overlooked is making the training course interesting for the sales people attending. Poor instructers and a monotonous programme will greatly undermine the process of knowledge transfer. Consequently, great care should be given when designing the structure of the programme for the variety of training methods used and the active involvement of the delegates.

Lectures
Lectures are frequently the most effective proven core training method. However, they should not be too long; one and a half hours without a break is the longest practical time span. Just because the lecturer is talking does not mean that the delegates are still listening. Another important point regarding lectures is that this does not mean dictation from a manuscript or a prepared overhead. The emphasis should be on delegates obtaining a 'real-time' understanding of the information from listening and thinking, not writing. Hard copy of each lecture should be available at the end of each training module.

Video
Sales training is a pragmatic subject, the skills required and the errors that are made can be effectively demonstrated on video film. The best known films are in the Video Arts productions associated with John Cleese, Connie Booth, John Standing and Bernard Cribbins. Interspersing lectures with a short video adds a great deal to the variety and consequently the interest. They can be particularly effective for the first session after lunch when delegates are likely to be a little drowsy.

Role plays
Putting into practice the skills and knowledge gained from a lecture and demonstrated by a video is an important part of the learning process. In role play the people on the sales training course take turns at 'role playing' sales person and customer. The other members of the course either watch from a position behind the 'sales person' or from another room using a video monitor. At the end of the sequence the 'sales person's performance is discussed and evaluated by delegates and the instructor. Both good and bad aspects of the performance receive comment. An example of a role play evaluation form is shown in Figure 7.1.

Case studies
Sales cases studies are a useful method of helping sales people understand the strategic and planning aspects of selling. The people on

Participant . . . .   Call No . . . .
Instructor . . . .   Date . . . .

	Excellent	Good	Satisfac.	Weak	Unsatisfac.	Comment, where appropriate
PREPARATION						
Pre-Call Organisation						
Strategy and Objectives						
Lookahead						
Reference sells						
Aids						
TECHNIQUE						
Opening						
Use of Questions						
Listening						
Creating interest						
Establishing Need						
Seeking Agreement						
Selling Benefits						
Objection Handling						
Using Aids						
Future Plan						
Summary and Close						
Flexible/Resourceful						
Control						
Selling the Company						
PERSONAL						
Rapport						
Presence						
Level						
Expression						
Enthusiasm						
Self Confidence						
Instils Confidence						
Sensitivity						
Professionalism						
KNOWLEDGE						
Application						
Industry						
Products						
Competition						
Company Policy						

	Excellent	Good	+	Satisfactory	–	Weak	Unsatisfactory
OVERALL GRADE							

Further Comment
. . . .
. . . .

Figure 7.1 Call evaluation sheet

the training course are presented with a situation history usually including details of business problems that can be resolved using the company's products. However, additional difficulties are then introduced involving competitors' activity, customer personalities and budget restrictions. The course members are expected to produce a strategy for winning the sale including specific product proposals and countering effectively the competitive offering. At the end the actual historic result is usually explained by the instructor.

Quizzes and tests

Quizzes are a good way of getting the brain functioning at 9am. The people on the sales training course may have had less than their full complement of sleep if case study work or presentation preparation is expected to be undertaken outside normal working hours. The most popular quizzes are of a general knowledge and 'Trivial Pursuits' variety.

Tests are designed to provide positive feedback as to how well the delegates are absorbing the course information. It is better if they are written and act as a mini-examination.

7.4.2 Field training

Any idea of 'sitting-with-Fred' and learning by watching and listening is out of vogue in the 1990s. However, there is something to be said for spending a week with an experienced sales person who then acts as a supervisor for a period of three to twelve months. The supervisory role (remunerated by an additional salary allowance) takes the form of assistance with territory planning, prospect identification, organizing in-house demonstrations, producing direct mail letters, handling difficult prospects and producing selling proposals. The advantage of this approach is that it provides the young sales executive with access to experience without overburdening the sales manager. It also gives 'management' experience to senior sales staff in preparation for a more senior appointments later in their careers.

Job rotation

Certain types of job rotation can provide useful field training experience for sales people. Perhaps the most useful, is experience in marketing – providing the sales person with an insight into new product planning, consumer market measurement, planning the advertising and the promotional strategy, brand management and customer service.

Another popular form of job rotation is to use experienced sales people as training instructors for a period of one or two years. This provides the sales trainer with the opportunity to improve presentation skills and the chance to think carefully through all sorts of odd angles to selling that there is never time to do 'on territory'. It has been said that the best way to learn is to instruct. One very important point is that the instructor should be paid a salary comparable to what he or she would have earned on territory, that is including estimated commission payments. If this is not carried out only the 'also-rans' will be prepared to accept this sort of assignment.

7.5 Career planning

In the same way that a professional sales person plans the strategy for winning the sale against the competition, it is also wise for the sales person to have a career plan. Without a plan and preoccupied with short-term objectives it is easy to drift into a backwater or just be overtaken by more ambitious individuals.

Most companies have different grades of selling positions reflecting the experience required and size of sales budget to be achieved. They might be described as:

- Junior sales executive.
- Sales executive.
- Senior sales executive/major accounts.

The sales management responsibility usually operates at two levels, though different companies grade 'district', 'area' and 'region' in a different order. These might be

- District sales manager (managing five to ten sales people).
- Regional sales manager (managing three to seven districts).

The top selling job is usually director status and sometimes combines the responsibility for the marketing function as well.

7.5.1 Sales executive or sales manager

Clearly, one decision that needs to be made is how far into the management grades does the individual sales person wish to proceed (if they are able). After district sales manager (in the notation used) the scope for face-to-face selling is much reduced. The sales manager job is frequently 75 per cent sitting at a desk or round a table in a meeting. This is very different to spending 80 per cent of the time out of the office meeting customers, prospective customers and driving the length and breadth of the sales territory.

As the sales manager's job is different to that of the sales executive, so are the skills required. The most successful sales person does not always make the best manager. Some people have to accept that their skills lie in selling and not management. If this is the case then the difficulty should be acknowledged and accepted as quickly as possible. In companies where selling success is appropriately rewarded there should not be a significant earnings difference between a very successful sales person and a moderately successful district manager.

7.5.2 Selling or marketing?

Many young sales executives ponder if they should gain formal marketing experience during their career. The answer is a clear and emphatic yes for two reasons: first the knowledge and experience gained will prove very useful in selling jobs. Second, it opens up another career path for the future.

Most people who work in selling work very hard indeed, the pressure is constant if sales budgets (or quotas) are to be achieved. Consequently there is relatively little time for 'brainstorming' sessions, detailed new product planning, correcting a product brochure that has technical errors and measuring the exact size of the markets for consumer products. Experience in these areas is essential for senior management positions. It can only be obtained usually by a secondment to a marketing department.

Different companies organize the marketing department in different ways, but the major functions are usually:

- market development planning,
- new product development,
- brand/product management,
- market and consumer research,
- advertising and promotion,
- PR, and
- customer relations.

7.5.3 Second careers

Many companies regard selling as a young person's job. The sales executive profiles presented in chapter 6 frequently specified that the age be between 28- and 35-years-old, sometimes up to 40. Consequently the question arises as what to do for the next twenty or twenty-five years? There are a number of alternatives, the most popular are consultancy, training, recruitment and to start a business in a completely different field.

Consultancy

Many sales executives and managers 'retire' from corporate employment in their late 30s or early 40s. They then use their specialist knowledge gained over fifteen or twenty years to advise their former employers and competitors on a part-time basis. The advantages to the clients is that they have an expert when they need them. This avoids the cost of a full-time salary and fitting another senior person into the management structure. From the sales person's point of view it provides an opportunity to 'change down a gear' while maintaining an acceptable income.

Training

Training is another popular area that is frequently combined with lecturing at colleges and polytechnics where the Chartered Institute of Marketing courses are offered.

Many companies have decided against employing their own staff trainers or taking experienced sales people 'off territory' for a spell to instruct new recruits and less experienced sales people. Using outsiders is both practical and cost effective.

Recruitment

There is a continuous shortage of good sales people in almost every industry. The skills required are specialized and take several years to develop, then after ten or fifteen years the person is either promoted into senior management or pursues an alternative career. Many of those who are successful are so busy working to maintain that success that they fail to spot job opportunities with other companies.

From the employer's point of view screening would-be applicants is a major overhead. Personnel departments are generally not qualified to act as more than a post box and sales managers can struggle to sort through hundreds of direct applicants.

Employing an experienced recruiter to deal with the response solves a major time problem and also provides an element of confidentiality to the prospective employer. The recruiter places the advertisement, handles the response, conducts the interviews and presents the client with a short list of the best half a dozen candidates.

Starting a new business

Many former sales people and sales managers start their own business after fifteen or twenty years as a salaried executive. Many do very well, as the skills required to run a small business are very similar to those necessary to manage a sales territory. The techniques for selling, marketing, administration, pricing, producing reports, communicating and persuading people to work with you are very much what they were when working for their employers for all those years.

8
Essential selling skills

Together with certain key personal characteristics essential for success in selling are a number of basic skills that must be thoroughly learnt and tested. These skills can be acquired by mastering the following:

- Knowledge about the product, the market, the company.
- Technique: the method and procedure for selling effectively.
- Practice at the application of the sales techniques.
- Feedback from an acknowledged expert in selling.

In this chapter, the part played by technique will be explored in considerable detail. The approach taken focuses on five clear objectives that provide the structure to a single sales interview or indeed a whole campaign. The sales executive needs to learn thoroughly and to understand these key objectives. Once this has been done, the executive needs to learn to spot the particular cues for applying the appropriate selling skill. These skills have been carefully formulated for the achievement of each objective in the selling sequence that ends with making the sale.

8.1 Selling objectives

These may be conveniently examined in the form of a pyramid: starting from the base, it is necessary to:

Rapport (in the context of selling) is essentially a meeting of the minds on one or two marginal topics such as sport, a hobby, a news event, the local traffic conditions or the weather.

Without this firm base on which to build, no sale is secure. With rapport alone, however, there is still no sale, so the next block of our pyramid is:

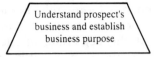

This means understanding the prospect's job (perhaps not the full description, but the important aspects), the prospect's objectives both official (i.e. a level of computerization, say a fixed asset register) and unofficial (no risk of failure) and directing the sales message towards their achievement. The third objective is to:

After discovering what the prospect needs to make the business more effective and profitable, we now have to:

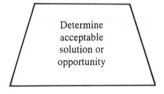

Once the solution has been determined, the next step is to get agreement from your prospect and:

There is one vital objective missing. At all stages in the sales cycle, the sales executive has to handle the inevitable objections which are based on misunderstanding, scepticism or doubt. We will examine later in the chapter why these are there, what causes them and how they should be handled if the sale is to be achieved.

8.2 Cues for using selling skills

The sales executive who has thoroughly mastered the skills of the profession will be alert to certain cues both stated and implied by the prospective customer. At the beginning of the discussion the sales person may gather that the prospect is a little uncertain why they are talking. The sales executive is trying to establish rapport, but if the prospect is clearly impatient, move rapidly onto the second objective. This need not mean that the interview has been inexpertly arranged: people can be very busy, and at the start of the discussion they may need to be reminded of what has previously been agreed.

For example they might say:

- I don't know much about your company.
- Why did you fix this meeting?
- What do you think you can do for me that my existing supplier cannot?
- How can I help you? I am very busy.
- What do you want to accomplish today?
- I am all ears.

These are examples of the cue of uncertain purpose, which match up against the sales person's objective to establish what is the business purpose of the person sitting on the other side of the desk.

As the discussion proceeds, it is quite likely that the prospect may make statements that indicate an unclear need, or may express uncertain attitudes:

- I am not sure that we can use this product of yours.
- I am told that our present supplier is as good as anybody else in the market.
- I do not think that I fully understand why your product is better for us.
- I have known XYZ Ltd. for five years; they always seem very reliable . . .

The objective at this stage is to discover a business need that is not being adequately fulfilled by an existing supplier, or perhaps one not being fulfilled at all. When a clear need is identified then the objective is to 'determine an acceptable solution'. This is a way of satisfying the prospect's needs in a way which uses your company's products. The sort of cues to look out for here are:

- Ah, yes, that seems to be a good idea.
- That would save money over the year.

- Regular delivery is important.
- I have always been unhappy about . . .
- I should be grateful if you could do . . . for me.

In a smooth and progressive sales dialogue without the difficulty of overcoming objections, which will be examined later, the sales executive needs to spot the moment when the prospect has accepted the solution proposed but needs to be 'closed'. Examples might be:

- Your plan makes a lot of sense, but I am afraid it is a bit too expensive.
- I like the way you have approached the problem.
- I think what you are suggesting is feasible.
- I can see what you mean about delay causing problems later in the year.
- There's no point in waiting until . . .

In summary, there are four types of cue to look out for in a straightforward sales dialogue. They are expressions of: uncertain purpose, unclear need, a clear need, and of a feeling that the solution that has been proposed is acceptable. The next section focuses on the skills that should be used to achieve the objectives on hearing the cues. (See Table 8.1.)

Table 8.1 *Summary of cues and sales objectives*

Cue	Objective
Reluctance to get straight down to business	Establish rapport
Uncertain purpose	Establish business purpose
Unclear needs/attitudes probe – closed probe	Explore needs/attitudes
Clear need	Determine acceptable solution
Accepted general solution	Commit to action plan

8.3 Selling skills

Various selling skills are used to achieve specific objectives in the structured sales plan as the sales executive picks up on the cues from the customer. At the beginning of the sales interview, it is likely that the prospect will show no immediate desire to get down to business. This is the cue for 'sensitive conversation' to establish rapport. The key to this conversation may be in the various paraphernalia in the prospect's office (photographs of some past sporting achievement, contemporary prints, holiday souvenirs, tribal masks or just a collection of briar pipes). The knack is to find the prospect's favourite subject and encourage conversation about it for a few minutes while you, the sales executive, listen thoughtfully.

After a few minutes, the prospect will become aware of the fact that this is not the main purpose of the meeting and will say something indicating some uncertainty about the purpose of the meeting. The sales objective at this second stage is to establish in your mind a clear understanding of the prospect's business purpose. The skill to be used is to make a statement of general benefit to the prospect. This can be done in two ways:

1 *Refer to a probable need*
- In our last conversation you suggested . . .
- Other companies in a similar position . . .
- Based on your proposed initiative in . . .
- From what I know about . . .

2 *Tell how you can help*
- We have a number of products that can . . .
- We are specialists in . . .
- With a number of other clients we have . . .
- We differ from most of our competitors in that . . .

The advantage of and the main reason for the general benefit statement is that it follows the prospect's train of thought, and, it is to be hoped, provides a smooth transition to the business topic. It also locates the sales executive in the position of an empathetic problem-solver, ready to bring a range of products and years of experience to the assistance of the prospect. It also serves to focus on your company's particular sphere of competence.

Why do you have general benefit statements

- They follow the customer's train of thought.
- They give a reason for the customer to talk to you.
- They provide a transition to a business topic.
- They identify your company's particular competence.
- They demonstrate credibility.
- They zero in on the most significant perceived needs.
- They focus on improvement opportunities.
- They define your business in beneficial language.
- They position you as a problem-solver.
- They illustrate empathy.

- They position the firm's history and your personal experience as a benefit.
- They signify intent.
- They open the door.

The next stage in the interview strategy is to explore the prospect's needs and attitudes. This is best approached by the technique of 'probing', which is asking specific questions designed to encourage the other person to tell what he thinks about certain aspects of his/her work.

There are two sorts of probes: 'open', used to clarify a point, e.g. 'To what do you attribute the recent decrease in your profitability?', and 'closed'. Closed probes are used only to confirm a detail, such as 'Are you saying that only vehicles converted to lead-free petrol will be considered?'

Open probes are generally more efficient than closed probes for getting information because they are designed to encourage the respondent to explain something in detail. The closed probe, on the other hand, can generally be answered with 'yes' or 'no', and the sales executive has to be ready with another question.

Once clear needs start to emerge, the objective is to determine an acceptable solution using the company's products or services. The skill for doing this is to propose a general solution. This is deliberately a little vague, because the sales executive still has to elicit the prospect's views on the finer details. The way to do this is by:

- Restating the need, e.g. 'I understand you will require delivery by 1 April?'
- Presenting options, e.g. 'Were you thinking of the booted version or the hatch-back?'
- Expanding on the benefits, e.g. 'Of course, if you order twenty or more within a three-month period, we pay for the delivery and insurance. This will reduce the effective cost by £179 per vehicle.'

It is important to appreciate that proposing is the first overt selling skill that has been examined in this structured interview process. It needs to be handled with considerable tact. A good sale is a collaboration between the sales person and the customer. Both sales executive and buyer should feel the essence of a mutually beneficial partnership. When something of more than token value is bought, the customer should be aware of entering into a business relationship with the seller. This relationship, if based on trust, mutual respect and joint commitment, can not only result in a high level of customer satisfaction, but the prospect of additional sales in the future.

The fifth skill in the structured interview is triggered by a statement to the effect that the prospect has accepted the proposed solution to the as yet unfulfilled need. The skill is 'recommendation'. The objective is to commit the customer to a plan of action. The cue statement may be one of these:

- That seems to be the answer.
- I like the sound of that idea.
- I think we have covered all the key issues.
- That should do the job.

The skill of recommending also comes in three parts:

- Support the acceptance. 'I think that is a good choice, Mr Johnson.'
- Make suggestions. 'Might I suggest that you take the conversion to lead-free petrol option at no extra charge.'
- Expand with benefits. 'With the average price of lead-free petrol at 18p per gallon cheaper than 4-star leaded for twenty cars, it could save your company more than £6,000 per year.'

See Table 8.2 for a summary of the above points.

Table 8.2   *Summary of cues, skills and sales objectives*

Cue	Skill	Objective
Reluctance to get straight down to business	Sensitive conversation	Establish rapport
Uncertain purpose	State general benefit • refer to probable need • tell how you can help	Establish business purpose
Unclear needs/ attitudes	Probe: • open probe • closed probe	Explore needs/ attitudes
Clear need	Propose general solution: • restate need(s) • present options • expand with benefits	Determine acceptable solution
Accepted general solution	Recommend: • support acceptance • make suggestions • expand with benefits • overcome objections	Commit to action plan

8.4 Useful remarks

At almost any time during the structured sales interview the prospective customer can make what may be called 'a useful remark'. It might be something like:

- I have had some excellent service from your company in the past.
- I am not looking for a one-off deal, but a more permanent business relationship.
- I have been comparing prices, and considering the additional features of your product, you really are very competitive.

This is an opportunity to progress the dialogue usefully and increase the chances of a sale. It should not be wasted. The objective is to build a personal relationship between the prospect and the sales person. The skill involved is to 'support' the useful remark by agreement, paraphrasing what the prospect has said and then expanding on the useful remark (see Table 8.3).

Table 8.3

Cue	Skill	Objective
Useful remark	Support • agree • paraphrase • expand	Build a personal relationship

Examples of words and phrases for supporting a useful remark

Agreement
- 'I am glad that you feel . . .'
- 'Other customers find . . .'
- Smile encouragingly.
- Nod, sage-like, with eye contact.
- 'Absolutely.'
- 'Right.'

Paraphrase

- 'If I understand correctly, you are saying . . .'
- 'The point is, then, . . .'
- 'Then you are saying that if . . .'
- 'In other words . . .'

Expansion

- 'One of the things we do find is . . .'
- 'Not only that, but also . . .'
- 'Moreover . . .'
- 'Taking this one step further, . . .'
- 'That reminds me of another . . .'
- Enthusiasm.

8.5 Overcoming objections

The skills explained so far have concentrated on allowing the sales executive to establish a good working relationship with the prospect, helping with identification of the prospect's needs and then getting agreement of specific requirements. Alternatives, and how their benefits might satisfy the prospect's requirements, have also been considered. However, at any moment within the structured interview, objections may be raised. These must be dealt with in a proficient manner, because they are neither criticism of the sales executive or the company's products, nor are they an indication of personal obstinacy. For the most part objections are genuine reservations about the product or service being offered. A part of the sales person's message has not been taken on board. If the sale is to progress, the objections must be skilfully overcome.

Objections may be of three distinct types: misunderstandings, scepticism, or the identification of a perceived drawback. Some typical objections might be the following.

Misunderstandings

- I thought we would need a smaller version of this.
- We cannot spare two people for two months to install this.
- You can not offer a systems approach.

Scepticism

- How is this compatible with our existing system?
- I don't believe we can get a payback within a year.
- Have you ever worked in our industry before?

Drawbacks

- Your costs are higher than your competitors'.
- I don't want to wait six months for delivery.
- It wouldn't make sense to use you because you don't have a local representative.

The skills needed for dealing with these objections are shown in Table 8.4.

Table 8.4

Cue	Skill
Misunderstanding	Explaining
Scepticism	Proving
Drawback	Offsetting

For each skill there are steps to follow for the correct application of the skill (see Table 8.5).

Table 8.5

Cue	Skill	Steps to follow
Misunderstanding	Explaining	Provide correct information Expand with benefits
Scepticism	Proving	Offer proof Expand with benefits
Drawback	Offsetting	Re-focus on all considerations Compare pros and cons Draw conclusions

Examples of words and phrases for explaining

Provide the correct information

- In fact the model 1600cc economy engine will give an average mpg of 27 in town and 42 on a run at an average speed of 60mph.
- Included in the fees are all costs for the preparation of course material and the hire of the video recorder.

Expand with benefits

- The effect of this will be to reduce your petrol costs by 8 per cent over the fleet you are running at the moment.
- So in fact the quotation is within your budget. There are no hidden extras to worry about.

Examples of words and phrases for proving

Offer proof

- Actually, I have some figures here published by the Motor Agents Association/the AA/the CBI/the Inland Revenue.
- Let us review the total costs of the last training course that we ran for you . . .

Examples of words and phrases for offsetting

Refocusing on all considerations

- Let's look at the total situation.
- I think it would be helpful to look at all the issues affecting this decision.
- As I understand it, what you really want to accomplish . . .
- Your objective in all this is to . . .
- Putting this whole thing in perspective, . . .

Compare pros and cons

- On the one hand . . . on the other hand.
- While it's true that . . . what you gain from this is . . .
- You would have to . . . but in the end you would . . .
- The net return on this investment is . . .

Draw conclusions

- It seems to me that . . .
- The positives seem to outweigh . . .
- This seems to net out in favour of . . .
- Although I see your point of view, I would strongly suggest . . .
- That problem is pretty small compared to the advantages of . . .
- Yes, other offers are less expensive, but we can start immediately, and time does seem to be critical . . .

8.6 Obtaining prompt acceptance

It is worth paying particular attention to the final stage of committing to an appropriate action plan in the structured interview. Despite having successfully negotiated so far, it is still possible for the inexperienced or untrained sales executive to walk away from the meeting with nothing tangible.

Given a choice of doing something now or postponing action, most people will take the latter. Making decisions is stressful – what if the wrong decision is taken? The consequences might be terrible! So the sales executive needs a skill to overcome the prospect's subconscious preference for delaying a decision without resorting to undue pressure. Remember this is a consultative sell, and maintaining and building a relationship which results in the prospect wanting to buy is a more powerful strategy than the momentary pressure from a coercive sales tactic.

As before, there are customer cues to look for which relate to the appropriate skill (see Table 8.6).

Table 8.6

Cue	Skill	Steps to follow
Acceptance	Close	Support acceptance Request commitment
Delay	Project	State disadvantages of delay State advantages of proceeding immediately

Remember that at some point in the sales conversation, the customer will give some cue that he or she accepts your recommendation. This acceptance cue not only means that the objective of determining the acceptance solution has been attained, but also that the prospect is ready to move towards a commitment. This means that they are prepared to agree to some action leading towards the implementation of the solution that has been worked out together. Closing is not just taking an order: it requires agreement to some action from the other party. This action might be a visit to a reference customer, agreement to a survey starting, the transfer of paper records to magnetic media or the production of a press release to announce the contract. The act of doing something positive will help reinforce the idea that the course of action decided on is the best one.

Part Three   Sales Channels

9
Selecting the sales channel

The sales channel is the route taken by goods through the selling process. It starts with the manufacturer or supplier and goes right through to the purchase by the ultimate user or consumer.

Selecting the most appropriate sales channel for a product or service is extremely important for three reasons. First, the channel must be capable of taking the goods to the marketplace; second, the prospective customer must feel comfortable with the method, style, and choice of the place where the sale is made. Third, the costs of effecting the ultimate sale should be based on sound commercial judgement.

However, there are other influences affecting the chosen channel which are largely outside the control of an individual company. Some of these are due to the distribution infrastructure which can occur where wholesalers achieve a position of power and influence over an extended period of time. Another factor is convention: many people would be wary of purchasing expensive jewellery from a street vendor or door-to-door sales person, for example. This would not be anxiety about value or price so much as concern about the history of the items on offer.

9.1 Marketing strategy and channel selection

Sales channel selection is a sub-set of the business sales and marketing strategy. The strategy will comprise a plan and methodology for achieving the company's goals or objectives. Thus if a company objective calls for a 60 per cent share of a particular market, the sales channels selected will generally be very different and probably far greater in number than if the target were a 0.5 per cent market share. In the first instance the targeted objective will only be achieved by massive market exposure. In the latter case a very selective market skimming exercise might well achieve the sales objective in terms of quantity, at the same time fulfilling highly profitable financial objectives.

On other occasions, manufacturers may have to compromise between the sales channels they would prefer and those that are available. Any market or industry will tend to have a number of established intermediaries and a new entrant may have to use the existing structure unless it has the capital and business volume to develop its own vertical markets. Indeed, if it cannot do the latter, the prospective entrant may possibly have to work very hard to persuade the established structure to take yet another product in an already well-filled line.

9.2 Consumer characteristics and the choice of sales channels

It has already been stated that the channels selected must be acceptable to the purchasing public. It is now appropriate to be more specific. Market segmentation principles should be applied to the question of sales channels selection. The objective is to make available the company's products and/or services to the required numbers of targeted groups of prospective purchasers. The logic is quite clear: different groups will have different preferences and habits regarding their preferred purchasing methodology. Consider the following examples.

Example A
Someone living in a rural district twenty miles from a large town or hypermarket and without private transport might well purchase a considerable range of items from mail order catalogues. Thus, if a geographical segmentation study shows that a significant percentage of targeted consumers are rurally based and without their own means of transport, i.e. pensioners, and purchase patterns suggest mail order catalogues have high levels of sales, then they should be one of the channels used.

Example B
A connoisseur pipe smoker with a preference for some of the more unusual Dunhill or US brands will never be able to obtain supplies from a corner shop. The wholesalers who supply the corner shop do not stock these exclusive brands. They are only available from specialist tobaconnists, of which there are possibly seven or eight in the Central London W1 postal district: Desmond Sautter of Mount Street, Astleys in Jermyn Street, Davidoff on the corner of Jermyn Street and St. James's Street, the Snuff Box in Charing Cross Road, and perhaps two or three others. Regional towns and cities will tend to have one specialist

supplier. The other alternative is to open a direct account with the tobacco company (if they will supply you).

The characteristics of the consumer public have a major influence on the choice of sales channel. Where the market is large and widely dispersed, or if consumers purchase a product in small quantities, long channels will be used because of the relatively high unit cost of servicing low value orders. In these circumstances it is likely that each company's product will be sold from the same retail outlet as their competitors'. The product will be supplied to the retailer through the wholesaler or distributor network because the manufacturer finds it prohibitively expensive to service small value accounts. The manufacturer consequently refuses to supply a retailer direct unless the order has a minimum value of perhaps £500.

This presents the retailer with a cash flow problem, a stock volume problem and perhaps a shelf-life problem if the products deteriorate before they have been sold. The retailer could of course attempt to persuade consumers to purchase these products in quantity. This, however, generally requires the inducement of a price discount and retail margins are such that the affordable discount may not seem sufficiently attractive for the consumers to change their purchasing habits. Consequently one manufacturer may decide to have two or more complementary sales channels according to the value of the customer's order.

9.3 Sales channel costs

Generally speaking the shortest channels are the most expensive for the manufacturer in terms of an overhead cost that is borne before the calculation of the net profit. This is where a sales force is used to sell the product directly to the end user in the case of capital goods and to a national or regional retail chain for consumer goods.

Example A – short channel

	£'000	£'000
Total sales revenue		10,500
Direct costs		
Raw materials	3,700	
Direct labour	1,050	
Direct production expenses	1,900	
	6,650	

Operating costs
Marketing	700	
Distribution	150	
Selling	1,050	
Administration	200	2,100	8,750

Net profit before Corporation Tax   1,750 (16.7%)

Example B – longer channel

	£'000	£'000
Sales revenue (to distributors)		8,950
Direct costs	6,650	

Operating costs
Marketing	300	
Administration	50	
Selling	50	400	7,050

Net profit before Corporation Tax   1,900 (18.1%)

In the example, the manufacturer accepts a lower selling price by using a distributor who in turn expects to make a profit, but the distributor is also responsible for the majority of the costs associated with distribution, selling and marketing. However, the manufacturer has the advantage of a smaller investment in the sales channel and may obtain payment sooner where the distributor is contracted to payment within a fixed period.

9.4 The product

Generally, low cost, low technology products are better suited to longer channels where the overheads of each organization in the channel can be allocated over many manufacturers' products. This also enhances the position of each organization in the market because they are able to provide a wide range of complementary products to cater for a similarly wide range of purchase requirements. This is made possible because the sales people at each level in the channel will require only a general, rather than specific knowledge of each supplier's product. This is sufficient because the products are by definition neither complicated to operate nor difficult to understand.

Multiple retailers attempting to sell Amstrad microcomputers using basic grade retail staff have experienced many problems. The product provides neither the margin nor the volume to employ a specialist sales person and a knowledge of the standard range of stationery products is not relevant to computers, however low in price they may be. There are many amusing stories told by those with a knowledge of computers about the attempts of the uninformed to sell to the ignorant in this retail environment.

Desk-top computers are an interesting example of the development of new sales channels in response to changes in the price of technology. The modern desk-top computer built to IBM 286 specification and retailing for well under £5,000 has more power and storage space than equipment sold for £100,000 ten years ago. A net present value calculation of £100,000 in 1979 compared with £5,000 in 1989 provides the explanation. A product selling at £5,000 on an average margin of 27.5 per cent cannot support the overheads of a large organization without high-volume sales. These high-volume sales are not only infrequent, but where they do arise, the seller is under great pressure to discount because the buyer is aware of the heavy competition between only slightly differentiated products.

This is the reason why in 1982 and 1983 the companies making and assembling small computers decided to sell them through third-party organizations. IBM Approved Agent and ICL Traderpoint are examples of this response.

9.5 The number of intermediaries in the channel

Another consideration for companies is the appropriate number of middlemen to use at each stage in the channel level. Three broad strategies are possible. *Intensive distribution* is where the product is stocked in as many outlets as possible. This is particularly the case with convenience, fast-moving consumer goods (fmcg). Consider for a moment the number of retail outlets in any high street where Coca-Cola or Cadbury's chocolate may be purchased (supermarkets, off-licences, cinemas, tobacconist/newsagents, cafe bars, sandwich bars and some bakery shops).

Exclusive distribution is where the number of intermediaries at any stage in the channel structure is deliberately limited. In the UK, care must be taken not to do this on the basis of exclusive geographical territories, because this conflicts with the Restrictive Trade Practises Act (1976). Exclusive distribution often goes with the requirement not to carry competing lines for that product market sector. This restriction frequently applies to new cars, some types of household electrical goods (Currys and Dixons often have UK exclusivity to products) and exclusive tailoring – men's Chester Barrie suits for example. Exclusive distribution channels have the effect of enhancing a quality product's image, making higher profit margins possible.

Selective distribution is a half-way-house between intensive and exclusive distribution. The manufacturer has the dual advantage of control over a manageable number of outlets and at the same time the ability to maintain a substantial market-place presence, generally at a lower cost than with intensive distribution channels.

9.6 Other influences on sales channel design

There are also a number of what might be called secondary influences on the structure of sales channels. These are the competition, the company itself and the influence of what might be called the economic and legal environment.

Particularly in the retail market, sales channel design is strongly influenced by the competition. There are many shops that see a physical proximity to Marks & Spencer as being an important trading factor: customers going to shop in Marks & Spencer may well see something of interest in their shop window as they walk past. Indeed, Marks & Spencer have capitalized on this fact and have a separate property division whose job is to buy up enough high street frontage for their own requirements and for other stores on either side. These sites are then sold at a profit to other retailers wishing to locate in adjacent positions.

In other industries the exact opposite is the case, where a company might choose a completely different sales channel to differentiate it from the competition or because it cannot compete on the competitor's terms. Examples of this are the various mail order catalogues of which Argos seems to be the best established.

The company's characteristics also play a significant part in the range of sales channels available to it. For example, the company's size determines which markets it may approach and its ability to recruit the appropriate distributors. The width of the product mix also exerts an influence. The wider the mix (that is, the more products a company has to offer consumers), the greater the company's ability to deal directly with customers particularly in the fmcg market-place. Companies in the industrial market-place, however, are more likely to go direct or through a single intermediary level as they almost certainly have fewer customers than their counterparts selling in the retail market-place.

The business environment generally exerts two types of influence on a company's choice of sales channel. The law in many countries is designed to prevent the establishment of monopolies. A company that has sole manufacturing rights might be prevented from also buying a large distribution network. Lord Young's recent investigation into the 'tied house' position of the five national UK brewing companies is an example of concern in this area of monopoly. Similarly, a foreign country may be restricted from owning more than a minority shareholding in a domestic company. Second, the prevailing economic climate may have some effect. When conditions are depressed, producers may approach the question of sales channels and distribution in the most economical manner consistent with achieving their objectives. When the economy is stronger, strategies involving a greater investment may be selected.

9.7 The functions of the sales channels

In many ways the sales channel performs for fast-moving consumer goods the functions of a sales person in the capital goods and industrial market-places. The reason is that the nature of the product, its relatively low purchase price and its mass market appeal make the channel a more practical method of distribution. Viewing the sales channel in this way, it should be easy to understand the contribution it can make towards the flow of information, market research, data concerning product design and sales promotions, as well as the actual physical distribution and display of the merchandise.

It can also be helpful to view the sales channel in the form of several other flows: the physical flow describes the movement of products from manufacturer to wholesaler to retailer to customer. The title 'flow' describes the ownership route and in particular, where and under what conditions the transfer of ownership takes place. This is particularly important when selling abroad, where the overseas customer may default on payment or in the domestic market in the case of damaged goods. The payment flow is also of particular importance to exporting and is discussed in section 9.8.

9.8 Channels for export markets

The task facing the international seller is that sales channels and distribution systems within foreign countries vary dramatically. These local variations must be superimposed on the alternatives that already exist as a result of the product's perceived characteristics (perishability, unit value, weight, size) and consumer purchase practices (is the product a necessity or a luxury with a regular or infrequent purchase cycle?). In addition, some countries impose certain legal restrictions on product distribution. Finally, the activities of any competition should also be considered.

The final choice between the various alternative sales channels will generally be a balance between budgeted distribution costs on the one hand versus the degree of control of the sales and marketing effort on the other. Channel costs quite typically fall into two types – the capital or initial investment cost and the cost of managing and maintaining the system or network of which a major element is the margin taken by the intermediaries.

There are four principal types of overseas sales channel although most are capable of some local variation. The relative cost and benefits of each are outlined in Table 9.1.

Generally, where the value of an individual order is high, perhaps in excess of £250,000, and particularly where the product is technically complicated, a company is likely to sell direct using its own sales and marketing expertise with a local agent. Where the potential for the level of business is greater, a joint venture or subsidiary might seem a preferable and worthwhile investment. High-value, high-volume orders of consumer retail products can also qualify.

9.8.1　Indirect export

This generally involves institutions called 'export houses', which are organizations specializing in the handling and financing of British exports and international trade not connected with the UK, though they themselves do not manufacture. There are three main types, each offering a slightly different service.

Export merchants resemble domestic wholesalers with overseas interests and methods of distribution which can include agents, sales people and sometimes local offices. The advantage to the manufacturer is that the merchant takes legal title to the goods and is responsible for all the documentation and risk.

A confirming house finances the export transaction by paying the seller before the goods leave the UK. In return, a commission is received by the confirming house for taking the short-term credit risk that was unacceptable to the producer. Manufacturers' export agents take care of the distribution in the export market but the principal must handle the export finance, the credit risk, shipping, insurance and documentation.

Table 9.1   *Alternative export sales channels*

	Initial Investment	Recurring costs	Degree of control	Profitability	Timing of payment to UK company
Indirect export	None	High distribution margins	Low	Generally low or modest	Immediate
Direct export	Low	Low corporate costs and dealer margins	Some	Modest	Several months depending on sales cycle
Joint ventures	Low	Training/quality control	Some/more	Modest (licence fees are normally between 2 and 7 per cent)	Six or twelve monthly licence payments
Overseas manufacturing subsidiary	High	The idea is that these should be modest	Absolute within local government sanctions	Potentially high, though repatriation may be restricted	Annually

Sometimes an established company will allow another to use its own overseas distribution network in exchange for a commission payment. This is called complementary marketing.

9.8.2 Direct export

It is not essential to use an intermediary: indeed, many types of industrial products are sold direct to overseas countries such as those types of consumer goods sold through a department store group or a mail order house. Sales to local and national governments are also frequently direct.

Where a company does not have its own overseas offices, a commission agent is frequently used in addition to the corporate sales and marketing team. The advantage to the exporter is the agent's local knowledge and experience at a low initial investment cost. Another alternative is to use a distributor or stockist who purchases and then re-sells the exporter's products. As the volume of business increases, a branch office might become financially feasible depending on the restrictions imposed by local law, particularly employment legislation and the implications of local contract law. The branch office does, however, involve initial capital expenditure and a continuing overhead irrespective of the subsequent short-term volume of sales.

9.8.3 Joint ventures

This term covers five different types of 'partnership' with an overseas organization: licensing, franchising, industrial (manufacturing) co-operation, contract manufacture and management contracts. The major advantages to the exporter are the avoidance of market entry barriers (import quotas or tariffs), a reduction in freight charges and a much reduced cost of initial investment.

Licensing allows overseas organizations to use a UK company's knowledge and technical know-how (whether or not covered by a patent) in return for an agreed remuneration. The disadvantage of this from the licenser's viewpoint is that the licensee may become a competitor at the end of the agreement.

Business format franchising requires the franchisee (local operator) to carry on a particular business under a format or system established by the franchisor (UK company in this case). The franchisee can use the franchisor's trade name, trade mark, good-will and know-how, while the franchisor is entitled to exercise continuing control over the way in which the franchisee carries on the business. The franchisee is not only expected to make a substantial personal investment in the business but pay the franchisor a regular percentage (usually 10 per cent) of the turnover. The financial advantages and disadvantages are similar to those for licensing.

Industrial co-operation agreements are generally long-term specialization agreements entered into by two companies from different countries with the object of sharing the costs of a certain project. Well-known examples are Concorde, the European Airbus, the Westland helicopter issue and the channel tunnel.

Contract manufacture is a financial halfway point between licensing and a direct investment in an overseas manufacturing or process capability. It is a long-term contract for the manufacture or assembly of a product. A particular financial advantage is the limited local investment which is free from the subsequent risk of nationalization or expropriation.

The management contract is similar to a long-term consultancy agreement where an overseas operation is managed in return for fees and sometimes a share of the profits.

9.8.4 Overseas manufacturing subsidiary

Manufacturing a product in another country is likely to involve a substantial capital investment and a higher element of risk than generally exists in the home market. Unilateral nationalization without adequate compensation is perhaps greatest in certain developing nations.[1]

The first decision must be whether or not to invest abroad. Clearly a number of product market possibilities will present themselves with various rates of return and net present values. All these alternatives which meet or exceed the corporate criteria for such decisions (rate of return, market share) should then be ranked in descending order according to the country or product combination.

The second decision, which product should be manufactured in which country, should receive consideration above and beyond strict financial return.

Subsequent decisions revolve around the nature of the manufacturing capability, assembly or the complete manufacturing process. Assembly close to the market offers for many companies an attractive compromise between exporting and a complete overseas manufacturing capability. The advantages are lower freight costs, cost advantages reflecting lower rates of pay in the overseas market, lower or no import duties and indeed a certain amount of official patronage in some circumstances.

The fourth decision revolves around whether there are additional benefits from a joint venture with an organization indigenous to the market. In some third world countries this is the only effective option available as 100 per cent foreign ownership is discouraged. In some circumstances this is a very convenient and practical way to reach the market at a reduced capital cost. However, in other situations it can be a veritable minefield of intrigue, deviousness and outright skullduggery; or so it may appear to the UK or European partner.

A variation on this, representing effectively the fifth decision, is whether to buy a going concern in the overseas country or start up an entirely new operation. The former may be financially attractive if a suitable candidate can be discovered and a minimum amount of ill-feeling generated by the take-over.

Notes

1 The Export Credit Guarantee Department provides insurance against this eventuality in certain circumstances – though usually for a maximum of fifteen years and 90 per cent of any loss.

10
Technical selling to industry and government

10.1 Differences between consumer and industrial/government selling

The industrial market place comprises businesses that buy products and services in order to produce and sell their product. This market category includes businesses engaged in agriculture, mining, manufacturing, construction, transportation, communications, banking, finance, insurance, sport, medicine, defence and a vast range of services from consultancy to office catering and cleaning. Because these are organizations with a structure of authority and regulations, their performance in the marketplace is rather different from that of the individual consumer.

10.1.1 Fewer buyers

The industrial market for any product is usually made up of fewer buyers than for any consumer market. For example, a company selling a product to the financial services sector might define their market as:

- Banks
Clearing – head offices	160
Foreign (all)	473
Merchant	205

- Building societies – head offices   119

- Insurance
Brokers (Lloyds)	163
Companies – head offices	358
Stockbroking firms	708
Pension funds (companies with)	1,685

Total market   3,875 businesses

The gross potential consumer market for a product might be the adult working population of twelve million. Many companies selling products in industrial markets find that 80 per cent of their business is with fewer than fifteen organizations. The prime features of industrial selling is that there are fewer buyers but they can be very large and dominant. Marks & Spencer, for example, restrict their suppliers of products that have the St Michael label from selling to anybody else.

10.1.2 Geographically concentrated buyers

In England the computer industry is mainly located in the Thames Valley in the area of Slough, Reading and Newbury, so much so that the nickname 'Silicon Valley' is widely recognized. In the USA more than 50 per cent of the industrial buying power resides in seven states: New York, California, Pennsylvania, Illinois, Ohio, New Jersey and Michigan. Clearly this has implications for not only where sellers to these companies locate their offices, but also for sales territory allocation. The experienced industrial sales executive knows both the geographical territory and the key accounts where the sales target is achievable. The newcomers and 'apprentices' are generally left the lean pickings.

10.1.3 Professional purchasing

Industrial goods and services are purchased by professional buyers who make a career of the job. Decisions and money spent have to be justified to senior management. Committees are often formed where the product to be purchased exceeds £10,000. When over £100,000, detailed procedures are involved which can take many months or even years. Consequently, companies selling in this market need appropriately qualified and experienced sales executives if they are to compete seriously. This is the reason why senior sales executives in the computer industry can earn £50–70,000 a year when they reach target, which is often in excess of £1.5 million of equipment. The characteristics required have been detailed in chapter 6, and there are many companies chasing a pool of some 3,000–3,500 with the right skills and experience. As fast as youngsters qualify to go solo on territory, some of the older sales executives take promotion into marketing management or move on to a second career. The pace is relentless and few people over 40-years-old still have the enthusiasm for the long hours and the perseverance in the face of many difficulties.

10.1.4 Additional characteristics:

Reciprocity
Industrial buyers often choose suppliers who also buy from them. Several computer companies buy all their office furniture, lease their cars, book their travel arrangements and arrange their various insurance policies with companies that buy their computers.

Buying to very specific requirements
New products are frequently designed to meet the specialized demand from industrial buyers. This is feasible because of the large value of these orders and accepted because it is frequently the only way to have a realistic chance of winning the business. In the computer industry whole suites of programmes and ranges of desk-top terminals have been designed and built to meet the specific requirements of a particular customer. Quite often a separate company is formed to sell it to third parties in an endeavour to recoup some of the high development costs.

Leasing
Many industrial buyers are now leasing equipment rather than making outright purchase. This happens with cars, computers, heavy construction equipment, vending machines and temporary buildings. The advantages to the lessee are greater availability of capital, guaranteed good service (or the product is returned), the latest model and tax advantages (although these are subject to variation annually in the budget). Regional grants also can have an impact on the lease or buy decision.

10.2 Organizational buying procedures

Industrial buyers do not buy products and services for individual personal consumption: things are bought to make money, reduce costs or to meet various social and legal requirements as an employer in a certain industry. A creche may be designed, built, staffed and furnished so that a company may benefit from the employment of mothers of young children who may have gained many years' useful experience at their job prior to motherhood. Air-conditioning may be installed to increase staff comfort in hot climates, and an accounts department might be computerized to reduce costs.

Most industrial organizations (and government departments) devise a procurement process to buy their necessary supplies and equipment.

10.2.1 Recognition of a problem

This can be the result of internal or external events that focus the attention of someone on a better way of approaching a task or problem. For example, it is perceived that a largely manual process can now be effectively mechanized from the point of view of cost; an old machine breaks down completely; new products require new components; new legal or safety requirements mean new standards which the existing equipment cannot meet. Additionally, an enterprising sales person may create an opportunity by finding a new industrial user for a standard product from a mailshot, or even occasionally, and with great luck, from a cold call.

10.2.2 Need description

Once a need has been identified, the procurement process requires that it be quantified and costed precisely. Complex products will usually have a committee to evaluate fully all the perceived criteria. This is the time when the experienced industrial sales executive should start talking to the buying organization. Product experience linked to the applications where it has been successfully installed can be of help to the evaluation committee. From the sales executive's point of view, a professional impression may mean that certain key features of the product are built into the mandatory requirements of the buying specification. (It is singularly unfortunate for the competition if their products are subsequently found to be without these essential features!)

10.2.3 Product specification

The next step is to develop a product specification which prospective suppliers can be asked to tender against. This may be done in one of several ways depending on the product. Engineering components may be subject to a value analysis study to investigate the cheapest practical way of producing the required item. Computer requirements will be generally explored by a multi-function committee comprising users, technical experts, an accountant, a decision-maker, a buyer and an administrator under the title of a 'gatekeeper'. The job of the latter is to be the contact with the various selling organizations. In selling jargon this group is known as the 'decision-making unit' or DMU. Other products, for example computer software, may be specified by outside consultants. Whichever approach is used, the result is a product specification with a budgeted cost.

10.2.4 Supplier search

The buyer organization then assembles what it hopes is a comprehensive list of prospective suppliers for the product under consideration. Some of these will have already been consulted at the specification stage. From a sales point of view this is the normal time when it is possible to establish contact. It clearly provides those organizations with the opportunity to 'educate' the prospect regarding their product philosophy. Indeed, individual product features may still be incorporated in the buyer's product specification. This can put non-participating organizations at a considerable disadvantage because they are asked to quote against a specification that they have had no opportunity of influencing.

Lists of potential suppliers are quite easily compiled from trade directories, recommendations from professional organizations (the Chartered Institute of Marketing Consultants Register, the Defence Manufacturers Association and the HMSO list of approved suppliers) and companies enjoying a good reputation in the marketplace.

10.2.5 Invitation of proposals

At this stage a detailed specification of the buyer's requirements is sent to the chosen list of potential suppliers. The specification is frequently divided into 'mandatory' and 'desirable' requirements, timescales for delivery, and where relevant, deadlines for complete installation, a budget purchase price and full supporting documentation. This is to assist the suppliers with any necessary calculations regarding size or power of the equipment they are proposing. The response to this requirement document should be a professionally produced detailed report stating how the proposed product will meet the prospect's various requirements and quoting a price.

10.2.6 The short-list

Where the number of potential suppliers is large and the requirement technically complex and expensive, it is usual for the purchaser to produce a short-list of three or four proposals. These selected companies are then involved in a round of detailed technical discussions, presentations, demonstrations and pilot testing as to the suitability of their proposal for the buyer organization.

This is a critically important stage in the buying cycle because this is where the suitability of each proposal is carefully examined. In many instances new technology is involved and it is likely that in some cases what is being offered exists only in prototype form. Consequently the buyer may be forced to compare what actually exists now against what might exist in six months' time.

10.2.7 Memorandum of agreement

It is because of the complexities of these comparisons and the element of risk involved with unproven technology that most government departments in the UK and many private companies introduce another stage into the buying process. This is called the memorandum of agreement and is a legally binding document. It forces the short-listed companies to state unequivocally which equipment they are offering and to give a guarantee of the performance specification. In the event of a supplier being subsequently awarded the contract and the equipment underperforming, a suit for damages would result. This is to prevent the buyer from being left in the position of having to take on trust certain aspects of the supplier's proposals.

10.2.8 Tendering

This is the final stage of the pre-contract process. The remaining suppliers on the short-list (some have been known to withdraw) submit a formal offer of the equipment listed in the memorandum of agreement at a price below the maximum that has been agreed. It is not unusual for this price to have increased above that in the original requirement document, the reason being that the buyer is sometimes forced to accept that no supplier can offer what they want at the price they originally calculated. In this situation the buyer is left with the problem of reducing the requirement in some way, not buying at all or increasing the budget.

However, as a result of the memorandum, the buyer should be faced with a choice of three or four technically sound propositions, the final selection frequently being made on price alone. The competing suppliers are left to decide their final price and any additional benefits that they are able to offer above the essential buyer requirements specified in the memorandum.

10.2.9 Placing an order

Now at last the buyer organization has three or four tenders and the DMU makes a decision. In some instances, more than one supplier will be favoured, although in the case of purchasing a computer this is unlikely. Unexpected decisions can be made, however. They are not expected by the suppliers because they have been concentrating hard on winning the contract. In the dynamic environment of the outside world, new developments may have taken place during the eighteen months or so that the process has taken. Consequently, orders may be placed with more than one supplier as part-orders for 'live' testing.

Other factors may include 'call-off' contracts for the supply of consumable items over, say, a five-year period at a fixed scale of prices. Alternatively, the purchaser may ask for a larger quantity than was originally tendered for and new price negotiations may commence with the chosen supplier(s).

In summary, this is a challenging area where only highly experienced professionals succeed. Successful suppliers need to understand the vagaries of the market in great detail and maintain up-to-date assessments of competitors' capabilities. Personal contact and reputation matter a great deal as in some contracts there are political overtones where the result of winning or losing can mean jobs saved or lost.

10.3 The government marketplace

The government marketplace comprises the central government departments listed in Table 10.1, the 650 local authorities in England, Wales, Scotland and Northern Ireland and a few public corporations (British Rail, The London Transport Executive, Post Office, National Coal Board and the Nationalized Bus Company). The government departments and bodies listed in Table 10.1 have been divided into three priorities of potential market value for computer technology. When it is remembered that the National Health Service is the biggest employer in western Europe and is only part of the Department of Health, it is easy to perceive what an enormous market for goods and services the government sector represents.

10.3.1 Selling to government departments

Government buying practices are complex, time-consuming and frequently frustrating. However, contracts of a substantial size are often awarded and this supplies the motivation. A major reason for the weighty bureaucracy is that government agencies are subject to public review and any hint of impropriety is quickly publicized in a most embarrassing way by the media.

Table 10.1   *An analysis of government departments spending power*

Category 1
Ministry of Agriculture, Fisheries and Food
Ministry of Defence
Department of Health (including the NHS)
Department of Social Security
Department of Employment
Department of the Environment
Home Office (including the Metropolitan Police)
Board of the Inland Revenue
Department of Trade and Industry
Department of Transport
HM Treasury

Category 2
Cabinet Office (including CSO and Management and Personnel)
HM Customs and Excise
Department of Education and Science
Department of Energy
Foreign and Commonwealth Office
Northern Ireland Office
Overseas Development Administration
Scottish Office
Welsh Office

Category 3
Central Office of Information
Department of the Director of Public Prosecutions
Export Credits Guarantee Department
Forestry Commission
Her Majesty's Stationery Office
Land Registry
Lord Chancellor's Department
Manpower Services Commission
Royal Mint
National Audit Office
Department for National Savings
National Investment and Loans Office
Paymaster General's Office
Public Trustee Office
Office of Fair Trading

There are three methods by which a small firm can generally sell a product or service to the government. *Selling to the MOD* makes the following suggestions:

Sub-contract opportunities from a major defence contractor probably provide the best chance for a small business to become a supplier to the MOD. In an effort to reduce staff levels and associated costs, the policy is to place most contracts in the hands of a single prime contractor. The prime contractor is then left to choose the necessary sub-contractors.

As a rule the MOD does not intervene directly in the relationship between prime and sub-contractors. The MOD takes the view that it is up to small firms to convince the prime contractor as to the quality of their product and to offer them at a competitive price. Firms are expected to be registered by the British Standards Institution to British Standard 5750.[1]

The largest defence contractors are listed in *The Statement on Defence Estimates* published annually by HMSO. Annex 3 gives a list of these companies with their head office address and telephone number.

More than £350 million-worth of goods are purchased annually by defence establishments using delegated purchasing powers. These local purchases are generally subject to a lower level of assessment and consequently represent an ideal opportunity for small businesses to sell to the MOD. The establishments using this method of procurement are listed in Annex 4 of the *Statement on the Defence Estimates*. Direct contracts are also awarded by the Headquarters Contract Branch of the MOD. A significant number of these, particularly for maintenance and spares, are awarded to small firms. However, these firms must have satisfied the Ministry as to their commercial viability, technical competence and quality management systems.

Notes

1 British Standards Institution, Certification and Assessment Department, Quality Assurance Services, PO Box 375, Milton Keynes MK14 6LO. Telephone 0908 315555.

11
Franchising

Traditionally, companies either employed their own sales force or used distributors and agents to sell their products. However, the high incomes demanded by sales professionals and the increasing competition from developing countries with low-priced medium-quality products has forced many businesses to seek alternative ways of selling.

There has always been a great reluctance to pay sales executives not achieving target, and some companies have tried unsuccessfully to implement commission-only selling schemes. These schemes have only been successful in the insurance industry and where the selling cycle is very short. The sale must be capable of conclusion in a few days so that the sales executive can be paid his commission. Very few people are prepared or able to work for more than a few days without any certainty of financial reward.

However, the idea that hungry sales executives sell has always prevailed and companies have continued the search for reduced-cost methods of achieving the sale. Some companies approached this by reducing the skills required in the selling role to the repetition of a few structured questions. Other businesses have developed a successful formula – a fast food concept, car maintenance outside the customer's house, the cleaning of household fabrics in the home – but lacked the finance for expansion.

From these two different sources emerged the idea of 'business format franchising'.

11.1 Franchising explained

Franchising is a marketing-orientated method of distribution in which one person, the franchisor, grants a licence or a franchise to another person, the franchisee, which permits the franchisee to use the franchisor's trade name, trade marks and business system in return for an initial payment and further payments at regular intervals.

The parties

The franchisor is almost invariably a limited liability company. The franchisee can, however, operate as a sole trader, a partnership or as a limited company. The franchisor will require the franchisee(s) to sign an agreement so as to guarantee the performance of the limited company. This is to protect the franchisor from non-recoverable losses from the franchisees company which has limited liability protection.

Term and option to renew

The length of the agreement is likely to reflect not only the type of business but also the amount of the front end fee payable by the franchisee. While five years might be average, agreements are known to run from one year to fifteen or more. However, many franchisors will offer an option to renew the agreement on certain conditions.

Territory

Franchisees have an 'exclusive' territory in which to operate their franchise. This has been made more difficult since the Restrictive Trade Practices Act 1976 (see 11.2 below). It is, of course, a substantial advantage to the franchisees but a disadvantage to the franchisor, particularly if the franchisees do not work hard in the territory to exploit its potential on which the franchisor depends as much as the franchisee for his income.

The franchisor might also reasonably require the franchisees to demonstrate their commitment by achieving a certain level of performance, failing which he/she may take back part of the territory or remove the exclusivity from the territory, and that might result in other franchisees offering the franchisor's service in the same area.

Property

In some franchises the property from which the service or the products are offered can be of prime importance. The franchisor therefore may insist on controlling the property by taking a head lease and ensuring that the property reverts to him/her if for any reason the franchise should cease to operate.

Exclusive supply

The prime object of some franchisors is to distribute products which they themselves either manufacture or otherwise distribute. In these circumstances, the franchisee will be required to purchase the products exclusively from the franchisor. Provision should be made for circumstances where the franchisor is unable to supply.

Fees

Most franchises provide for two or three payments to be made by the franchisee to the franchisor. The first is an initial fee to cover the expense of setting up the individual franchisee in business and may include training, initial stock, shopfitting and a small sum to reflect the existing reputation of the franchise.

Most franchisors, however, for their principal income rely on regular payments for the continuing services they provide. These payments are made monthly or weekly and are normally calculated as a percentage of the gross income of the franchisee's business. Sometimes, however, where the franchisor exclusively provides products for sale in the business, income is derived from the usual mark-up on the sale of the products to the franchisee.

It is, of course, a matter of commercial judgement as to whether the amounts charged by the franchisor are reasonable, bearing in mind the services which the franchisor provides to the franchisee both on an ongoing and on a special basis.

Sale or assignment of business

Unless the amount of capital invested in the business is small, or the term of the agreement is very short, most franchisors now permit the franchisee, subject to reasonable terms and conditions, to assign or sell the business to a third party.

The franchise manual

It is not only impossible but highly undesirable for the franchise agreement to try to set out all the details of the franchisor's business system. All franchisors, therefore, will have a separate manual which specifies precisely how the business should be conducted. It will, together with the initial training course, impart the know-how and expertise necessary if the franchisees are to succeed, and the franchisor therefore has an obligation to update the manual with new material as the business develops during the course of the agreement.

The manual often contains a great deal of confidential information. Clauses restricting access to this information, and to prevent franchisees from passing on what they have learnt during the course of the Franchise Agreement, are both reasonable and desirable in order to protect the integrity of the franchise as a whole.

Franchisees benefit from the franchisor's proven business system and should therefore expect to follow the system precisely. The franchisor can react strongly to any breaches of obligations, as he/she has responsibilities to all the other franchisees too.

Disputes

However fair and reasonable the terms of the agreement, however great the initial goodwill between the parties, from time to time differences of opinion will arise. These are best resolved by direct discussions.

Some franchise agreements provide for arbitration. The British Franchise Association is always prepared to assist when disputes arise between members and their franchisees. Good franchisors will make the effort to communicate regularly with their franchisees as this provides one of the best ways of avoiding problems.

Franchising, while far from being a partnership in strictly legal terms, is very much a partnership in the everyday sense of the word, and depends on the commitment of both parties to comply with the spirit and the terms of the contract.

11.2 The franchise contract

The franchise contract is the legal document in which the proposed business proposition is written down in considerable detail. It must accurately reflect the promises made and it must be fair, while at the same time ensuring that there are sufficient controls to protect the integrity of the system. The franchise contract should:

1 Deal correctly, in legal terms, with the various property rights owned by the franchisor.
2 Provide the operational details and controls for the franchisee.
3 Provide the franchisee with security in his/her operations and in his/her ability to develop and sell a valuable asset.

The franchisor's proprietory interests
This section will deal with such things as trade marks, trade names, copyright materials and the franchisor's business system and know-how.

The rights granted to the franchisee
This will deal with operational aspects of the franchise and the formal granting of rights to use trade marks and copyright material.

Territorial rights
It is important at this point to mention territorial rights, since these can create practical problems where exclusive territorial rights are a feature.

First, there are the commercial considerations; these have caused many problems for franchisors over the years. It is very difficult to determine a territorial allocation which is fair to both parties, especially when the extent of the likely penetration of the market cannot be judged. Indeed, quite often, even the total size of the potential market cannot be estimated.

Many franchisors in the past who have chosen the exclusive territorial route have found that there was no effective way of ensuring that the potential of the area was fully exploited. The effect of this is to harm the whole network, because within the area a market and a demand is being created by advertising and promotion which is not met by resources. This is likely to encourage competitive activity, particularly as disgruntled or potential customers are not likely to look elsewhere within the same network for their requirements. The network thus gets a bad name. An obvious response is to suggest that performance targets should be established. Since the assessment of fair performance targets is, however, dependent on the same factors as have to be considered in defining a territory, the problem remains basically the same.

Second, there are the legal considerations. The introduction of exclusive territorial rights is likely to trigger the operation of the Restrictive Trade Practices Act 1976.

The agreement is then required to be registered with the Office of Fair Trading. The restrictive provisions have to be considered in the light of the interests of consumers to the exclusion of what is in the interests of franchisor and franchisee. The provisions of the agreement in which the Office of Fair Trading usually expresses an interest are those provisions which are designed to protect the network and the integrity of the system from being copied and exploited by departing franchisees. The Act also allows for the continuous monitoring of the agreement, and for the subsequent revival of interest by the Office of Fair Trading.

Many franchisors do not offer exclusive territorial rights for these reasons.

Terms of agreement

The contract will also specify the period of agreement. The basic principle to be adopted here is that the franchise relationship should be capable of subsisting on a long-term basis. There may be various reasons, including, where tied supply of products is involved, legal reasons, for agreeing on a relatively short initial period, say five years, but most franchise schemes allow for the franchisee to be able to exercise a right of renewal.

Franchisor's services

The nature and extent of the services to be provided by the franchisor to the franchisee, both initially and on a continuing basis, should be covered. This area of the contract will deal with the initial services, which enable the franchisee to be initiated, trained and equipped to open for trading. On a continuing basis, the franchisor will be providing services which should be detailed in the agreement including the possibility of developing and introducing new ideas.

The initial and continuing obligations of the franchisees

These will range from accepting the financial burden of setting-up in compliance with the franchisor's requirements, to operating accounting and other administrative systems to ensure that essential management information is available to both parties.

These systems will often be described in an operational manual to which the franchisee will be introduced in training and which will serve as a reference guide. The manual will be constantly updated as the system develops.

The operational controls imposed on the franchisee

The controls are to ensure that operational standards are properly controlled – failure to maintain standards in one unit can harm the whole network. Franchisees will rightly be alarmed if their counterparts fail to maintain standards and the franchisor allows them to continue in this way. The contract will contain the obligations and the manual will explain how the obligation is to be discharged.

Sale of the business

One of the reasons for the success of franchising is the motivation it provides to the franchisee, which comes with self-employment and the incentive at the end of the day of making a capital gain. For this reason, the franchised business should be capable of being sold. However, there will always be controls. If there are none, it should be a matter for suspicion. After all, if a franchisor is highly selective when considering applications for franchises, there is every reason to be equally selective about those who want to join the network by buying an established business from an existing franchisee.

The criteria by which a prospective purchaser will be judged by the franchisor should be set out in the contract. The procedure to be followed should also be provided in the contract. Some franchisors insert into the contract an option to buy the business if the franchisee wishes to sell. If such a provision is inserted in the contract it should provide for the payment of at least the same price as is offered to the franchisee by a bona fide third party. Any artificial formula which might enable the franchisor to buy at less than market value should be resisted, as it is clearly against the franchisee's interests.

Death of the franchisee

In this event, provision should be made to demonstrate that the franchisor will provide assistance to enable the business to be preserved as an asset to be realized, or alternatively taken over by the franchisee's dependants.

Arbitration

Arbitration is in reality private litigation using an independent arbitrator chosen by the parties. It has advantages in that the proceedings are private; the arbitrator chosen can be selected because of his/her special knowledge of the business that is the subject of arbitration; the timing of the proceedings can be fixed to suit the parties' convenience. The parties may establish the rules for their arbitration and save time and expense in so doing.

There are also disadvantages. Not every dispute under a franchise contract will be resolved by the decision of an arbitrator; for example, the franchisor will not want an arbitrator to judge whether quality standards and systems are being maintained. The franchisor's right to an injunction may be impaired if the arbitration agreement does not reserve those rights. The wrong choice of arbitrator may result in an unsatisfactory compromise decision.

Bearing in mind the long-term relationship involved, those areas where genuine misunderstandings can arise may be considered suitable for arbitration, for example fee calculations and rights of renewal.

Termination provisions

Invariably, there will be express provision for the termination of the agreement in the event of a default by the franchisee. Usually, the franchisee will be given the opportunity to put right minor remediable breaches so as to avoid termination, providing that he/she does not persist in making such breaches.

The consequences of termination will usually involve the franchisee in taking steps to ensure that he ceases to display any association with the franchisor. The franchisee will no longer enjoy the use of the trade mark/trade name and other property rights, owned by the franchisor. In addition, the franchisee will be under an obligation for a period of time not to compete with the franchisor, or other franchisees, nor be allowed to make use of the franchisor's system, or other methods.

11.3 The cost to the franchisee

It is important for the franchisor to provide the prospective franchisee with detailed financial information relating to the likely profitability of the proposed franchise. One of the requirements for membership of the British Franchise Association is that a pilot site should have been operated for at least a period of one year. Consequently, as an absolute minimum, audited accounts should be available covering this operation. Longer established franchise operations should have a wider range of historical financial information available relating to performance of existing franchisees.

Projected profit and loss account

An essential requirement for the prospective franchisee is a cash flow projection of the timing of the costs associated with operating the franchise and the expected revenue from sales over the same period. It is preferable to have these projections for at least the first three years, five years is even better. These statements will facilitate financial planning, because short-term finance may be required by the franchisee until sales revenue regularly exceeds the costs of running the business. Also it will allow the franchisee and his/her financial adviser to reach a judgement about the acceptability of the financial return from the investment of both labour and capital in the project.

Assuming that the prospective franchisee and their adviser/ accountant are satisfied with the profit and loss account projections, they should have the opportunity to check the assumptions on which the projections are based. This should take the form of actual evidence based on the original franchise and the results of market research.

Costs and overheads are relatively easy to control and forecast, but sales are dependent on a number of factors over which the franchisee has little influence.

However, market conditions, the propensity of consumers to purchase, the effect of competition, relative prices, the quality of the product or service and the effect of the franchisor's marketing and promotional activities can all be measured and quite accurately predicted by market research.

Projected balance sheet

This will be a useful document for estimating the future value of the business should the franchisee need to sell the concern before the term of the franchise expires. The balance sheet will identify the assets and likely liabilities of the business at various stages in the future and provide a useful indication of capital growth.

The commitment made by the franchisor

In return for the initial franchise fee and a percentage of the franchisee's turnover (frequently 10 per cent) the franchisor will provide essentially three services:

1 *A protected business format* which may be used exclusively by the franchisee in the business area or territory. This may include:

- A trade mark or trade name and the goodwill with which it is associated.
- A business format: a system recorded in a manual, which might contain some elements which are secret and confidential.
- In some cases, formula specifications, design drawings and operational documents.
- Copyright in some of the above items which are in written form and capable of copyright protection.

2 *Initial services.* The nature of these services will vary, bearing in mind the type of business. The general principle is that the franchisor's initial services (including training) should be sufficiently comprehensive to set up a previously inexperienced person in business to trade effectively, in accordance with the chosen franchise system, almost immediately.

3 *Continuing services.* Having established the franchisee in business, the franchisor now has the responsibility to sustain a continuing range of support services. These include:

- Performance monitoring to help maintain standards and profitability.
- Continuing update of methods and new innovations.
- Market research and development.
- Promotion and advertising.
- Benefit of bulk purchasing power.
- The provision at head office of a specialist range of management services.

In addition to the above, most franchise systems provide for advertising and promotion to be handled by the franchisor who will receive from franchisees a contribution for that purpose. The most common method of calculating the contribution is the same as for franchise fees, namely as a percentage of the gross sales by the franchisee – 4 per cent is a common figure.

In some cases a franchisor may include the advertising expenses in the franchise fee and undertake to spend a percentage of the fee on advertising and promotion. There are also cases where local advertising rather than national is more important and a franchisee may find the franchisor does not seek a contribution but imposes on the franchisee the obligation to spend a certain sum on approved local advertising.

12
Export selling

12.1 Reasons for export selling

The principal reasons why companies sell their products abroad are increased profit, increased market share and making an acceptable return on previous investment. However, strategically the diversification may offer a broader base less susceptible to the variances of a single market.

With countries at different stages of economic development, a product becoming *déjà-vu* in a western industrialized market may just becoming 'trendy' in a less developed economy. Car manufacturers have been very successful at extending the product life-cycle. Visitors to Iran will see large numbers of 1969–1970 Hillman Hunters – Austin Rover having sold the entire production line complete with spares and unsold stock to the government. Peugeot have done a similar deal with Tunisia and visitors there will see large numbers of 1960 style Peugeots being used by taxi-drivers.

The competition may be less severe accommodating more rapid growth than is available in the home market. At certain times, business in the domestic economy can be very expensive because rivals desperate for sales indulge in price-cutting exercises and heavy promotional campaigns.

Additionally, exporting may lead to joint venture activities with production at a lower cost than is available in the home market. This may give the company a useful choice of production centres removing single site dependability and any associated restrictions associated with that situation.

However, these reasons act only as a general background to the decision to sell abroad. Clearly, this decision should be based on a calculated return or profit on the initiative. Indeed the size of this minimum acceptable return might be more than would be required for a home market exercise because of the extra risk and uncertainty of trading abroad. Risk is defined in this instance as the situation where the returns from an investment are not known in advance with absolute confidence. Uncertainty is used to explain that more than one possible financial outcome may be the result of the investment.[1]

Having decided that there is business potential from selling abroad extensive market research needs to be undertaken in order to quantify this perceived potential (much of this information will be available from existing secondary sources). Five decisions then need to be taken:

- Sell abroad or not?
- Which market(s)?
- Which method of entry (direct, indirect, licensing)?
- What mix of products?
- The organization required?

12.2 Export selling has added difficulties

Some people might wonder why a separate chapter is necessary for export selling, after all there are certain principles that are applicable to any type of selling. The answer is quite simply that selling in overseas markets is more difficult because certain additional problems are encountered which generally do not arise in the home market. Things that can be taken for granted in the domestic market cannot be depended on when selling overseas. Many of these difficulties involve communications.

Postal communications
In the UK if you address a letter clearly and include the correct postcode and postage it will normally reach its destination within two days. This simple process may not be relied on when posting documents abroad. Letters to France frequently take four days, to the Republic of Ireland post can generally take one week to arrive. When posting letters and packages outside Europe this delivery can frequently be three or four weeks. The author has spent two years corresponding with business contacts in Zimbabwe and mail always took nearly four weeks and sometimes five to reach the destination in Harare. This is from one capital city (London) to another. If the destination was some town in the 'bundu', it could clearly have been longer.

Telephone contact
Using the telephone is certainly an alternative and international dialling to major towns in most parts of the world is not only possible but quite straightforward. In some areas there is of course an acute shortage of telephone lines so that many attempts may need to be made before a

connection is established. The major difficulty is the different time zones which make East to West communication more difficult. Even four and five hour differences require some adjustment (New York going west and Riyadh going east for example). However, when this becomes eight or nine hours (Los Angeles, Rangoon) for one party to contact the other in their office, the former is dialling from their home at 2am. The first few times it is of course quite novel, but after a while it becomes a considerable nuisance.

Facsimile

Facsimile is the technical communications product of the 1990s – many people running businesses from home even have one. It is certainly fast, relatively cheap and overcomes the problems of different time zones. Someone in London can send a fax as they leave their office at 6pm and their contact overseas will find it waiting for them when they arrive in their office the following day. This works well in Western developed countries, however, this technology is not widely available in third world countries. Quality is also still something of a problem, while it is perfectly acceptable for conveying information it is generally not of a high enough standard except in draft form for legal contracts nor does it lend itself to photocopying.

Telex

The old traditional method of speedy international written communication almost entirely made up of the word 'urgent' plus a few nouns and verbs frequently including logical gaps. This has the additional advantage of being widely available even in the poorer overseas countries. However, due to the rapid developments in fascimile technology many western companies have already discarded this more primitive method of communication.

Language

Because of Britain's Empire tradition, the expectation has generally been that the 'foreigner' would learn our language. Consequently, today British business people fall into two distinct categories: the largest group by far who are extremely amusing when they make any attempt to speak another nation's language and those who have language qualifications but no others which are developed to a professional standard. This latter group often find difficulty in securing employment in accordance with their intellect and general skills.

Language is a particularly important difference, because the avoidance of a misunderstanding or picking up a subtle hint can be crucial in negotiation. Where language is a barrier rather than a conduit, it can be used as an excuse for prevarication whenever one party wishes to avoid being held to a point previously agreed. In some overseas countries this type of 'back-sliding' has been developed into an exact science. Using interpreters is not an effective answer in these circumstances because unless they are experienced in business themselves they will find the logic of the elusiveness difficult to follow.

Culture
The culture of a nation or a group of people describes an expression of their way of life. It is learned behaviour passed from one generation to another and represents a code for living and working. Clearly anything as influential as this will affect consumption of goods and services. Only those products that are compatible with the code will be acceptable. Indeed for success the behaviour of the 'foreign' sales person will have to conform to the culture of the customer country. A particular example of this might include the status of women in Arab countries and Japan. In Saudi Arabia a woman is not allowed to drive a car. She may not even leave the country without a male relative signing a form to 'give permission'. Consequently, companies interested in selling to these countries must take these norms into account. This means no female executives can be directly involved in the business or negotiations. The selling message needs to address itself to the male as well as the female for products normally bought by women in western countries. Any messages suggesting 'freedom' and 'independence' to women consumers of the sort popularly used to sell cosmetics, shampoos and small cars in Britain would be totally unacceptable.

Other points to take into account might be the content for example of certain animal fats in the product. Indeed, one of the causes of the Indian mutiny in 1857 involved the rumour that the cartridges to be used in New Enfield rifles were greased in cow fat. This was objectionable to the Hindus for whom the cow is a sacred animal and equally objectionable to muslims for whom the cow is unclean. Consequently companies selling leather goods and food products need to take account of such factors.

Another aspect of culture can involve documentation of the law of contract and a European's strong preference to have agreements in writing. To a moslem insistence on this procedure can be insulting (if he does not understand western business procedures) because in a moslem's culture, a man's word is binding. Yet this is the exact opposite of the perceived business behaviour of some overseas nationals held by many westerners. It all serves to increase the pitfalls and scope for misunderstanding when attempting to sell in overseas markets.

12.3 Organizing for export selling

The key factor in organizing for export is authority and responsibility. Someone must be absolutely responsible for each product market whether the country is targeted or not. Someone must be responsible for responding to enquiries even if there is no current objective to sell in that market or country. Otherwise business will be lost. Also this responsibility should be as close as possible to the level where the selling is done – preferably first line management. A very flat structure is best (sales and marketing director, regional sales manager, export sales executive). Levels of authority should be precisely set and the chain of command prescribed.

Large companies selling multi-nationally tend to have complex structures based on function, region and/or product. Regional organization is the most efficient where the selling is to specific groups of countries (EEC, LAFTA[2]) or where the markets are in close proximity but away from head office (East Africa for example). The difficulty arises when the product line comprises very different products sold to different market segments. This will of course tend to favour a product orientated organization – but the result will then be different people selling different products in the same national market with customers unable to differentiate between the various product groups. Also opportunities may be missed that do not specifically fall into one specific group. Consequently, a regional organization is to be preferred because the responsibility is more precise and the authority likely to be more absolute.

12.4 Product decisions

Product policy is a key aspect of the marketing mix, essentially the choice is:

- improving product performance in existing markets,
- extend the product line or develop new products,
- sell existing products into new markets.

However, conditions in overseas markets can be very different to the home market – this may be the climate, cultural environment, economic development of the market, financial resources (hard currency = pounds, dollars, yen, deutschmarks), and life-styles.

Product modification

This question revolves around the additional sales that may be achieved if the product exactly meets the needs of key export market segments against the total cost of making the changes.

Mandatory product modifications are clearly those standards imposed by law – for example selling electrical products into France requires an Agrement Board Certificate. Safety factors also come under this heading.

Technical modifications are also essential to take account of local voltage requirements others may include fitting the steering wheel on the left hand side of the vehicle, double glazing and power heaters for cold climates and air conditioning in hot countries.

Local taxation may also exert an influence on the engine size of cars for example or the alcohol content of certain drinks. This may also have an effect on production methods, because reduced tariffs may be available on products assembled in the importing country.

Consumer taste is certainly a major reason for product modification, this may be prevailing trends based on popular culture in the case of fashion products, or in terms of foodstuffs traditional eating habits. Though in the case of hamburgers, western-produced films have successfully created a demand for McDonalds in places as far apart as Moscow and Tokyo.

Packaging

Different countries have different requirements and codes and the company selling in overseas markets should address this question. The costs involved are rarely as significant as those incurred in product modifications but may need to reflect the time taken in transit, the treatment that may be received in transit, climatic conditions and the consumption rate by the end user.

The promotional aspects of packaging also merit consideration – for example individual packs for certain products in low income countries and in others prevalent fashionable colours need considerations because they can be very different from those in the home markets.

Labelling

Every country tends to have its own requirements and regulations but the usual essentials are: brand name, manufacturers name, description of what is inside, weight, country of origin and use by date (where appropriate). This label of course has an additional job which is to attract consumers and encourage a regular pattern of repeat purchases. This will require the additional skills of a graphic designer and copy writer except where the brand is an international one (Kit Kat, Marlborough, Coca Cola or Johnnie Walker for example).

Trade mark piracy

Protection of a successful and well-known brand name is rarely straight-forward. It is even more difficult internationally because some countries are heavily involved in brand imitation and piracy. Trade mark piracy is the registration of brand names by third parties not connected with the home market owner or the export market distribution. The idea is to extract payment from the 'legitimate owners' of the mark and brand.

Registration of each brand in every country in the world (some 170) can be unacceptably expensive just on the off-chance that at some future stage export to that country might be proposed. Filing and registration in most European countries starts at £400–£500 per class of good per brand name or trade mark. Searches against third party marks are an extra cost as is countering any opposition representing other vested interests.

12.5 Additional requirements for an export sales executive

In Chapter 6, the key characteristics for success in selling were identified as perception, perseverance, effective communication skills and social sensitivity. The export sales person requires these and additional characteristics developed to a high level in order to be 'self-sufficient' away from the 'support systems of head office'. Even though intercontinental communications are continuously improving, the export sales person is frequently alone and out of immediate contact with colleagues and management back home.

Decisiveness

The export sales executive should be capable of making decisions for him or herself on the spot without constant referral back to head office. Overseas customers will obviously exploit this angle to the maximum knowing that the sales executive is anxious to make the sale. Variations to the usual terms of payment, delivery, product specification or volume discounts will be demanded in a constant attempt to negotiate a better deal. The only way that the sales executive can stop the 'merry-go-round' of constantly changing requests is to ask for a list of absolute requirements – second, he/she should request agreement that if these requirements are fulfilled the contract will be signed within a specified (short) time period. It is then a question of deciding oneself or making contact with the specified head office decision-maker for confirmation or variation of the terms.

Product and commercial knowledge
The export sales executive needs to be knowledgeable about all aspects of the products being sold by the company in the overseas market. This may involve the entire list of the following items:

- Product details:
    technical specification
    any computer requirement
    required software
    new developments proposed
    applications experience of using products
    details of relevant competitors products
- Support/service availability
    spares requirement
    level of service offered/required
- Project management service
    what is involved and when
- Pricing policy
    terms of payment and when
    currency
    delivery procedures
- Distributor/franchise terms
    down payment
    training
    fees
    advertising/promotion policy
- Legal aspects
    UK law of contract/foreign/mixture of both[3]

Linguistic ability
This is important because the sales executive is not only able to follow what is being discussed, but commands respect and demonstrates professionalism.

Health
Travelling is physically demanding with normal patterns of work, relaxation and sleep disrupted. In addition the climate is different, the food and drink can be strange and exotic and even the most carefully laid plans disrupted.

A robust constitution is essential to withstand the rigours of international business life. Hosts are normally keen for the visitor to try the local gastronomic delicacies which can be very different to the head office executive dining room: Scandinavian soused herring washed down with copious quantities of aquavit, a French five course meal accompanied by several glasses of a 'grand cru'; or a selection of Indian curries or a Japanese meal supported by rice wine. While immensely enjoyable at the time it requires considerable time afterwards for rest and recuperation.

Suddenly arriving in dry and hot climate or a particularly humid climate, a wet climate or a cold climate can also affect, the health, comfort and general well-being of the export sales executive.

Dependability
Senior management must be able to rely on the export sales executive to do the work without any form of close supervision. Clearly, the temptations can be considerable with the company financing all the travel, accommodation and living expenses. However, notwithstanding this, the market research must be completed, prospects' requirements ascertained, sales prospects prepared and reports for head office completed.

Cosmopolitan attitudes
It is also necessary for the export sales executive to integrate and identify with the local people and business contacts. Resolutely drinking tea at four in the afternoon demanding Keiler marmalade at breakfast and having dessert before the cheese is not the way to approach extended periods as the guest of another culture. This is not to say that the extremes of the local national costume should be worn but a noticeable effort to try and appreciate the local way of life is important.

12.6 Countertrade

Exporting companies may find themselves involved in counter trade. This is an 'umbrella term' used in reciprocal trade to cover various commercial arrangements that include: barter, counter purchase, offset, buy back, evidence accounts and switch trading. The common theme is that the export of goods into the importing country is entirely dependent on the acceptance of reciprocal exports by the exporter. The usual reason being that the original importer lacks the 'hard currency'[3] or the commercial credit required to pay for the imported goods. It is also used as a device to expand the sales of domestic industries particularly agriculture and mineral extraction.

Barter – is the direct exchange of goods between trading partners. All other forms of counter trade involve money and third party commitment.

Compensation is where the seller from the industrialized country agrees to take full or partial payment in kind from the lesser developed country (LDC). Any company going into a 100 per cent goods for 100 per cent goods deal is considered to be in a weak negotiating position or naive. Selling the 'compensation goods' may prove quite difficult and usually a third party (trading house) would be involved. Clearly, the prudent exporter will only accept quality, re-sellable goods and have a contract with a buyer before agreeing to the compensation trade.

Counter-purchase is where the exporter commits to buy (or transfers the right to a third party) products from the importing country ranging from 5 per cent to 100 per cent of principal export deal. The advantage to the original exporter is immediate full payment or standard specified credit terms, where settlement of the counter-purchase obligation is only due when a buyer has been found and a contract signed.

Buyback is where a seller of capital equipment or technology agrees to accept products manufactured with the equipment supplied in part or full payment for the plant itself.

Offset is where exports to a country include components made by the importing country. Originally a feature of defence and aircraft contracts, it is now extending to other industries.

Switch trading is where for example Brazil has a large credit surplus with Hungary. This surplus can be 'tapped' by a third party so that Spanish exports to Brazil might be financed by the sale of Hungarian goods to India. The manipulations of the trade are known as 'switch' or 'swop' deals because they frequently involve switching the documentation and destination while in transit.

Evidence accounts occur where companies with significant levels of continuing business in certain key markets may be obliged to arrange counter-purchase exports from those markets at least equivalent to the import of their own products. An 'evidence account' is established to facilitate the complex calculations.

Notes

1 For a full explanation of the calculations involved in making selling and marketing investment decisions, see Taylor, A. and Steward, K. (1990) *A Financial Handbook for Sales and Marketing Managers*, Cassell, London.

2 Latin American Free Trade Association.
3 'Hard currencies' are the internationally accepted pound sterling, US dollar, West German mark and Japanese yen. UK exporters generally expect payment in pounds or dollars.

Part Four   Planned Selling

13
The planned selling process

This chapter is about the technique of professional selling. It explains in detail the typical sales cycle practised by the author in his days as a minicomputer sales executive and later as a strategic marketing manager. This experience was gained with the companies EMI Medical, NCR, ICL and McDonnel Douglas Information Systems. The typical value of the sales sought and won during this period was in the range of £200,000–£500,000. The cumulative total during the nine years was in excess of £12 million. The principles of this structured technique are applicable to a wide range of selling activity and can be used and adapted for many products with a sales value of more than £500:

1 Every sales campaign must have a strategy for winning.
2 Every action taken must have specific objectives.
3 These objectives are achieved by following an agreed method and procedure.

13.1 Preparing to sell

Every contact with the prospect, whether it is a meeting, a demonstration, a presentation or the submission of a report or proposal, can advance or retard the chance of making a sale. A poor showing at any one of these points of contact can jeopardize that possibility irreparably. Therefore the professional takes great care to maximize the advantage that may be gained from these contacts. This is achieved by:

1 Preparing the sales campaign with care.
2 Planning the objectives.
3 Using a proven method and procedure to achieve these objectives.

13.1.1 Preparing yourself

The very first step in the selling process is for the sales executive to prepare himself for winning the contract.

Appearance

To present a professional image, the sales executive must dress in a conventional businesslike way. Fashion items for the most part should be avoided unless of course the industry is creative, where these eccentricities are expected. In standard commerce, convention is very important. Mannerisms and posture are also important. This means adopting a businesslike attitude, displaying a large element of self-respect and confidence. The higher the value of the business under consideration, the more importance there is attached to this protocol. As a rule of thumb, don't wear party clothes if the business is valued at more than £500. Finally, no sunglasses, no chewing gum and no cigarettes – leave all that in the car!

Attitude

It is important that the sales executive is enthusiastic about the products on sale and takes an obvious interest in what the prospects have to say about their business. A disciplined approach is essential to the effective management of a sales territory.

Business knowledge

The way to achieve sales is to relate your company's products and services to the prospect's needs. This requires an understanding of how the business operates at several levels: operator, supervisor, manager, technical adviser, accountant and director. Don't forget the business sales executive is selling solutions to business problems, and different businesses can have different problems.

Market knowledge

Next, the sales executive needs to know about the market he/she is selling into: the key organizations or companies, their decision-makers, whose equipment they use, why they use your competitors, who are the competition, what are their products, details of their product specifications and finally the trends in this marketplace – what problems will the prospects be facing tomorrow, what technological, legal, economic and socio-cultural developments are emerging?

Knowledge of company procedures

All companies have their own 'culture' and procedures. As a sales executive aspiring to the 'bonus club' or 'million pound round table', you should gain familiarity with these customs and norms: they are important for getting others in the prospect's company involved in helping you win the business. Ignorance of these cultural factors can alienate those who might be of great assistance in winning that sale.

13.1.2 Preparing to sell

An industrial sales person with a territorial, product, or vertical market responsibility will generally obtain business from making additional sales to existing customers and finding new companies to sell his/her company's products. The sales executive's business target will reflect this mix: all existing customers with their additional business potential will be listed, as will new prospects who have been identified. This information will usually be detailed in a 'territory plan' produced so that the area sales manager can forecast ahead and monitor the sales executive's performance. Each customer will be listed with details of address, telephone number, names and job titles of decision-makers and influencers, and details of their past purchases from your company. The forward business prospects should be summarized on one or two sheets of paper for planning and control. The summary might look like Table 13.1.

Table 13.1

Company name	Equipment	Value	Expected purchase date	Probability of sale	Value × probability
Z Machine Tools Ltd.	AB 716-2	£10,000	Jan 91	0.70	£7,000
Bank of U	AB 716-4	£20,000	Mar 91	0.60	£12,000
ABC Corp.	2 × AB 716-4	£41,000	Apr 91	0.40	£16,400
XYZ Ltd.	AB 716-2	£10,000	May 91	0.50	£5,000
		£81,000			£40,400

Identifiable sales in the first six months of 1991 are a possible £81,000. If the sales executive's target for this period is £250,000, there is a lot of work to do in finding some additional companies to whom sales can be made. The question is how to go about finding new business prospects. Some of the more usual sources are:

- References from existing customers.
- Direct mail replies.
- Exhibition leads.
- Coupon responses from display advertising.
- A predecessor's territory records.

- Delegates attending company seminars.
- Friends and associates.
- Telephone sales canvassing.

These are all fairly passive sources relying for the most part (except the direct mail) on other people to pass the information to the sales executive. There is, however, something positive that each sales executive can do: a systematic search to identify businesses in a predetermined segment of the market. These segments can be cut by geographical location, SIC code (standard industrial classification) or turnover, etc. The information is available from a range of business directories or their equivalent on-line business databases. Some of the largest and best known business on-line databases are:

- ICC Information Systems Ltd., 16–26 Banner Street, London EC1Y 8QE. Tel 071 253 0063.
- Financial Times Business Information, 126 Jermyn Street, London SW1Y 4UJ. Tel 071 925 2323.
- Reuters Ltd., 85 Fleet Street, London EC4P 4AJ. Tel 071 250 1122.
- Kompass On-line, Reed Information Services Ltd., Windsor Court, East Grinstead House, East Grinstead, West Sussex RH19 1BR. Tel 0342 315213.
- Extel Financial Ltd., Fitzroy House, 13–17 Epworth Street, London EC2A 4DL. Tel 071 251 3333.

13.1.3 Prequalifying

A good sales executive always keeps the prospect list topped up with new leads. Part of each week should be devoted to this task. This is far more effective than doing nothing when busy, and a massive effort when the prospect list looks unlikely to produce target level business. The sales executive should persuade his/her company to subscribe to one of the on-line databases mentioned above, and for a couple of hours each week should search for and download details of a few companies in the targeted market segment.

It will be necessary to 'prequalify' the companies searched for according to some of the following criteria:

- Is the head office in another person's territory?
- Is the company part of a group?
- Is the profit record healthy?
- Is the business technology or labour intensive?
- Is the company an identifiable prospect in terms of the products or services sold by your company?

The prequalification should of course be undertaken outside the main selling hours of 9am–1pm and 2pm–5pm.

13.2 Making the approach

The objective at this stage of preparing to sell is to decide whether this company has the potential for a sale. In other words, does their business potential justify the time and effort involved in mounting a campaign? This process is called 'qualifying' the suspect. When qualified, the suspect company becomes a prospect.

13.2.1 Evaluating the business potential

The essential questions revolve around the company's need for the products and services that your company can sell to them:

- Do they have the need?
- Can your product meet their need?
- Can this be done in a cost-effective way?
- Do they have a policy for buying this type of product? If so, is it open to include your company?
- Is the need recognized?
- Has the buying process started?
- Is there a competitor's product already installed?
- Who in the organization is responsible for these decisions?
- Are they accessible?
- Is there finance available for the purchase?
- Is the timescale of interest? (A decision that will not be made for two years is less interesting than one to be made in six months.)

13.2.2 The person to approach

One golden rule in selling is to do the business at the most senior level possible, where the decisions count for something. The objective is to discover who this person is, sell to them, overcome any objections and ask for the order. The danger with selling at a junior level is that the person may resist your subsequent attempts to meet the decision-maker in person. This is a real problem because the subordinate will probably lack the sales executive's skills to present the benefits of the product lucidly to superiors, and the sale can be lost. Hence, the rule is to deal with somebody in authority. This is of course easier when the product or service under consideration is expensive. If the products are inexpensive then you must attempt to sell volume which can either be many of one product or several of many products. In each case the total price could be substantial.

13.2.3 The method of approach

There are three methods of approaching the suspect: by telephone, by letter and making a 'cold call'. Cold calling has declined as a viable approach for making contact over the past twenty years. People in business are generally very busy, and not receptive to the 'hail fellow, well met' visit without an appointment.

The telephone is also intrusive in this context and should really be used only to find out who is the right person in the organization to contact. If in the process of doing this the sales executive speaks to the person he/she will be writing to, then he/she should either take the opportunity to qualify the prospect a little more, or say that he/she was thinking of writing to ask for an appointment to discuss such-and-such a perceived need.

An example of what the letter might look like is shown in Exhibit 13.1.

13.3 Opening the sale

On an opening call when the sales executive meets the prospective customer for the first time, he/she must be aware of first impressions and make certain that the ones made are favourable. Winning the prospect's respect and confidence at this stage is extremely important.

13.3.1 Plan the call objectives

First establish the needs. Is the prospect interested? Can he/she see the need? Next, qualify the prospect. Can your company's products meet the needs? Third, identify and understand the prospect's decision-making process: who decides, what are the criteria, what is the timescale and who if any are the competition? Finally, the sales executive should be attempting to get an agreement to some plan of action: an agreement as to who does what next.

13.3.2 Pre-call preparation

Before the meeting there are a number of things that the proficient sales executive will attend to in order to maximize the chances of reaching a positive position at the end of the initial encounter.

Exhibit 13.1

Mr A. B. Snook BSc, MIPM
Training Director
Gulf Chemicals plc
Inner Circle
Regents Park
London NW1 4NS

Dear Mr Snook

I have read with a certain amount of interest about Gulf
Chemicals' recent acquisition of several smaller chemical
businesses as reported in the business press. I was wondering if
you had considered how the different financial reporting
systems might cause difficulty for purposes of consolidation
and ultimately control.

For example, do all the cost centre managers thoroughly
understand the terminology, objectives and procedures of
Gulf's monthly reporting system? Clearly a specially prepared
training programme might be of benefit.

KSA has helped many clients to identify and resolve business
problems through carefully designed training programmes.
These have proved very cost-effective, particularly in the
busy post-acquisition period.

Should you wish to take this a step further, a one-hour meeting
might serve to identify the specific areas where KSA might make
the greatest contribution. Perhaps I could telephone your
secretary next week to arrange a convenient time to meet.

Yours sincerely

K Steward

Keith Steward

The first thing to do is to prepare some opening statements that grab the prospect's attention, saying clearly why the meeting has been called. A professional start to the meeting will gain the prospect's respect.

Another point of preparation is to make sure that any visual aids that might be required are ready. These aids should be chosen to make a strong visual impact and avoid lengthy explanations. They may include brochures, photocopies from technical manuals, sample reports, editorial on the product or even a desk-top flip chart.

Any foreseeable objections should be anticipated and counters prepared in advance (explain, offset and prove). It would be foolish to fall at the first hurdle.

Finally, prepare some reference sales: note down a few customers where the purchase of the company's products has been a great success. Avoid where possible a direct competitor to the new prospect (that may backfire) and check with the company being used as an example (if it is one of his/her customers that is being quoted) that all is well. Finally, it can be a good idea to summarize these points on a call plan for easy reference during that first meeting (see Exhibit 13.2).

13.4 Strategies for decisions

Asking the right questions will help the sales executive find out the prospect's 'basis of decision' at that time. However, at this stage the experienced sales executive is wary of the various difficulties yet to be encountered:

• Has this person the money?	M
• Has this person the authority?	A
• Has this person the need?	N
• Do the company's products have an area of uniqueness?	A
• Are the competition involved?	C
• What is the timescale?	T

MANACT is something that a wise sales person will bear in mind when planning a sales strategy for an identified prospect. It is a useful method of qualifying a suspect and deciding whether they are worth much time and effort.

The next task is to identify all the managers and directors who might be involved in making the decision. This might include the chairman, managing director, finance director, technical director, sales and marketing director, departmental manager and ultimate users. Each person who is party to the decision needs to be met and their attitudes

Exhibit 13.2

CALL PLAN		
COMPANY	CONTACT NAME	POSITION
CALL OBJECTIVES		
OPENING STATEMENT		
POSSIBLE OBJECTIONS	COUNTERS	

AIDS
☐ Foils
☐ Flip (Full size/Desktop)
☐ Brochure
☐ Report Format
☐ Screen Format
☐ Other

Reference sell
Co.
Address
Tel.   Checked with local office
Contact   OK to use

Use the reverse of this form for your visit report.

and point of view noted. If possible their basis of decision in favour of one product or another should be discovered.

The sales executive should also establish exactly what the product is to be used for. An office computer might be used for: sales ledger, purchase ledger, nominal ledger, asset register, payroll and the provision of management accounts. How much does this currently cost? What are the drawbacks of the existing system?

Remember that the ultimate basis of decision will be which supplier can match the prospect's requirements most specifically. This may involve price, particular product features, perceived quality of service, logical expansion path, size, design, ease of operation and speed of delivery. The sales executive has to identify these key criteria and make certain that the company can meet them precisely. If not, the sales person must place doubt on the importance of the criterion which the company cannot attain. For example, price: if your company only supplies a quality product, you must work with the prospect to justify the benefit to his company of buying a superior product rather than taking the cheapest on the market. Selling business solutions is largely about convincing the prospect that he/she has a particular set of needs which match the benefits of the product the sales executive has available. Clearly there are limits to what may be achieved in this area, and the experienced sales executive does not get involved in a situation where the prospect's needs are vastly different from what his/her company can offer.

Identifying the basis of decision is crucial to the sale strategy because:

- It indicates the selling activity necessary to prove that a particular company can meet the needs.
- It prevents the prospect from opting for a competitor's product on the grounds of lower cost.
- It looks professional.
- It can provide the opportunity for making the 'unique selling proposition' (USP).

The following checklist will help the sales executive to recognize what the position is in the sales campaign and what needs to be done to get a decision.

1 Is the opportunity qualified?

- Is there a genuine business need for the type of solution offered by your product?
- Does the prospect recognize the need?
- Is the prospect sufficiently determined to go ahead with this type of solution?

- Do you believe that the solution can be justified:
    on quantifiable cost savings/increase in profits?
    on unquantifiable benefits to the business?
- Is the finance available?

2 *Have you identified decision-makers and recommenders?*

- Do you know who will make the decision?
- Whose recommendation will the decision-maker seek?

3 *Have you agreed the decision criteria?*

- What does the prospect want from your product?
- Do you know why he/she will buy from your company?
- Does he/she know why he will buy from your company?
- Have you got agreement to the basis for the decision?

4 *Have you identified competitive activity?*

- Who is involved, or who could be?
- Who has been rejected, and why?
- Which decision-maker and/or recommender is susceptible to competitive influence?

5 *Have you defined the sales strategy?*

- Have you defined the specific action you need to close the sale?
- Have you scheduled these activities?
- Have you agreed a decision timescale?
- Have you scheduled your own time?

6 *Have you made full use of your resources?*

- Have you demonstrated your company's solution?
- Has the prospect visited a reference site?
- Have you presented to the staff or the would-be user department?
- Have you presented to the decision-maker/recommender?
- Have you involved technical support staff?
- Have you scheduled the resources that may be required?
- Have you agreed a staff training plan?
- Have you agreed an implementation plan?
- Have you outlined a plan for continuing executive contact on a formal basis?
- Have you thought about using the company's senior management?

7 Does the prospect agree to the feasibility of your company's solution?
Is it:

- Financially justified?
- Technically feasible?
- Practically feasible?
- The right time to proceed?

8 Do you have the agreement of all the key recommenders/decision-makers?

- Have you satisfactorily answered all objections?
- Does your proposal acknowledge agreement?

9 Can he/she sign your contract?

- Does the decision-maker have the authority to sign?
- Have you cleared the contract fine print with the prospect?
- Have you asked for a signature?

10 Are you mentally prepared for the sale?

14

Implementing the plan and making the sale

It is now time to start progressing the sale towards that final moment when the prospect signs the contract. In order to do this a number of meetings will take place between the sales executive and the prospective buyer. In sales jargon these meetings are referred to as 'sales calls', and as such they need to be planned in advance. These calls are very important to the sales executive because they present the opportunity for gathering facts, establishing prospect needs, presenting sales ideas, providing statements of capability, scoring points over the competition and generally creating a professional image. Because the call is so important in terms of making a sale, the structure has been broken down into component parts for analysis.

14.1 The structure of a sales call

A sales call can be broken down into five components:

- Plan call
  objectives
  opening statement
  anticipate objections
  sales aids
- Opening
  create impact
  summarize
  state purpose
- Body
  question
  listen
  sell benefits
  use aids
  handle objections

- Summary and close
    confirm understanding
    establish agreement
    future plan
- Future plan
    follow-up
    reappraise strategy

The call plan is vitally important to successful selling: it is essential to plan the objectives of the call, otherwise there is nothing specific to aim for. Without an objective the call can become a chat and as such is useless.

Second, you must prepare an opening statement. This is an opportunity to grab the prospect's attention and commence a useful structured dialogue. Any sales executive who starts with 'Well, how are things?' deserves to get thrown out for being crass and unprofessional.

Third, you must anticipate possible objections to any claims and prepare a response. Experienced politicians when they are interviewed on the television have been rehearsed by colleagues to minimize the possibility of making a gaff or seeming not to know the answer. The sensible sales executive does the same.

Finally, you should prepare any visual aids that might be an advantage – a picture or diagram may explain a concept more clearly than a thousand words.

Create impact

In the opening minutes of a sales call, the sales executive should endeavour to create interest and establish rapport, then summarize the relevant background and clearly state the purpose of the visit. It is very important that the customer knows what the sales executive is hoping to achieve. In an ideal situation they may both have the same objective and may conveniently work together. Alternatively, the prospect may say that what the sale executive hopes to achieve is impossible. This at least saves time and wasted effort. Indeed, the prospect may suggest what is realistically achieveable, and this may still be of interest.

However, in the event that this does not happen and the purpose of the call is accepted, the sales executive can proceed to the 'main body' of the call, keeping the call objectives firmly focused. In general terms these should comprise:

- identifying the prospect's interests and needs,
- identifying and appraising any competitive activity,
- establishing the prospect's basis for making a decision,
- qualifying him/her for a sale of your company's products.

Asking questions

In the body of the sales call, the sales executive gathers facts, identifies needs, presents ideas, discusses alternative solutions and answers any objections. This is achieved by asking questions, listening to the answers, selling benefits and handling objections skilfully.

It is important to remember that some prospects may be difficult to deal with because they have a dominant personality and terse manner. These people require great sensitivity and skilful handling. Using the above techniques is a sure way to overcome these difficulties.

Asking relevant questions is not only a way of obtaining information but also of controlling the direction and pace of the meeting. Questions can also serve to put the prospect at ease by getting him involved in the discussion. Making him/her think out the answers to penetrating questions will help them to relax. Questions can also be used to seek agreement. Getting the prospect to say 'yes' will also assist the smooth flow of the call. Finally, questions should be used to get commitment: 'If XYZ Ltd does this will you support the proposal?'

Listen to the prospect

Having asked a question, it is essential that the sales executive listen to the answer carefully. It can be very annoying when someone does not appear to be listening to what you say. Annoyed prospects do not give business to those who have caused the annoyance, so the sales executive should keep an alert posture, maintain eye contact, make a note or two, nod in agreement and avoid doodling and stifled yawns.

Let the prospect finish speaking before asking the next question: do not talk over the last part of the answer. Listen to the answers: if they reveal a new area of interest, follow it up with a new line of questions and abandon the carefully prepared list of questions if they no longer seem relevant. Finally, do not be afraid of a little silence when waiting for the answer to a question. The prospect is probably thinking – have the courtesy to wait in silence.

Selling benefits

In most instances people buy a product for what it will do for them, rather than what it is, that is the benefits of ownership or the pleasure of consumption. The exceptions are usually prestige items with a particular brand name: a Rolls Royce car: a painting by Van Gogh or Picasso; a Rolex watch for example.

A benefit is an actual advantage from ownership or usage and it arises by satisfying a need. The sales executive's task is firstly to identify the need, then to select the benefit that meets that need. The benefit must be clearly stated in language that the prospect will understand and be directly related to the identified need.

This is more difficult than is at first apparent, and the reason is this. Engineers and marketing specialists design products with features because they are tangible and they can be specifically designed and created. Products are then made to a specification which should be based on thorough product market research. The fact sheets which a company produces list these features in great technical detail, which is useful to the prospect when making a buying decision, but frequently they need translating into specific benefits that relate to particular needs. The sales executive must provide that translation service to maximize chances of closing the sale. Table 14.1 shows examples of products, a feature and a potential benefit associated with that feature.

When selling benefits, endeavour to quantify them wherever possible in terms of time and money saved for the tangible benefits (i.e. increased revenue, reduced costs, fewer operators, fewer rejects, less wastage). The unquantifiable benefits should be presented in terms of reduced risk because your product offers improved customer service, better

Table 14.1

Product	Feature	Benefit
Saloon car	Aluminium bodywork	1 Will not rust 2 Lighter than steel, so higher performance for engine size
	2-litre engine	More power = less strain from driving because of reduced noise and higher cruising speeds
Kitchen units	Solid wood door	1 Quality finish possible 2 Handles do not pull out 3 No danger of peeling veneer on edges
XX Financial modelling package	Integrated ledger systems	1 management accounts can be produced without re-keying data 2 saves money and time = better quality information = better operational decisions = (hopefully) greater profits

management control of variables, easy expansion in the future, an established supplier etc. The credibility can be increased by quoting reference customers. See Exhibit 14.1.

Using sales aids

Visual aids can be valuable selling tools, particularly if the product is complex or the application novel or particularly technical. Examples are: brochures, manuals, technical write-ups, graphs, cost-benefit calculations, plans, photographs and slides. They can be very useful

- to clarify any complicated technical point,
- to reinforce a benefit,
- to act as an *aide memoire* to the prospect,
- to bring the sales executive into closer contact with the prospect (this can serve to reduce the barrier between 'us' and 'them').

Having claimed some advantages to sales aids, it is as well to be aware of the dangers of their indiscriminate use. Handing across a brochure can be the biggest conversation stopper. It can be difficult to compete with and indeed the prospect might assume all the relevant information is in the brochure and use this as a reason to terminate the interview.

The lesson is to be wary of introducing distractions unless they are controllable: for example keep hold of any brochure or chart and go round the side of the prospect's desk to point out the detail in question. When demonstrating something use a pen and not a finger as a pointer, and put the material away after it has been used. If the prospect wants a copy leave it behind at the end of the meeting or send one through the post with a covering letter or report summarizing the main points covered during the meeting.

Handling objections

On course for making a sale it is quite usual to encounter objections that are expressed by the prospect. This is nothing to be afraid of and merely represents the usual anxiety that most people have when spending money or making a major decision. The three major types of objection have already been identified (drawback, misunderstanding and scepticism). Here, some general procedures will be presented as to how to deal with all these objections effectively, then specific techniques will be used to deal with specific objections when they are used.

First, when presented with an objection, pause (even if you have a reply ready): it lets the prospect know that the remarks have been listened to. It also shows respect for the point of view expressed which is important in a situation which could degenerate into confrontation if not handled carefully. In some instances, the prospect may answer his/her own objection because having spoken it aloud it sounds trite or may go on to reveal real concern in greater depth.

Exhibit 14.1 Summary of benefits

Need								Feature	Benefit
Financial management tools	Operations management tools	Growth capacity for future requirements	Minimum disruption to business	Proven supplier capability	Reliable service to users	Supply of hardware and software	Best value for money		
			✓					Availability of support from number-cruncher systems	Removes risk of not understanding how it works ∴ implemented more quickly
				✓				Many number-cruncher users of production packages	Reduces risk of not working because 'bugs' not identified
			✓					Operator diagnostics and aids (e.g. 'Help' command)	Reduces time in effecting repair ∴ less downtime
✓	✓							User programmable systems	Saves money, user can do it himself quickly ∴ saves time
✓							✓	Financial modelling packages	Faster analysis of financial data – better quality decisions – less risk, more profit
			✓		✓			Hardware and software reliability features	= less down time = less disruption = greater operational benefit

The next point concerns having the correct attitude, which requires a calm, confident response demonstrating that the objection has been given serious consideration. When the objection has been countered, the sales executive should ask if the prospect is satisfied with the reply. If 'yes', then it is reasonable to ask for some commitment by a 'trial close'.

A 'trial close' is a practice close that is presented casually so that if the prospect has another objection there is scope to counter this too before the 'final close'. The final close is what it says and should only be used when a positive response is the only one possible.

The three main types of objection listed in Chapter 9 are presented again in Table 14.2 with some additional variations:

Summary and close
Summarizing is a sales technique in its own right: indeed, in a court of law the judge summarizes the evidence for the jury before they adjourn. The point is to get definite agreement to what has been negotiated in the preceding discussion and make back-tracking difficult.

Failure to summarize risks the prospect forgetting the points that have been agreed. Furthermore, it provides the sales executive with an opportunity to recap and bring out any hidden objections, to establish agreement to conclusions and commitment to future action.

Of course, the really professional course is to confirm the summary in writing. It should be beautifully presented and correct in every detail. Avoid overstepping the mark by seeking to impose agreement on what has not been fully discussed. This risks a hostile response. Finally, remember to put in writing only what can be substantiated in practice: what is written can be filed and produced at a later date. Failure to meet the claims could result in breach of contract.

14.2 Selling the company

At any point in a sales campaign the sales executive could be confronted with the statement, 'You have succeeded in convincing us that we need a computer, but why should we buy one from your company?' The answer to this question is to present verbally some succinct reasons why they should buy from ABC Limited or Numbercruncher Systems. This should be followed up with written confirmation of the points and any available supporting documentation. The following are some suggested headings:

Table 14.2 *List of major objections*

Objection	Skill	Steps to follow
Misunderstanding	Explaining	Provide correct information Expand with benefits
Scepticism	Proving	Offer proof Expand with benefits
Drawback	Offsetting	Re-focus on all considerations; compare pros and cons to draw conclusions
Hidden objection	Listen and question tactfully	The objection must be brought into the open where it can be dealt with according to type
Delay	Question why? Use tact	The reasons for a reluctance to proceed must be uncovered before it can be dealt with
Specific reason (e.g. price)	Re-establish needs and benefits	Present price in terms of value for money and put it in proportion in terms of the cost of failure
Flimsy or fatuous objection	Ignore it totally	Pause Continue with dialogue
A fact (difficult to explain successfully)	Postpone discussion or acknowledge objection	Offer to discuss later Re-focus on other benefits Agree with prospect Offset
As yet unspoken but expected imminently	Forestall	Acknowledge objection Offset

1 Numbercruncher products

- Competitive price/performance ratio.
- Proven technology that is both modern and reliable.
- The product supplied can easily be upgraded as the buyer's organization expands.

2 Numbercruncher service

- The products are readily available from operational production lines.
- Installation is by company-trained specialists.
- There is an education and training school for customer employees to gain experience using the product.
- An on-line support service is available.
- Highly trained field engineers are available to maintain the hardware.

3 Confidence in Numbercruncher Systems

- The company is committed to customer satisfaction (member of the Institute of Customer Care – see chapter 5).
- Large number of UK customers (references given).
- Respect for company supported by the press (examples included).

4 Value

- Investment in Numbercruncher reduces the risk of 'unforeseeable costs' due to technical problems with the product or inexperience in implementation.
- Cost savings achieved by existing customers are documented.

5 Numbercruncher sales team

- Professionals committed to selling working solutions – sales executives, field engineers, technical support specialists and management.

14.3 The proposal

This is a detailed document of the company's offer of goods and services to the prospect. it should not include anything that has not been discussed with the prospect and should not be sent unless complete. Any points of uncertainty arising during preparation should be discussed with the prospect prior to going into print.

Producing a written proposal is a skilled job and cannot be undertaken for the first time without personal guidance and a template on which to base the document.

Content

The detailed outline of the content of an actual proposal prepared by the author for a £750,000 computer system is included as a guide for technical products of a capital nature (see Exhibit 14.2). Clearly, paragraphs can be added or discarded to reflect the product or industry concerned, but the main headings should be applicable across a wide range of applications. A final note on this particular proposal, which ran to fifty-five pages plus brochures and supporting documentation: it was produced in two weeks by two people responding to a prospect want description of 512 pages.

Exhibit 14.2   *Contents of a proposal for a £750,000 computer system*

Where a technical brochure already exists, use it as an appendix rather than have the information wordprocessed. However, it is not advisable to place the brochure in the main body of text as this will interrupt the flow of the presentation. The correct place for brochures is at the back of the report as appendices; however, refer to the appropriate appendix in the text so that the reader can refer to it if desired. Generally speaking, brochures, data sheets, standard legal contracts, itemized schedules of equipment, system flow charts and details of existing customers being used as a reference sale should be placed in clearly labelled appendices.

When the proposal has been written and wordprocessed, choose a moment (or half an hour) to sit down quietly and read it from cover to cover. This reading through should stimulate some thoughts about the document and who is going to read it. These thoughts can be expressed in writing in a management summary, a covering letter or indeed both. An example of the covering letter is shown in Exhibit 14.3.

Exhibit 14.3

Maurice Simpson FCCA
Finance Director
Casey Mouldings plc
Isleworth Trading Estate
Brentford
Middlesex TW3 3TW

Dear Mr Simpson

I am pleased to submit Numbercruncher's proposal for a computer-based solution to Casey's production scheduling difficulties. In doing so, I should like to thank your Management team for their co-operation during the past six weeks. I am confident that the time spent in helping us to define objectives, and in vetting our proposals, will prove to be time well spent.

Scope of the proposal: We have identified the areas which show the greatest scope for improved administration and control systems as:

  (i) the elimination of constraints on the supply of goods – to the consumer marketplace and the improvement of customer service in general

  (ii) the introduction of new financial control systems to reduce costs and to improve the control of prices and profitability

Page 3 of our proposal contains a complete list of other considerations which we agreed would form the basis of your decision for a computer system.

Recommendation: That Casey Mouldings order a Numbercruncher System 10 for delivery in April of next year. The implementation plan on page 13 shows that we can introduce systems to satisfy these business requirements within two years.

This is the plan which we agreed with you on August 17th, and it also has the concurrence of Mr Johnson, Ms Peacock and Dr Snow.

The Financial Investment: The estimated cost of the Numbercruncher products and services amounts to an initial one-time charge of £122,750 to cover the necessary hardware application programme packages and programming services. Thereafter the annual cost of support and maintenance is estimated at an average of £5,000 p.a. over the first three years. Set against these costs are your estimates of operation savings showing payback on the initial investment by the end of Year Two, and a cumulative net return before tax by the end of Year Three of £84,000.

A detailed analysis of costs and expected savings appears in Section 7. These are the figures agreed at our meeting on August 17th.

Benefits: In choosing a Numbercruncher system, Casey Mouldings will gain considerable benefits which cannot be expressed in financial germs. Among them:

The System 10 grows with your business. You may add or replace equipment with minimum disruption and no conversion costs.

Numbercruncher support services that are widely acknowledged for their professionalism:

– short delivery time
– local customer centres for total installation support
– Numbercruncher's bespoke software services
– Education and training for all levels of staff and management

The confidence in Numbercruncher products and services expressed by:

– 30 local customers using System 10
– 450 customers in UK
– The independent statements of customer executives (Mr Marshall, Ms Peacock and Dr Snow)

A Numbercruncher support team which takes customer service as its number one objective.

Conclusion: We have tried to demonstrate to your satisfaction that Numbercruncher can satisfy your decision criteria, and that the combination of our Numbercruncher hardware and support services represents the best return on your investment.

Finally, might I say that if we are to keep to the scheduled dates on the implementation plan, I shall ask you to place an order for the equipment and give the go-ahead for the pre-installation activity when we meet next on Monday September 3rd.

Yours sincerely

Keith Steward
Sales Executive

Style

The proposal should be written in the third person, grammatically correct and easy to read. Avoid unnecessary technical detail in the main body of the text, saving that for specific clearly identifiable appendices. Consider who is going to read it and what their main points of interest are. This means that the text should be divided into chapters, each with a heading, and within these chapters sections should also be clearly labelled.

It is important to avoid unnecessary verbosity by keeping sentences short and making regular use of paragraphs. Pay attention to page layout and appearance, starting major sections on a new page.

Accuracy

It is important that the proposal is checked for accuracy from a technical viewpoint, that the prices quoted are correct and add up, that the VAT is accurately calculated, that there are no omitted extras, and finally that production and support groups can deliver in the timescales quoted. Over-optimism with timescales and incorrect prices can cause problems. Even when the contract has been signed, the customer can still decide not to take delivery or attempt to hold the supplying company to an incorrect low price. Whatever the result, the sales executive has problems – the least of which will be the late payment of any commission.

14.4 Closing the sale

Closing the sale is achieving some action that will result in the prospect's signature on an agreement or order form. It is a technique that will be used many times during the course of selling. It represents the sales executive leading the prospect through a sequence of events that culminates in an agreement to buy.

Closing must be done with confidence although the fear of rejection can make it difficult sometimes to say the words. The anticipated embarrassment of rejection and disappointment can be acute. The author is able to recall having said to the trainee sales executive during sales training 'role plays', 'That's just what I want', to be met with the reply 'Or you could have the green one!' Such was the degree of tension that the young would-be sales executives had closed their ears to what they really wanted to hear.

But if the prospect does say no, there must be an objection. So there is now a reason for discussing the objection. When the sales executive has overcome the objection, the close can be repeated: the prospect is asked for commitment again. If the answer is still no, the process should be repeated. If it leads to a final no, then the sales executive may have to face up to a lost campaign. This is not the end of the world: no one ever suggested it was possible to win them all. It is better to find out sooner than later.It will release time to devote to other sales campaigns where the chances of success might be higher.

Whenever you feel apprehensive as a sales executive, you should remember that the prospect knows why you are in his/her office. The prospect is expecting to be asked for a commitment when all the questions have been answered. Fumble around and you will lose respect and possibly the sale. It is most unwise to expect the prospect to volunteer and ask for the agreement, just as your dinner guest at a restaurant is unlikely to ask for an invitation into your home afterwards for 'coffee'. Indeed, a positive approach at this stage will command respect. So ask for the order in a natural and confident manner; then shut up.

Asking the question puts the prospect on the hook. One more word will let him/her off it. The sales executive may feel pressure building up if the silence continues, but it must be ignored – the sales executive must stay silent. It is also important to keep a distance. Extra pressure should not be applied by too close physical contact. Eye contact should be maintained, but the sales executive should sit back and avoid a tense posture, looking relaxed but confident.

14.4.1 Methods of closing

The assumptive close
This is one of the most graceful techniques for making a sale and can be highly effective. It requires a positive attitude on the part of the sales executive, a good understanding of the structure of a sales interview, adroit objection handling and the assumption that purchase is virtually a foregone conclusion.

Success is very much dependent on thorough preparation: qualification – MANACT (money, authority, need, area of uniqueness, competition and timescale), good product knowledge and a clear understanding of the prospects needs. There is nothing to lose by assuming – if the prospect is not yet ready, you will be told. If the assumption was made in a tactful non-pressurized way – nothing will have been lost and another assumptive close can be made a few minutes later.

The assumptive close can effectively be made by asking a carefully worded question that only has relevance if a purchase can be assumed.

- Will you be paying cash or charge card?
- When did you want delivery?
- What completion date did you have in mind?

Forced-choice close

This is a method of attempting a trial close, by asking the prospect to chose between two alternative products for which the benefits have already been clearly explained:

- Was it the blue or the dark green that impressed you the most?
- Were you thinking of one dozen or two?

The strength of this technique is that it obliges the prospect to make a positive choice between the two viable alternatives. Whereas the question, were you thinking of buying the green one?, can more easily result in a negative response – just because the sales person has misjudged the preferred colour.

Another point to bear in mind is to avoid offering too many choices or giving so many explanations that the prospect is tired and confused by all the detail. When that happens the prospect postpones making a decision and the opportunity is lost. It is much better to identify the prospect's wants and restrict the choice of products offered to two or maybe three.

Open question . . . pause technique

An open question is one where it is difficult to respond with a simple 'yes' or 'no'. The concept behind this approach is to help the prospect realize that he/she has all the information required to make a decision. The pause (which is extremely important) is to apply a little gentle pressure to move him/her towards that important commitment.

'Mr Armstrong, what is your reaction to the demonstration?' After asking the question, it is abolutely essential to remain silent and give the prospect an opportunity to think and make the first comment. Interrupt and the 'spell' is broken and the discussion moves away from the unanswered key question. After asking the question, shut up and look purposeful, confident and business-like. Avoid staring at the prospect but do not be afraid to look at him/her.

The yes, yes, yes technique

This technique is based on obtaining a progressive sequence of multiple acceptances towards the penultimate question which is asking for the order. Here is an example:

Sales executive: Did you notice how the . . .
Prospect: Yes I did.
Sales executive: Would you agree that . . .
Prospect: Yes I would.
Sales executive: If I could prove to you . . . would you be interested?
Prospect: Yes, of course.

The contingency close technique

This is where the sales executive agrees to do something contingent on the prospect agreeing to buy. It has the advantage of applying a little pressure and avoiding the sales executive going to extra trouble to no avail. Examples might be:

- If I can get you on to the 10.30 flight and into the Royal Palace Hotel is that a deal?
- If I wordprocess the main points of our discussion today, and confirm delivery on the 29th at the standard price and bring the document to your office on Thursday morning will you sign the contract now?

The future close technique

This is a device that sets a deadline whereby the terms of business change against the customers interest at some date in the future. The disadvantage of delaying is usually a price increase, or lack of availability (through rationing or perishability or some other supply problem). This technique needs to be used with discretion because some buyers object strongly to this type of pressure.

'Special-offer' close

This is usually part of a sales promotion campaign. It is generally better only to do this as part of a tactical plan unless it is part of a 'clearance sale of end-of-line items' or slightly damaged stock. It can create a difficult precedence if not carefully managed.

'Puppy-dog' technique

This technique is named after the way of selling puppies to people who are undecided – leave it with them for a few days, and they will not be able to bear parting with it. The idea is generally applied these days to items of equipment lent for 'evaluation purposes'. If the prospect with the item on trial is impressed then they order a quantity.

The counsellor close

This technique is dependent on the sales executive having developed a sound trusting relationship with the client. Technical selling uses this device because the customer is frequently dependent on the sales exeuctive for technical advice and guidance.

The last one

This approach operates on the basis that some people only deciede that they need something when it is not available or when somebody else is determined to have it. It can legitimately be used when stocks are running low and certain customers are known to be dependent on immediate supply. The technique should be used with care because it is a favourite of the disreputable and might jaundice the sales executives or the company's reputation.

Summarize the benefits

The author first recalls learning this approach as an undergraduate working part-time selling index-linked life insurance in the late 1960s. Quite simply the sales executive, towards the end of the presentation, offers to summarize the benefits for the prospect of making the purchase. These can be tabulated on a sheet of paper for maximum effect. Once that has been done – a comment such as 'well that seems pretty conclusive' should complete the sale. It is important not to introduce new ideas at this stage because that will only provoke discussion rather than encourage commitment.

Ask for the order

Finally, ask for the business: 'May I have your order please?' or 'When can we start?' Then look meaningful, but keep quiet. Remember after asking a question . . . keep silent until you have an answer.

15
Sales forecasting

Traditionally, businesses have made those goods and services which they had the knowledge and resources to produce, and once the products were completed, the sales force was turned loose on the unsuspecting population. Sales people and managers were given their targets or quotas and accountants calculated the break-even point, carefully allocating overheads in the preferred manner.

However, in very few instances was any serious attempt made to quantify the size of the market in terms of what the consumer needed or wanted and to calculate the potential volume of sales. All the skills and effort had been applied internally to the organization without attempting to consider two very important factors: the consumer, and the competition.

In this chapter the concept of market segmentation is presented as a technique for measuring and analysing the potential total sales of a product in the marketplace. The wide availability of direct mailing lists means that this technique may be used with great precision. Each potential customer (in industrial markets) is identifiable by name and address from the mailing list.

Once prospective customers have been identified and the buying cycle has begun a highly pragmatic technique for forecasting the value of the potential sales is required. One such technique is explained which is suitable for industrial product and high-cost consumer durables. Once the number of potential customers exceeds 300–400 this method becomes rather cumbersome.

The final section of the chapter looks at the market for fast moving consumer goods. Here it is quite impossible to consider individual consumers and buying decisions because the numbers are so large. However, statistical theory can be of great assistance in the form of time series analysis. This is a sophisticated method and can be very accurate.

15.1 Measuring the market

Measuring the total market for a product or service is like painting a picture with a very broad brush. It serves as a starting point in the analysis, the reason being that the demand specification is so generalized as to be particular to only a very small percentage of buyers. Consumer requirements differ, and many people are seeking to purchase additional benefits above and beyond the basic product.

The UK market for housing is a good example (albeit somewhat out of its usual context) because of the vast amount of precise analysis that has been done on this subject. First thoughts might put this market as the total population (some 54 million people). Further analysis might reveal the fact that some people prefer to live in towns, while others live in rural areas. Other variations occur in the type of accommodation (house or flat) and whether the inhabitants are the owners, in the process of purchasing the property, or tenants.

Indeed, so much work has been done in this area that 'a classification of residential neighbourhoods' (ACORN) has gained widespread acceptance as a market segmentation grid. The rationale is that similar neighbourhoods will be populated by people with similar demographic and social characteristics representing similar life-style features. These in turn will be translated into purchase habits for products and services.

Table 15.1 shows the twelve basic ACORN groups and Table 15.2 a list of thirty-nine relatively homogeneous ACORN types, made by subdividing the groups on a local basis.

Table 15.1   *1981 ACORN profile UK ACORN Groups*

		1981 population	
		Thousand	*%*
A	Agricultural areas	1811	3.4
B	Modern family housing, higher incomes	8667	16.2
C	Older housing of intermediate status	9420	17.6
D	Poor quality older terraced housing	2321	4.3
E	Better-off council estates	6977	13.0
F	Less well-off council estates	5033	9.4
G	Poorest council estates	4049	7.6
H	Multi-racial areas	2086	3.9
I	High status non-family areas	2248	4.2
J	Affluent suburban housing	8515	15.9
K	Better-off retirement areas	2248	3.8
U	Unclassified	389	0.7

Source   ACORN User's Guide. CACI Market Analysis Division

Table 15.2 *ACORN types*

			1981 population	
			Thousand	%
A	1	Agricultural villages	1376	2.6
A	2	Areas of farms and smallholdings	435	0.8
B	3	Cheap modern private housing	2210	4.1
B	4	Recent private housing, young families	1649	3.1
B	5	Modern private housing, older children	3121	5.8
B	6	New detached houses, young families	1405	2.6
B	7	Military bases	282	0.5
C	8	Mixed owner-occupied and council estates	1880	3.5
C	9	Small town centres and flats above shops	2157	4.0
C	10	Villages with non-farm employment	2463	4.6
C	11	Older private housing, skilled workers	2920	5.5
D	12	Unimproved terraces with old people	1352	2.5
D	13	Pre-1914 terraces, low income families	762	1.4
D	14	Tenement flats lacking amenities	207	0.4
E	15	Council estates, well-off older workers	1916	3.6
E	16	Recent council estates	1393	2.6
E	17	Council estates, well-off young workers	2615	4.9
E	18	Small council houses, often Scottish	1052	2.0
F	19	Low-rise estates in industrial towns	2538	4.7
F	20	Inter-war council estates, older people	1668	3.1
F	21	Council housing for the elderly	827	1.5
G	22	New council estates in inner cities	1080	2.0
G	23	Overspill estates, high unemployment	1730	3.2
G	24	Council estates with overcrowding	868	1.6
G	25	Council estates with worst poverty	371	0.7
H	26	Multi-occupied terraces, poor Asians	204	0.4
H	27	Owner-occupied terraces with Asians	578	1.1
H	28	Multi-let housing with Afro-Caribbeans	387	0.7
H	29	Better-off multi-ethnic areas	916	1.7
I	30	High status areas, few children	1129	2.1
I	31	Multi-let big old houses and flats	822	1.5
I	32	Furnished flats, mostly single people	297	0.5
J	33	Inter-war semis, white collar workers	3054	5.7
J	34	Spacious inter-war semis, big gardens	2677	5.0
J	35	Villages with wealthy older commuters	1534	2.9
J	36	Detached houses, exclusive suburbs	1250	2.3
K	37	Private houses, well-off elderly	1200	2.2
K	38	Private flats with single pensioners	842	1.6
U	39	Unclassified	389	0.7
Area total			53,557	100.0

Source *ACORN User's Guide.* CACI Market Analysis Division

15.2 Market segmentation

In section 15.1 segmentation was presented as an approach for measuring demand in a realistic way by attempting to distinguish between different types of consumption in the market for housing. In this section, the generally accepted alternative methods for segmentation will be examined; for consumer markets they are: geographic, demographic, psychographic and behavioural.

Geographic segmentation
This is a method of dividing a total market based on significant regional differences that will have an effect on consumer requirements. This method is generally of lesser significance in European countries than in the USA, because demographic divisions based on nationality differences tend to override the geographic distinctions. For example, differences in the market for package holidays between France and Germany are probably as much to do with custom and national characteristics than geographical location.

However, in the UK, the following factors are relevant: rural and urban in terms of home central heating, for example with oil being used in rural areas and gas in urban areas. This may be explained by the fact that laying a gas main in high population density urban areas is a sound economic proposition. Furthermore, many flats in urban areas would find it a nuisance to make room for a 500-gallon oil storage tank which in rural areas fits conveniently into an obscure corner of the garden.

Demographic segmentation
This is probably the easiest concept to understand: essentially it means that consumption is examined under all the categories included in anti-discrimination legislation and a few more (age, sex, family size, family life-cycle, income, occupation, education, religion, race and nationality). Another advantage of demographic segmentation is the availability of the information from census data. It is also substantially accurate, although clearly there is degradation as the data can be up to ten years old.

Multivariable demographic segmentation is an extension of this, and offers some interesting prospects for analysis. This is partially demonstrated in Table 15.3. Clearly, target groups would have been more precisely identified, and their requirements understood and the appropriate product marketing plans effected, if the ACORN and socio-economic classification (A, B, C1, C2, D, E) had been overlaid on the age, gender and family commitments classifications as illustrated in Table 15.4.

Table 15.3 *Types of entertainment consumers want to have in a pub*

Base: 647 pub visitors	All (%)	AB* (%)	C1 (%)	C2 (%)	DE (%)	Acorn group			
						E,F,G (%)	I,J,K (%)	C,D (%)	Other* (%)
Food bar (for snacks and pub meals)	54	72	62	46	47	42	65	55	54
Separate play room for children	40	32	38	42	42	32	42	42	45
Beer garden	39	38	46	34	38	34	43	34	45
Live music (say two or three times a week)	32	17	32	33	36	37	25	36	29
Play area outside for children with swings, apparatus etc.	31	31	30	32	32	28	30	26	42
Juke box	24	11	21	24	31	29	19	27	17
Dart board	23	13	21	26	27	31	17	21	23
Pool table	23	16	17	21	31	32	16	21	19
Board/table games e.g. dominoes, draughts, chess, Trivial Pursuit	17	11	19	18	18	21	13	16	18
Video juke box	15	5	11	16	20	21		12	11
Large-screen TV set	10	1	10	11	14	14	7	16	5
Other types of pub game e.g. bar billiards	10	4	8	11	12	13	6	12	8
Fruit machine	9	7	7	10	12	16	5	8	7
Games machine e.g. Pacman and Atari types	7	3	6	8	8	11	4	7	5
None of these/don't know	9	10	10	8	10	10	13	8	7

* Denotes low sub sample.

Source BMRB/Mintel

Table 15.4   *Frequency of pub visiting*

Base: 938 adults	2–7 days a week (%)	About once a week (%)	Less often than once a week but at least once a month (%)	Less often than once a month (%)	Do not visit nowadays/ don't know
ALL	20	16	13	20	31
Men	29	19	11	16	25
Women	11	13	11	16	36
Housewives	7	11	16	28	38
Other women*	34	23	10	6	26
Married	15	16	15	25	29
Unmarried	28	15	10	12	35
Child	23	19	12	21	25
No child	17	14	14	20	34
15–24	37	20	11	11	21
25–34	25	24	14	18	19

35–44	16	20	19	25	21
45–54	19	9	13	32	26
55–64	13	10	12	26	38
65+	5	10	10	14	61
AB	18	10	18	21	34
C1	21	17	13	26	22
C2	19	21	16	18	27
D	22	14	9	22	33
E	17	13	11	14	47
Acorn group					
E,F,G	21	19	10	14	36
I,J,K	24	11	14	20	31
C,D	18	18	17	23	25
B	17	13	13	26	32
Other	10	17	19	27	29

* Denotes low sub-sample

Source   BMRB/Mintel

Psychographic segmentation

This recognizes that demographic segmentation can have serious limitations because not all people in the same demographic group behave in the same way or have the same purchase preferences. Psychographic segmentation attempts to look at consumers in terms of social class, life-style and personality.

A study by William Wells[1] distinguished between eight male life-style groups: the quiet family man, the traditionalist, the discontented man, the ethical highbrow, the pleasure-orientated man, the achiever, the he-man and the sophisticated man. 'The ethical highbrow' is described as 'a very concerned man, sensitive to people's needs. Basically a puritan, he is content with family life, friends and work, interested in literature, religion and social reform. As a consumer he is interested in quality, which may at times justify greater expenditure. He is well-educated, middle or upper socio-economic status, mainly middle-aged or older'.

A different study by Daniel Greene[2] identified five female life-style groups: the home-maker, the matriarch, the variety woman, the Cinderella and the glamour woman.

Behavioural segmentation

This is the approach where buyers are divided into different groups according to when, how or why they use or purchase a product or service. Most types of travel are divided into business and leisure (purchase occasion), with further sub-divisions according to budget. Segmentation according to the benefits sought from a product has been applied to many consumer products, but perhaps toothpaste is one of the better-known examples where some people select their toothpaste brand in the hope of preventing bad breath whereas others are more concerned about preventing dental decay.

User status (non-users, potential users, first-time users and ex-users) is another useful basis of segmentation. Usage rate is also commonly used and the analysis shown in Table 15.3 is a good example taken from a report produced by Mintel called *Leisure Intelligence*.

The overriding importance of segmentation is that it provides an analytical framework for managers to develop a strategy and prepare budgets that reflect likely levels of purchase reponse.

15.3 Measuring the segments and calculating future demand

Having decided on the most relevant segmentation strategy, calculating total potential demand is the next stage in the analysis. However, forecasting potential demand is not the ultimate objective: it is merely a stage in the process. What is of fundamental interest to sales executives is the demand for their products and when that demand will be. In most markets there are several suppliers, therefore it is reasonable to assume that each supplier will obtain a share, however, small, of that market. Estimating the size of that share of the market over several time periods is the object of this exercise.

Measuring the segments is less difficult than initially imagined. This is because it is likely that much of the work may have already been completed.

Indeed, the task in question may be that of finding out where this information can be obtained, rather than engaging in new primary research.

There are a number of good sources for this information, all of which can be found in a good specialist library which may be part of a university or college or the reference department of a public library. Examples of these in Central London are:

- The Postgraduate Business School Library, in Sussex Place, Regents Park.
- The Westminster University Library in Riding House Street, W1.
- The Westminster Central Reference Library in St. Martin's Street, WC2.

It is also helpful to become familiar with the various data sources; a comprehensive guide is included in chapter 4 of *Marketing Research for managers*[3], which includes details about government, company, industry and market sources. There is also the *Marketing Surveys Index*[4] which is a monthly publication listing all published marketing reports and surveys.

When measuring the segments in any market, there are likely to be three primary sources of data or marketing intelligence:

- An omnibus survey (if one exists) giving the basic data on market characteristics related to product attributes. The Market Research Society will have details.
- Syndicated research services providing on-going research and audits of certain markets, sponsored by 'syndicates' of businesses interested in the particular market.
- Secondary desk research, much of which will be available in the specialist libraries and through on-line databases, of which there are currently some 3,000 in the UK. Many of the specialist business libraries subscribe to one or more of these databases.

It is probably easiest to explain this using a real example. In September 1987, the author was involved in an analysis of the market for coin-operated amusement machines. Fairly quickly this was identified as some 70,000 public houses (28,000 free and 42,000 tied houses)* operated by five large national and sixty-two regional breweries and an unknown number of other outlets. How to identify them, quantify them and obtain their names and addresses easily and cost-effectively? The answer was to approach *one* direct mailing list broker who was able to supply all the details in Table 15.5 except the fast food outlets, which came from a secondary source. A total of 133,600 prospective customers neatly segmented by type of outlet.

Table 15.5   *Clubs for sports, recreation and entertainment etc.*

	Numbers
Aero clubs	153
Amusement arcades	759
Art galleries and museums	1,357
Billiard halls	178
Bingo halls	400
Bowling clubs	2,156
Camping sites	1,421
Caravan sites:	
all	5,200
over 75 berths	1,781
Cinemas	619
Concert halls and theatres	1,154
Entertainment officers – municipal	163
Film-producing companies	134
Studios	59
Football clubs:	
professional	130
Golf clubs:	
all	1,822
leading	780
Greyhound tracks	60
Gymnasia and health clubs	393
Holiday camps	178
Leisure centres	299
Leisure and recreation officers – municipal	476
Marinas and moorings	195

*Changed since March 1992 following the report by the Monopolies & Mergers Commission.

Table 15.5   *Continued*

	Numbers
Night clubs and discotheques	528
Outdoor pursuit centres	67
Political party headquarters	870
Radio and television companies (including branches)	142
Record companies	228
Recording studios	40
Riding holiday centres	36
Skating rinks	87
Squash clubs	1,499
Stately homes	832
Swimming pools	383
Ten pin bowling alleys	45
Theatrical training schools	122
Working men's clubs	3,073
YMCA/YWCA	319
Yacht and sailing clubs	1,307
Youth clubs	1,307
Youth hostels	353
Zoological gardens	27

Other prospective buyers

	Numbers
British Rail Area Boards	27
Wine Bars*	1,013
Hovercraft and hydrofoil operators	3
Shipping lines	188
Fast food outlets*	7,173
Residential homes – elderly	5,026
Residential homes – handicapped	346
Restaurants	17,084
Nursing homes – private	327
Universities and colleges	204
Colleges of technology, art and further education	632
Building and engineering colleges	273
Teacher training colleges	172

Source   Key Postal Advertising Ltd., direct mail brokers who can supply the names and addresses printed on labels or envelopes for a rental fee.

* *Source*   Business Database Ltd.

Calculating future demand

Having examined the various ways of optimally segmenting the target market and analysed published data about the identified groups' purchase profiles, it is now possible to do the 'fine tuning' by new very specific research. There are four very practical ways of obtaining the information:

- Surveys of buyers' intentions.
- Obtaining the opinion of the sales force.
- Obtaining the opinions of experts.
- Test marketing.

Surveys of buyers' intentions for industrial products can frequently be undertaken by the in-house marketing department. A market research agency is probably better for consumer products because samples will be taken from a much larger buying population (a major difference in the techniques of consumer and industrial marketing reflects the smaller number of consumers in the latter).

The buying intention surveys are likely to include both qualitative and quantitative research. Qualitative research is usually exploratory or diagnostic, involving relatively small numbers of people. They will often be selected to represent the previously identified segments. The survey will attempt to obtain impressions regarding the group's response to the product. Quantitative research is concerned with larger numbers of people. The results obtained are quantified on a previously agreed basis to indicate the numbers and proportions of sample members who fall into different response categories. A degree of statistical significance is then attributed to the results within the confines of a known margin of error.

Asking the sales force their opinion has a number of attractions. First, successful sales people have a very precise appreciation of their market and its requirements. Without this they are not successful. Second, it will have good motivational implications. All too frequently the sales person is presented with a product that has clearly been dreamed up in some ivory tower with scant regard for the highly competitive sales environment. However, this is not to say that the sales force commitments should be taken down and etched in stone, because they are likely to be highly subjective, representing an individual's requirements in a particular territory at that moment in time. However, checking the sales person's story with selected customers, particularly when matched against an appropriate 'lost order report', can verify the testimony.

Companies can also obtain input to their demand calculations from experts. These may be specialists employed by the City institutions, universities, marketing consultants, dealers and the appropriate trade associations. This can be a particularly valuable input, particularly when the various opinions are compared and the opinion of one party commented on by another.

The fourth approach, test marketing, is the ultimate way to obtain good feedback on prospective sales success. A situation resembling a sub-set of a total market is created and the product is then sold with the full benefits of advertising, promotion and PR but on a miniature scale. The results are then measured and compared against the competition and reasons for the success or lack of it formulated. These results can then be upgraded to provide an indicative forecast of likely sales for the total market.

15.4 Forecasting potential sales in industrial markets

The first consideration when forecasting potential sales is to understand the likely effect of certain macro-economic influences, such as government legislation (for example enforced wearing of seat belts, pensions legislation): will it affect these particular business sectors? Second, there are industry trends to be examined: is demand for this type of product increasing or declining? Third, the reputation of the company should be considered: does the name mean quality?

The next step is to examine the sales territory and segment either geographically, by product type or by major account – whichever makes the most sense – and start to identify potential buyers by name. Make a list of their names, what you think they will buy, and how much of it. For example, a Ford dealer's car sales executive might have these prospects:

Customer	Expected sale	Order value
ABC Ltd	Granada	£14,000
HLM plc	2 × Escort	£15,000
RTY Ltd	4 × Sierra	£36,000
ICK Ltd	2 × Fiesta	£10,000
KLN plc	6 × Orion	£41,000
	Total:	£116,000

Any sales executive presenting the above as a *sales forecast* would be naive for two reasons: one, there is no indication when the sale will take place, and two, there is no assessment of the certainty with which the forecast is made. On the question of timing, most businesses operate a forecast in months for the immediate future and quarters further ahead.

Consequently, the anticipated sales figures might be more usefully presented as shown in Table 15.6.

The next step is to attempt to estimate as accurately as possible the degree of certainty of orders. Failure to record any value at all for the potential sale is to understate the worth of a large amount of sales effort. Similarly, recording the potential sale at its full value before a firm and legally binding contract has been signed is seriously to over-estimate the value of the business prospect.

Table 15.6   *Sales forecast spread between months and quarters*

Customer	Expected sale	Jan	Feb	Mar	Qtr 2	Qtr 3	Qtr 4	Total Year
				Order value (£,000)				
ABC Ltd	Granada			14.0				
HLM plc	2 × Escort		15.0					
RTY Ltd	4 × Sierra				36.0			
ICK Ltd	2 × Fiesta	10.0						
KLN plc	6 × Orion					41.0		
Period forecast		10.0	15.0	14.0	36.0	41.0		116,000

The percentage chances of obtaining the business should be made according to company guidelines as to what is expected to be in place for, say, 60 per cent (see Table 15.7), and when it is, say 60 per cent, you multiply the likely order value by the success factor, so £14,000 for the Granada goes in the forecast as £8,400 (£14,000 × .60) and may be called thet expected value factor.

The reworked Table 15.8 clearly shows the situation when the chance factor has been included in the calculations.

15.5 Forecasting potential sales in consumer markets

Because of the large numbers of buyers and the immense difficulties of identifying individuals, the technique explained in Section 15.4 is not suitable for forecasting the sales of consumer products. Instead, a technique from the management science of statistics is used which bases its calculations on total sales of a territory or sales area. it does not attempt to examine individual sales.

Table 15.7   *Suggested order chance indicators for capital products*

(%)	
Not more than 5	Vague interest. Second meeting arranged
Not more than 10	Firm interest. Agreement to continue with investigation
Not more than 15	Confirmation of interest at Board level
Not more than 20	Terms of reference and basis of decision agreed
Not more than 30	Investigation completed and findings agreed with customer
Not more than 35	Proposal submitted
Not more than 50	Short listed
Not more than 60	Verbal confirmation of intent
Not more than 70	Board approval
Not more than 80	Letter of intent
Not more than 90	Contracts submitted for signing
Not more than 100	Order signed

Table 15.8   *Forecast sales by month and quarter after applying the expected chance indicator to the selling price*

Customer	Expected sale	Chance Factor (%)	Jan	Feb	Mar	Qtr 2	Qtr 3	Qtr 4	Total forecast sales
				Expected order value (£,000)					
ABC Ltd	Granada	60			8.4				
HLM plc	2 × Escort	60		9.0					
RTY Ltd	4 × Sierra	20				7.2			
ICK Ltd	2 × Fiesta	60	6.0						
KLN plc	6 × Orion	80					32.8		
Period forecast			6.0	9.0	8.4	7.2	32.8		£63,400

Time series analysis attempts to analyse a series of data items (for example the previous year's sales figures) so as to differentiate between the underlying trend in the data and the various seasonal fluctuations. The technique also isolates certain random variations from the date. These by definition are not regular or predictable and if included in the sale forecast without justification would only reduce accuracy.

Table 15.9 shows a simple time series recording the sales of some peat products by quarter (three months) over five years (column 2). Column 3 shows the total sales for each year. Even casual observation should

Table 15.9 *Sales of peat products*

Year	Quarter	Sales (£'000)	Annual total (£'000)
1	1	1,508	
	2	3,852	
	3	2,875	
	4	1,151	9,386
2	1	1,610	
	2	3,961	
	3	2,936	
	4	1,268	9,775
3	1	1,725	
	2	4,254	
	3	3,312	
	4	1,386	10,677
4	1	1,836	
	2	4,954	
	3	4,122	
	4	1,251	12,163
5	1	1,874	
	2	4,316	
	3	3,425	
	4	1,438	11,053
Total			53,054

Source Whitehead P., and Whitehead G., 1984 *Statistics for Business*, Pitman, London.

perceive that there are fluctuations in the sales, for the sales in quarters 2 and 3 are always higher than the sales in quarters 1 and 4.

These figures suggest a strong indication of a seasonal product. There is also a progressive increase in the level of sales in the same quarter in successive years with only two exceptions (Q2 years 4 and 5, Q3 years 4 and 5). In order to forecast any future sales from these figures it is necessary to identify the trend of the sales; this is the long-term underlying pattern of the figures. The method of doing this is to calculate the quarterly moving average.

15.5.1 The quarterly moving average

This is calculated by adding together the sales of the first four quarters and dividing the total by four. Thus:

$$1,508 + 3,852 + 2,875 + 1,151 = 9,386$$
$$9,386 \div 4 = 2,346.5$$

which is the four-quarterly moving average. To calculate the next one, drop off the first figure (1,508) (Q1 year 1) and substitute in its place Q1 year 2 (1,610); thus:

$$3,852 + 2,875 + 1,151 + 1,610 = 9,488 \div 4 = 2,372$$

This is done each quarter until column iv on Table 15.10 is completed. An important point to note is that the average for these quarters falls between the third and fourth quarter for each year. This means that the four-quarterly moving average cannot be compared in the strictest sense with the quarterly figures in column iii.

15.5.2 The centred trend

To avoid this technical difficulty of non-comparability, the four-quarterly moving averages are averaged again, thus the average of the first two figures in column iv becomes the first figure in column v in horizontal line with the Q3 actual sales figure. This average of the two four-quarterly moving average figures is called the centred trend.

$$2,346.5 + 2,372.0 = 4,718.5$$
$$4,718.5 \div 2 = 2,359.25$$

Again, dropping off the first figure (2,346.5) and adding the next four-quarterly moving average figure (2,399.25):

$$2,372 + 2,399.25 = 4,771.25$$
$$4,771.25 \div 2 = 2,385.625$$

Table 15.10 *Analysing sales to discover the trend*

i	ii	iii	iv	v	vi
Year	Quarter	Sales (£'000)	Four-quarterly moving average	Centred trend	Variation of the actual from the centred trend
1	1	1,508			
	2	3,852			
			2,346.50	2,359.25	+515.75
	3	2,875			
			2,372.0	2,385.625	−1,234.625
	4	1,151			
			2,399.25		
2	1	1.610		2,406.875	−796.875
			2,414.50		
	2	3,961		2,429.125	+1,531.875
			2,443.75		
	3	2.936		2,458.125	+477.875
			2,472.50		
	4	1,268		2,509.125	−1,241.125
			2,545.75		
3	1	1,725		2,592.75	−867.75
			2,639.75		
	2	4,254		2,654.50	+1,599.50
			2,669.25		
	3	3,312		2,683.125	+628.875
			2,697.00		
	4	1.386		2,784.50	−1,398.50
			2,872.00		
4	1	1,836		2,973.25	−1,137.25
			3,074.50		
	2	4,954		3,057.625	+1,896.375
			3,040.75		
	3	4,122		3,045.50	+1,076.50
			3,050.25		
	4	1,251		2,970.50	−1,719.50
			2,890.75		
5	1	1,874		2,803.625	−929.625
			2,716.50		
	2	4,316		2,739.875	+1,576.125
			2,763.25		
	3	3,425			
	4	1,438			

Source Whitehead, P., and Whitehead, G. (1984) *Statistics for Business*, Pitman, London.

When the centred trend has been calculated it can be plotted on a graph (see Figure 15.1). It shows a relatively smooth line with steady growth over the years when the seasonal fluctuations do not distort the picture. It is worth noting that there was an unusual increase in sales in year 4, followed by a drop in year 5. It would be usual for a marketing or sales manager to provide an explanation for this using their knowledge of the business. Year 4 might have been a particularly hot summer encouraging more people to develop their interest in gardening. Alternatively a competitor may have stopped trading or there may have been an increase in home ownership as the result of some government policy.

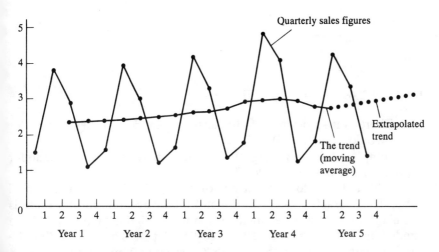

Figure 15.1   The trend in sales of peat products
Source   Whitehead, P. and Whitehead, G. (1984) *Statistics for Business*, Pitman, London

15.5.3 Extrapolating the trend

Extrapolating the trend is where the data pattern for the past few years (sales of peat in this example) are extended in a logical sequence for the next year or two. This can be used for forecasting purposes, though in order to obtain accurate quarterly predictions the seasonal variation needs to be accurately calculated.

15.5.4 Seasonal variations from the trend

The first step is to calculate the variation between central trend and the actual figures. The first quarter for which this is possible is Q3 year 1.

Referring back to Table 15.10, the centred trend in Q3 (column v) is 2,359.25 compared to actual sales of 2,875 (column iii), the variation of the actual from centred trend is therefore + 515.75.

In Q4, the centred trend is 2,385.625 compared to actual sales of 1,151: the actual sales are therefore − 1,234.625 of the centre trend. It is necessary to repeat these calculations for each quarter until column vi is complete.

Clearly these variations whether positive or negative could be affected by random as well as seasonal influences. The random influences can be eliminated by averaging them away. This is done by averaging the figures for each quarter.

Thus for Q3 over the five years, there are the following figures:

Year 1	+	515.75
Year 2	+	477.875
Year 3	+	628.875
Year 4	+ 1,076.5	
Total	+ 2,699.0 ÷ 4 = 674.75	

Note. There is insufficient data to calculate year 5 Q3 (sales figures for year 6 would be required).

To complete this averaging, similar calculations need to be made for quarters 1, 2 and 4 (see Table 15.11).

The third step is to make any necessary corrections to the seasonal trend. The averaging calculation is not totally accurate in that there is still likely to be a small element of random variation (which has been divided but not eliminated). The correction depends on the fact that the four-quarterly variations should sum to zero (the figures from which an average has been calculated should be equally spread around the average). The average of the quarterly variations is (from Table 15.11)

Q1 − 932.875	Q2 + 1,650.96875
Q3 − 1,398.4375	Q4 + 674.75
− 2,311.3125	+ 2,325.1875

The difference is −5.59375, which divided by four = 1.3984, each seasonal variation needs to be adjusted by +1.398 as a correction factor:

Q1	Q2	Q3	Q4
−932.875	+1,650.969	+674.750	−1,398.438
+ 1.398	+ 1.398	+ 1.398	+ 1.398
−931.477	+1,652.367	+676.148	−1,397.040

Table 15.11 *Seasonal variation (£'000)*

Year	Quarter 1	Quarter 2	Quarter 3	Quarter 4
1	–	–	+515.75	−1,234.625
2	−796.875	+1,531.875	+477.875	−1,241.125
3	−867.75	+1,599.5	+628.875	−1,398.5
4	−1,137.25	+1,896.375	+1,076.50	−1,719.5
5	−929.625	+1,576.125	–	–
Totals	−3,731.5	+6,603.875	+2,699.0	−5,593.75

Average quarterly deviation:

$$\text{Quarter 1} \quad \frac{-3,731.5}{4} = -932.875$$

$$\text{Quarter 2} \quad \frac{+6,603.875}{4} = +1,650.96875$$

$$\text{Quarter 3} \quad \frac{+2,699.0}{4} = +674.75$$

$$\text{Quarter 4} \quad \frac{-5,593.75}{4} = 1,398.4375$$

15.5.5 Random variations

Random variations in sales figures can arise from many reasons; the result of changes in government policy, environmental conditions, the sociocultural environment, the economic climate or indeed a change in the management policy of the firm toward its customers.

The random variation is calculated by subtracting the seasonal variation from the deviation from the trend. In Table 15.12 much of the detail from Table 15.10 has been reproduced, however, if column vi is subtracted from column v this produces the random variation (shown in column vii).

For Q3 Year 1 this is + 515.75 − +676.148 = −160.398. The expected seasonal variation was 676.148, which is the same for all third quarters, however, the actual variation was +515.75. Consequently something must have happened to reduce the variation (i.e. sales were higher than expected because of the seasonal variation). This negative random variation was −160.398.

Table 15.12   *A full-time series analysis*

i	ii	iii	iv	v	vi	vii
		Sales	Centred	Deviation	Seasonal	Random
Year	Quarter	(£'000)	trend	from trend	variation	variation
1	1	1,508	–			
	2	3,852	–			
	3	2,875	2,539.25	+515.75	+676.148	−160.398
	4	1,151	2,385.625	−1,234.625	−1,397.040	+162.415
2	1	1,610	2,406.875	−796.875	−931.477	+134.602
	2	3,961	2,429.125	+1,531.875	+1,652.367	−120.492
	3	2,936	2,458.125	+477.875	+676.148	−198.273
	4	1,268	2,509.125	−1,241.125	−1,397.040	+155.915
3	1	1,725	2,592.75	−867.75	−931.477	+63.727
	2	4,254	2,654.50	+1,599.50	+1,652.367	−52.867
	3	3,312	2,683.125	+628.875	+676.148	−47.273
	4	1,386	2,784.50	−1,398.50	−1,397.040	−1.46
4	1	1,836	2,973.25	−1,137.25	−931.477	−205.773
	2	4,954	3,057.625	−1896.375	+1,652.367	+244.008
	3	4,122	3,045.50	+1,076.50	+676.148	+400.352
	4	1,251	2,970.50	−1,719.50	−1,397.040	−322.46
5	1	1,874	2,803.625	−929.625	−931.477	+1.852
	2	4,316	2,739.875	+1,576.125	+1,652.367	−76.242
	3	3,425	–			
	4	1,438				

Source   Whitehead, P., and Whitehead,G. (1984), *Statistics for Business*, Pitman, London.

Similarly in year 4, Q3 the expected seasonal variation was + 676.148. However, the actual variation was 1,076.5 thereby increasing the deviation from trend by +400.352. This is to say that the sales were £400,353 more than might have been expected in this quarter. Clearly the possible reasons for this random variation need to be analysed by sales and marketing managers. Analysis of these random variations and the finding of acceptable explanations is important if accurate sales forecasts are to be achieved from the previous sales figures.

Table 15.13 *De-seasonalized data*

i Year	*ii* Quarter	*iii* Sales (£'000)	*iv* Seasonal variation	*v* De-seasonalized data
1	1	1,508	−931.477	2,439
	2	3,852	+1,652.367	2,200
	3	2,875	+676.148	2,199
	4	1,151	−1,397.040	2,548
2	1	1,610	−931.477	2,541
	2	3,961	+1,652.367	2,309
	3	2,936	+676.148	2,260
	4	1,268	−1,397.040	2,665
3	1	1,725	−931.477	2,656
	2	4,254	+1,652.367	2,602
	3	3,312	+676.148	2,636
	4	1,386	−1,397.040	2,783
4	1	1,836	−931.477	2,767
	2	4,954	+1,652.367	3,302
	3	4,122	+676.148	3,446
	4	1,251	−1,397.040	2,648
5	1	1,874	−931.477	2,805
	2	4,316	+1,652.367	2,664
	3	3,425	+676.148	2,749
	4	1,438	−1,397.040	2,835

Source Whitehead, P., and Whitehead,G. (1984), *Statistics for Business*, Pitman, London.

15.5.6 De-seasonalized data

Table 15.13 shows the previous years' sales figures in the most useful form for forecasting future sales. First, if the seasonal variation has a negative sign (as in Q1 and Q4), it means that actual sales are below the trend. De-seasonalizing the data is achieved by adding the variation to the actual sales figure.

This produces the figure that the sales might have been if the adverse seasonal influence had not taken place.

Q1 year 1 sales £1,508 + seasonal variation − £931.477
= de-seasonalized sales of £2,439.

Where the seasonal variation has a positive sign (Q2 and Q3), the actual sales have exceeded the trend in these quarters. De-seasonalization is achieved by deducting the variation from the actual sales achieved. This produces the result that the sales should have reached without the favourable seasonal effect.

In Q2 year 1 sales were £3,852 − seasonal variation + £1,652.367
= de-seasonalized sales of £2,200.

Extreme caution must be exercised when making sales forecasts even from such carefully prepared data as there is absolutely no guarantee that the trend will continue. All forms of environmental influence − political, economic, socio-culture, physical, technical − could affect future sales. However, sales and marketing managers with first-hand experience of their industries should attempt to superimpose assessments of these influences on to the de-seasonalized data. This could give a very useful indication of future sales.

Notes

1 *Journal of Marketing Research* (1975) **May**, 196–213.
2 *Journal of Marketing Research* (1973) **February**, 63–69.
3 Crouch, S. (1984) *Marketing Research for Managers*, Heinemann Oxford.
4 Published by Marketing Strategies for Industry, Mitcham, Surrey.

16
On territory

16.1 Something to aim at

The most difficult situation is where a newly employed sales executive starts work as part of a sales team that is selling a new product in a territory that has not been well covered for some months. The sales manager requires some form of target against which the sales executive's progress may be matched, however, as there are so many unknown variables. A sales quota as such is impossible on day one.

16.1.1 Targeted general objectives

One way to start is for the manager and the sales executive to agree some targeted general objectives for the first three or six months against which a bonus is paid on achievement. The objectives should be varied and general yet achievable in some part if they are to provide motivation for a real sales effort. Examples for a computer sales executive selling to industry might be:

- obtain an order from a manufacturing company,
- obtain an order from a light engineering company,
- sell a system for process control,
- sell a stock control system,
- sell a computer-assisted manufacturing (CAM) system,
- sell a network of micro computers,
  sell a system with twenty terminals,
  produce a detailed territory sales plan.

Each of these objectives should carry a bonus payment which might be £500 as compensation for a difficult 'cold start'.

16.1.2 Nominal sales quota

In addition to the targeted objectives, the new sales executive will be required to have a sales quota which will represent a portion of the area manager's target. To attempt to decide this in ignorance of the potential within a territory is close to madness, so a provisional total should be selected to be reviewed after three months. At this stage the sales executive should have completed a first draft of the territory sales plan for the year.

16.2 Getting started

Even when selling a new product to a sales territory that has not been worked for some months, the new sales executive should have access to some records left behind by a predecessor. This can be a good place to start looking for prospects. Where these records are incomplete in the sales office, a service department might be able to assist. In the case of computers, this could be engineering field maintenance. Go and see one of the managers and request a print-out of all the companies in your territory where there is a maintenance contract. This information can be the basis of the new sales executive's first contact with the territory because there will be a company name, address, contact name, position, telephone number and equipment details for each installation. A telephone call to each person listed, followed up by selective visits, will start to produce information on sales potential.

Draft territory plan
Here is an actual example produced by the author in January 1985 for a client, attempting to demonstrate that they were rather short of certain essentials if they were seriously to address the manufacturing sector of the computer market.

1 *Objective*
Sell £500,000 worth of XX series computers before 30 September 1985 (delivery, installation, acceptance and payment may take a minimum of three months). Failure to sell within this time frame will mean non-achievement of quota.

2 *Target market*
Manufacturing industry in Hertfordshire and Middlesex.

3 *Strategy*

   3.1 Five of the seven requirements of MANACTS are quite straightforward and easily achieved by an experienced government salesman:

      M – Have they the money?

      A – Do the people that you are speaking to have the authority to place an order?

      N – Do they **really** need the computer?

      A – (See below).

      C – (See below).

      T – Is their time scale the same as ours (see 1 above).

      S – Does the sizing suit out products?

   3.2 The second A is 'Areas of Uniqueness': what do ABC have that nobody else has? Unfortunately, being a little out of touch with the product line, I find it easier to look at what ABC do not have!

      i No special applications software (that I know of).

      ii No scientific compilers (Pascal, PL1, RPG2, APL, Prolog, Level II Cobol, C, Ada, Sibol, etc.).

      iii No Fortran.

      iv Limited networking capability (Ethernet? Oslan?)

      v Communications to other suppliers' computers?

        IBM 2780/3780 – Yes

        CO3 – No

        DEC – No

        PICK – No.

      vi Development environment: 4th generation?

        Unix – No.

      vii DP and WP on same processor?

   3.3 C = competition: vast: everybody is there.

     Alternatives:

      i Plough the base (probably being done).

      ii Find somebody pro-ABC (for whatever reason).

      iii Find somebody who needs to connect to another ABC installation.

      iv Find somebody in the process of throwing out a competitor.

      v Use a good personal contact.

   3.4 *Tactics*

      i Pilot site for evaluation, when accepted, and a minimum of three others single tender.

      ii Provide some software that does not exist anywhere else speculatively.

      iii 35 per cent + discount on hardware.

      iv Obtain third party marketing agreements with software houses who commit to ABC.

　　v Fast response to a crisis: at McDonnell Douglas in 1984 a mini
　　was placed in the Fox search HQ (Dunstable Police Station)
　　free of charge, on the basis that payment would be discussed
　　when the 'bugg--' was caught.

Identifying new prospects

This involves decisions regarding 1 the type of business, 2 the
geographical area, and 3 the source of the basic information.

　　If the answer to the first question is light engineering and
manufacturing industry, the geographical area required is Hertfordshire
and the nominated source the Kompass Directory of Company
Information, then it is a question of scanning the directory for prospects.
Selection by type of business is assisted by the standard industrial
classification (SIC) codes which are given to each listed company. In this
case companies of interest are numbers 37, 38, 39, 40 and 47. (See Exhibit
16.1.) Exhibit 16.2 is an example of what information is likely to be
available.

Exhibit 16.1　Guide to main industrial groups – Kompass

01 Livestock	21 Beverages
02 Agricultural Products	22 Leathers, Furs and their Products. Footwear
03 Horticulture, Aquatic Plants	
07 Agricultural Services	23 Textile Industry
08 Forestry	24 Wearing Apparel and Made-Up Textile Goods, Umbrellas, etc.
09 Fresh Fish and other Sea products	25 Wood and Cork Products
11 Coal and Peat	26 Furniture
12 Ores	27 Cellulose, Paper and Board Industries
13 Crude Petroleum and Natural Gas	28 Printing and Publishing
14 Quarrying	29 Rubber Products
	30 Plastics Products
16 Precious and Semi-Precious Stones, Uncut	31–32 Chemical and Oil Industries
19 Minerals	33 Non-Metallic Mineral Products
20 Food and Tobacco	34 Basic Metal Industries
	35–36 Metal Products

37 Electrical, Electronic, Data Processing and Nucleonic Equipment

38 Precision Equipment; Measuring, Testing, Optical, Photographic, Cinematographic, Medical and Surgical Equipment

39 Transport Equipment, Infrastructure

40 Hydraulic and Pneumatic Equipment, Steam Machines, Engines, Pumps, Compressors, Refrigeration, Heating and Air Conditioning Equipment

41 Agriculture, Horticulture and Forestry Equipment, Food, Drink and Tobacco Equipment

42 Chemical, Rubber and Plastics Plant and Equipment. Mechanical Preparation of Materials. Collecting and Processing Equipment for Industrial and Domestic Refuse. Water Treatment Equipment. Packing Machinery

43 Textile, Clothing, Leather Industry and Shoemaking Equipment

44 Pulp and Paper Industry. Printing Office Machinery and Equipment

45 Mining and Quarrying, Oil and Gas Extraction Equipment. Stone and Earth. Ceramic and Glass Industry Equipment. Mechanical Handling Equipment. Road Making, Building, Offshore and Underwater Equipment

46 Heavy Industry and Metal-Working Plant and Machinery

47 Metal, Woodworking, Special Purpose Machinery and Machine Tools. Industrial Robots

48 General Mechanical Engineering Sub-Contractors

49 Watches, Jewellery, Souvenirs and Religious Articles, Brushes, Wigs, Advertising and Display Articles, Labels, Games, Toys, Musical Instruments, Vending Machines, Office Equipment, Camping and Life Saving Equipment

51 Public Works

52 Building Contractors and Auxiliary Services

53 Building Services Contractors

56 Public Utility Services

61 Importers/Exporters, Brokers, Large Purchasing and Selling Organizations, Department Stores

62–65 Wholesale Distributive Trades; Consumer Goods

66–67 Wholesale Distributive Trades; Investment, Office, Building and Hospital Equipment and Supplies

68 Wholesale Distribution; Transport Equipment and Installation

69 Hotels, Motels, Restaurants, Catering, Conference Centres, etc.

71–73 Land Transportation

74 Sea Transportation, Ports

75 Air Transportation, Ports

76–77 Transport Services, Goods Storage

78–79 Communication Services, Radio and Television	84 Technical Services, Engineering
	85 Various Services, Research
80 Administrative, Personnel and Real Estate Services	86 Training
81 Commercial Services	88 Economic and Professional Organizations
82 Financial and Insurance Services	89 Entertainments Industry
83 Leasing/Renting Services	

Exhibit 16.2

HERTFORDSHIRE

HAWKER SIDDELEY DYNAMICS ENGINEERING LTD

Address	Bridge Road East, Welwyn Garden City, AL7 1LR
Tel	0707 331299
Turnover	£20–£30 million; fixed assets £3284k ROCE[1] 16.8% NPBT[2] £1772k
Business	37, 38; manufacture of specialized electronic equipment for the control and supervision of machinery plant & processes. In particular, controls for aviation & industrial gas turbines etc.
Executives	T.J. Buckle (MD); B.H. Gilroy (FD); P. Brett; W. T. White (Production)

1 ROCE = return on capital employed
2 NPBT = Net profit before tax

As an alternative to looking up the information in a reference dictionary, it is also available as a computer print-out from Kompass or ICC Information Services.

Once the 'raw company data' have been obtained, it is worth a telephone call to establish the identity of the person responsible for buying the products you are attempting to sell. Indeed, it is probably worthwhile trying to speak to this person on the telephone to introduce yourself, to inquire whose computers the company uses, for what purpose and whether ABC's product has ever been considered. An answer in the form that the company uses competitors' equipment and is committed to them for the foreseeable future will prevent the sales executive from wasting time. On the other hand, an interested response could be the opener for a meeting or at least an indication that someone might read the brochures.

Brochures

The next item the sales executive should address is the question of brochures, technical data sheets and the documentation of successful installations that may be used as a reference by potential customers. Every market segment requires a certain amount of specially prepared literature to demonstrate the vendor's capability and serious commitment.

The product brochures should be full colour high gloss articles with general details about the product range and a statement about the company. They should be complemented by data sheets of detailed technical information for the computer professional so that comparisons may be made to competitors' offerings. Finally, case histories are the neat way of demonstrating competence and experience in certain areas where a 'true success story' is written up and printed as a leaflet.

Without this sort of promotional material, the sales executive's task is made more difficult because there can be a question-mark regarding credibility. While the marketing department usually takes responsibility for the production of this material, the experienced sales executive should ensure that the resource is devoted to selling requirements.

In-house resources

When productsd cost £10,000 or more, it is essential to be able to demonstrate unequivocally that the claims made by the sales executive are real. One way of doing this is to have an office-based resource that can demonstrate what the prospect is being asked to buy. In the case of computers, this requires a processor, disk drives, printer and workstations. Technical staff are required to load the system and lead the prospect through the software that is usually the reason for the purchase.

This resource needs to be budgeted, installed and a level of demonstrable competence acquired before any attempt is made to present to the customer. The experienced sales executive will organize some practice demonstrations to ensure that all skills are up to standard.

Reference sites

These are customers who are sufficiently pleased with their purchase to be prepared to receive visits from representatives from other organizations to see how well their installation performs. This sort of facility from an existing customer can be very helpful when attempting to sell. That organizations are prepared to do this is very often part of the personal relationship that should be established between the host manager and the sales executive. The sales executive new to a territory should visit these reference sites as a priority to ensure that they are satisfied with the service that they are receiving from the supplier; otherwise they may refrain from the full-blooded enthusiasm that is so useful next time they receive a visit from prospective purchasers of the suppliers' equipment.

Where the reference sites are considered no longer useful (for whatever reason), replacements should be found as soon as possible.

16.3 Territory planning

Having come to a realistic agreement with the sales manager as to what is achievable (in the absence of much solid information) and completed certain essential preparatory work, it is time to start selling in earnest. Where a territory has been fallow for a period or where a company is new to a market or trying to make a big impact where in the past it has had only fragmentary success, it can be very useful to produce a capability statement.

Capability statements
This type of document can be used as an introduction to a sales proposal or tender document or used as a direct mail message to identified key decision-makers. Exhibit 16.3 is an actual example prepared by the author a few years ago. The supplier's name has been substituted for that of a fictitious company.

Exhibit 16.3

**THE NATIONAL HEALTH SERVICE AND
NUMBERCRUNCHER INFORMATION SYSTEMS LTD (NISL)**

1 *Background*   Numbercruncher Information Systems Ltd is now the third, or possibly even the second largest supplier of computer systems to the National Health Service (NHS). Numbercruncher equipment is currently being used by Regional and District Health Authorities, Family Practitioner Committees and several hospitals. The total value of Numbercruncher systems installed in the NHS runs into several million pounds.

---

2 *Aims and Objectives* The aim of this paper is to keep the Regional and District Health Authorities informed of Numbercruncher's activities in the NHS and briefly to set out Numbercruncher's capabilities of meeting the systems needs of the NHS by the provision of products which comply with the NHS Devolved Management Responsibility policies.

3 *Numbercruncher's key marketing thrusts to the NHS*

1 Integrated stores information system: national supplies system integrated with a pharmacy and dispensary system.
2 Direct input of pay and personnel.
3 Competitive tendering and monitoring for the support services.
4 Financial systems for DHAs and RHAs.
5 Ambulance scheduling.
6 Pathology systems.
7 Works information management system.

4 *Systems development* Healthcare systems are at present developed on Numbercruncher computers in four different ways:

- By NHS staff (e.g. National Supplies Information System)
- A joint development by one (or more) Health Authority and Numbercruncher (e.g. Ambulance Scheduling and Control Systems).
- A private venture by Numbercruncher (e.g. Competitive Tendering and Monitoring for the Support Services).
- By enlisting the aid of a third party software house to assist with system development (e.g. Integrated Personnel System).

It is likely that all four methods of development will continue.

5 *Numbercruncher's outline of proposals to the NHS* Numbercruncher wishes to enter into a coherent pricing agreement with the NHS. It proposes to offer the NHS the maximum affordable discount against published list prices at all levels of delegated financial authority. NISL believes that the terms it will offer cannot be bettered consistently by any competitor prepared to provide the same level of after-sales service and the stability necessary for long-term commitment. In addition to a fixed price policy NISL would also wish to negotiate a standard contract that could be used with confidence by all Health Authorities. NISL believes that it is in the interests of both parties to do this.

6 *Salient background about Numbercruncher (NISL)* The following general points about NISL should be noted:

- R & D is UK-directed, and largely UK-based.
- All hardware is manufactured in the UK. A new factory costing £5 million has just been built in Berkhampsted, Hertfordshire, to supply the European markets.
- Current annual turnover in the UK is at the rate of some £70–£80 million. This is consistent with a continuing 30–35 per cent annual growth rate.
- Ownership of the company rests with Worldwide Inc., who are at pains to maintain the autonomy of the UK element of Numbercruncher, and are investing heavily.

– The company has a large specialized health group consisting of sales, support, marketing and product development staff dedicated to meeting the current and future needs of the NHS.

7 *Health Service-installed base*   At present, some 158 NHS sites use NISL computers and additional orders are imminent. Foremost among the applications in use is the Supplies Information System developed by NHS staff and funded by the Computer Policy Committee. The implementation of this system by Westpark and District HA won the Health and Social Service Review's Health Management Award. It has unquestionably repaid its initial investment many times over.

Other successful NHS systems include Ambulance Scheduling, Budgetary Control, Direct Input of Pay linked to Manpower Planning, Family Practitioner Committee, Pharmacy and many others listed in the Appendix at the end of this section.

These applications and the sites where they run are of obvious interest. It should also be noted that there are many other applications available which are relevant to the efficient management and control of any large organization. These products include systems labour organization accounts (DLO), contract monitoring, estate management, planned plant maintenance, time and attendance, etc., etc. These systems have already been installed in some eighty three Local Authorities (158 computers). In addition many departments of central government are adopting Numbercruncher systems; these include such disparate ministries as Defence, Environment, Agriculture and the Department of Health itself.

8 *Numbercruncher products*

a Hardware   It would be easy to fill many pages with descriptions of the hardware range, and the philosophy behind its design. However, NISL believes that a demonstration is more convincing than thousands of words and invariably this is the approach taken. As a general synopsis NISL fulfils the following requirements:

– Designed for decision support systems and management information systems;
– Offers:
  – Distributed data processing
  – Multi-functional Local Area Networks.
  – Personal computers linked to large installations.
  – Full operating system compatibility.
  – Co-existence with (and full transparency of operation to) mainframe installations.
  – High reliability (99.5 per cent up time across the installed base).
  – Coherency.

In short NISL hardware meets any NHS computing requirement, except where systems are required for advanced medico-scientific experimentation.

b Software tools   NISL has been aware for a long time that a major impediment to the development of efficient systems is the existence of factors which inhibit ease of use. With other systems, users commonly find that they have:

– No real-time capability.
– Situations where programming effort is substantially devoted to system maintenance.
– Difficulty in implementing system improvements because the specialist staff are too busy to take on new tasks.
– Thus, computer systems that do not meet users' real needs.

Particular attention has therefore been paid by Numbercruncher to making life simpler by the provision of certain software development tools. These can be considered in two groups:

Group 1
Representing the refinement of third-generation programming language techniques to make them as easy as possible. In this group are included:

– DATA BASIC: a simple programming language which has a natural affinity with the language increasingly taught in schools.
– PUSHTU: An easy-to-use enquiry language from which very complex enquiries can be derived.
– PROP: A user-definable set of pre-programmed instructions which enable the user to invoke a complex routine at a keystroke.
– REFERENCE: A user-friendly screen-resident 'help' facility which enables an unskilled or occasional user to generate ad hoc enquiries.

Group 2
The second group, which covers fourth- and fifth-generation programme language techniques, takes NISL's software a big step forward towards even greater user-friendliness and subsequently greater cost-effectiveness. However, there is a general distrust of the computer industry's offerings in this area. This is in part because of oversell by the industry, so that users are led to believe that the benefits are immediate and quantifiable without any effort on the user's part. This is a misconception. Any new technique involves a studious application of discipline, which in turn demands training. Well-trained analysts can, and do, achieve remarkable results, but a lack of this training, combined with an over-reach of expectation, can lead to problems.

The current leader in genuine fourth-generation languages is NISL's APP (Application Language Liberator). It has the following advantages when used by an experienced operator:

– Easy prototyping.
– Fast system development.
– Simple and on-line programme documentation.
– Very easy system maintenance.
– Great reduction in system overheads.
– Provision of facilities for multiple levels of security and access control.

- Very economical use of memory.
- Ease of use.
- Rapid response to user requirements.

In short, the disciplined approach to system development using APP pays off in the short term by permitting genuine reiterative prototyping, and in the long term by a significant reduction in life cycle costs because of the very great reduction in system maintenance. NISL now has a significant number of APP reference sites where this may be confirmed.

- Green language   This is Numbercruncher's first contribution to fifth-generation language. It permits the user to converse in free text with the database. In the short term we expect that the advantages this offers, in terms of ease of use and reduction in user training requirement, will make Green into an industry standard for enquiry languages.

c Communications   It is Numbercruncher's policy to ensure that:

- All NISL systems are compatible one with another.
- There is transparency to other systems, both mainframe and personal computers, in batch and interactive mode. This is standard, for example, for IBM and ICL protocols.
- A customer's particular needs are provided for, whether these are non-standard communications or a requirement for special software.

d Reliability and customer support:
- There are more than 2,600 NISL computer systems in use in the UK; system up-time is recorded as better than 99.5 per cent.
- Response to faults is generally achieved within one hour nationwide on the mainland and Northern Ireland.
- Engineers are both hardware- and software-trained.
- There is a full calendar of customer training programmes.
- All operating system upgrades are provided free of charge and forwarded to users on release. This has the advantage of maintaining compatibility across the product range.

9 *Summary*   Numbercruncher trusts that it has demonstrated in this paper that the company has:

- A commitment to supply the NHS with proven computer systems.
- A hardware range with reliability that is second to none.
- A comprehensive and innovative range of user-friendly software languages, and systems packages of great interest to the NHS.
- A thoroughly reliable, rapid-response, support organization.
- A firm financial base for its operations in the UK.

10 *Invitation*   NISL will be pleased to supply further information on any of its NHS systems and/or arrange demonstrations on request.

APPENDIX

APPLICATIONS FOR NUMBERCRUNCHER EQUIPMENT WITHIN THE NHS

1 *Medical systems*
   Cytology
   Radiology
   Microbiology
   Histology
2 *Medical support systems*
   Supplies information systems
   Pharmacy
   Dispensary
3 *Community health, patient care and administration*
   Family practitioner committee
   Master patient index
   Inpatient administration
   Outpatients
   Waiting lists
   Attendance analysis
   Bed statistics
   Primary care
   Child care
   Community health index
   Blood transfusion
   Patients' private moneys
4 *Transport and paramedical support*
   Ambulance scheduling
   Vehicle fleet maintenance
5 *Personnel, training and pay*
   Personnel records
   Direct input of pay
   Travel expenses
   Union returns
   Nurses' training
6 *General administration*
   Audit planning and controls
   Creditor payments
   Budgetary controls
   Capital projects monitoring
   Endowment ledger
   Office automation   wordprocessing
                       spreadsheets
                       financial modelling
                       data entry and validation
                       electronic mail
                       calculator
                       diary
7 *Applications currently being developed*
   Competitive tendering and monitoring of support services
   Works information management system.

Territory audit

An important part of planning the potential in a sales territory is knowing where you will not sell. As part of the process of identifying new prospects, you the sales executive will discover competitor installations. Make a systematic record of these and ask the manager in each case why a particular supplier was chosen and conversely why ABC Ltd. or Numbercruncher Systems were not. Just because other people in the company cherish their amateur status, there is real danger of missing the sales quota if an attempt is made to emulate these people!

After three months of serious prospecting for new business in a systematic manner and meeting any existing customers, a clear picture should begin to emerge of where the potential for short- and medium-term business exists. Also, it should be possible to identify who are the major competition, what advantages their products have and what sort of company favours their product. Write this up in the territory plan – it demonstrates that one sales executive is taking a professional approach. It will also save time in avoiding chasing after marginal business just because one of these companies is in the process of buying.

Calandar of major events

Produce a calendar of the major events taking place in the territory that are of relevance to business prospects. This will help the sales executive to plan resource requirements to obtain the business. Examples of these might be national trade exhibitions, county fairs, meetings of the chamber of commerce, technical exhibitions at universities or colleges, seminars organized by the marketing department, product launches, sponsorship venues and company hospitality events. Each of these occasions presents an opportunity to meet prospects by inviting them as guests.

Managing upwards

Most sales managers are experienced and competent former sales executives, so enlist their help by asking them to do specific 'management' tasks that may assist in winning a sale. Encourage them to take a prospect company's managing director to a concert where your company has a box, or to invite him to a select product launch preview where the relevant government minister is a guest speaker. Invite marketing specialists and technical experts to in-house demonstrations where they can meet the prospect over lunch. All of these people represent an extra resource that can be used in winning the sale.

16.4 Achieving quota

The achievement of a sales quota is the ultimate test of a sales executive. It is the culmination of all the preparation, planning, prospecting, proposal writing and selling during the year. Unfortunately, even when this has been done with great professionalism, there is no guarantee of a favourable result.

There are other factors that are largely beyond the control of the sales executive, of which money and politics are the most common. Even when the contracts have been submitted for signing, the buying organization can have a financial setback which means an immediate moratorium on all capital spending. The company could have been taken over, or a reciprocal deal could emerge to the detriment of the previous negotiations. Market confidence can be shaken by the result of a general election or external events in Europe or the Middle East, which might make companies decide to reduce expenditure.

It is here that perception is called on, the foremost of selling skills. Anticipation of events and market trends may enable the sales executive to out-manoeuvre the negative tide of events. Alternatively, the sales executive should work with a margin of 'cover', so that when one market is depressed another is buoyant. A mix of private and public sector, home market and overseas business, are examples. Regular customers are also desirable for any sales executive's business plan.

Second, dependable repeat business that flows month after month if good service is provided can be a most useful start to making quota. Also, existing users should be targeted for additional business: they will probably be prepared to give advance warning of any new requirements.

It is important to meet considerable numbers of business prospects. It is therefore essential to have an effective system for generating these 'leads'. Many selling jobs work on a conversion rate of one in four, therefore forty prospects can yield ten sales; one hundred and twenty prospects may mean thirty sales. It is important not to 'slow down' once it looks as though the targeted quota is going to be achieved.

It is also important to enlist the help of other people to make the sale: use the senior management of the selling company to establish contact with senior people of the buying organization. Establish contact through professional organizations, societies and clubs to help strengthen the links. Also, identify the buyer's basis of decision clearly and concisely as early as possible. This is to give senior management time to make the decisions that may be necessary to win the sale.

Summary of ways for achieving quota

- Have a mix of target markets, so that troughs in one may be compensated for by peaks in another.
- Give good service to regular customers.
- Target existing users of your product for additional business.
- Meet large numbers of prospects, because in many cases a percentage of the people contacted become customers.
- Use senior management wherever possible to forge links with the buying organization.
- Identify the prospect's basis of decision as early as possible.

17
Budgeting for selling

17.1 Budgeting explained

A budget is a financial and quantitative statement prepared and approved before the time period to which it relates. It is a statement of the policy to be pursued in the achievement of specific business objectives. A budget frequently includes details of projected sales revenue, the costs associated with the enterprise's operation and profit estimate.

A budgetary control system checks that individual executives adhere to the agreed budget policy of the business. Control is effected by the continuous comparison of actual results with budgeted performance. At regular management meetings decisions are taken and individuals instructed to take action to bring their costs or revenues into line with the budget statement. In some instances the causes are deemed to be outside company control and a revision is approved. An example of this might be an unforeseen increase in telephone charges or petrol prices. An example of a budgeted profit and loss account is shown in Table 17.1.

It is worth emphasizing that budgets are produced in advance of the defined time period. Time must be allowed for discussion, argument and ultimately agreement. The figures for each executive or department are then compiled into a master budget or plan to fulfil the directors' stated objectives for that time period, usually one year.

The budgets are drawn up in financial terms (a useful common denominator for comparison of both sales revenue and expenditure). Once the period covered by the budget has started each executive with responsibility for a portion of the budget should produce regular statements (weekly or monthly) showing the actual performance of their unit. These details are then collated by the management accountant into the management reports that are used as a basis for making decisions about the business direction. The following format is quite common:

Budget	Actual	Cumulative	Variance	%	Explanation	Action
Month 1	Month 1	year to date				and who

Table 17.1 Budgeted (or projected) profit and loss account QPS Ltd., for the period March 19X1–February 19X2

Sales	March (£)	April (£)	May (£)	June (£)	July (£)	August (£)	September (£)	October (£)	November (£)	December (£)	January (£)	February (£)	Total (£)
Product A	1,800	2,000	3,500	10,000	9,000	10,000	10,000	7,000	7,000	5,000	5,000	5,000	75,300
Product B	3,000	15,000	17,500	17,500	17,500	17,500	17,500	17,500	19,000	10,000	10,000	18,000	180,000
	4,800	17,000	21,000	27,500	26,500	27,500	27,500	24,500	26,000	15,000	15,000	23,000	255,300
COSTS													
Stock b/f	–	29,000	29,000	29,000	29,000	29,000	29,000	29,000	29,000	29,000	29,000	29,000	–
Direct Costs	33,000	14,900	17,900	22,500	22,000	22,500	22,500	20,000	21,500	12,100	12,100	19,100	240,100
Stock c/f	(29,000)	(29,000)	(29,000)	(29,000)	(29,000)	(29,000)	(29,000)	(29,000)	(29,000)	(29,000)	(29,000)	(29,000)	(29,000)
Rent/rates	350	350	350	350	350	350	350	350	350	350	350	350	4,200
Light/heat	150	15	15	15	15	15	15	150	150	150	150	150	990
Insurance	80	80	80	80	80	80	80	80	80	80	80	120	1,000
Telephone	100	100	100	100	100	100	100	100	100	100	100	100	1,200
Staff wages	80	80	80	80	80	80	80	80	80	80	80	80	960
Motor expenses	170	170	170	170	170	170	170	170	170	170	170	170	2,040
Sundries	80	80	80	80	80	80	80	80	80	80	80	80	960
Post/print/stat	500	25	25	25	25	25	25	25	25	25	25	25	775
Advertising	500	25	25	25	25	25	25	25	25	25	25	25	775
Legal	500	–	–	–	–	150	–	–	–	–	–	–	650
Accountancy	200	–	100	–	–	100	–	–	100	–	–	150	650
Depreciation	120	120	120	120	120	120	120	120	120	120	120	120	1,440
	6,830	15,945	19,045	23,545	23,045	23,795	23,545	21,180	22,780	13,280	13,280	20,470	226,740
Monthly Profit/(loss)	(2,030)	1,055	1,955	3,955	3,455	3,705	3,955	3,320	3,220	1,720	1,720	2,530	28,560
Drawings	(1,700)	(1,700)	(1,700)	(1,700)	(1,700)	(1,700)	(1,700)	(1,700)	(1,700)	(1,700)	(1,700)	(1,700)	(20,400)
O/D chg/int	(740)	(140)	(140)	(260)	(260)	(260)	(165)	(165)	(165)	(130)	(130)	(130)	(2,685)
Loan interest	(300)	(300)	(300)	(300)	(300)	(300)	(300)	(300)	(300)	(300)	(300)	(300)	(3,600)
	£(4,770)	£(1,085)	£ (185)	£ 1,695	£ 1,195	£ 1,445	£ 1,790	£ 1,155	£ 1,055	£ (410)	£ (410)	£ 400	£ 1,875

17.2 The objectives of budgetary control

Budgeting is part of the business planning process that forces executives to think ahead using their knowledge of the business to anticipate costs and revenues in a future time period. Writing these estimates on paper and passing them to the managing director or department head communicates essential information for planning and controlling the total business. This is ultimately achieved by comparing actual results with budget figures.

These points may be conveniently summarized. The objectives of budgetary control are:

- To obtain ideas and forecasts from those in charge of sections of the business.
- To collate the figures and co-ordinate the various activities of the business.
- To institute a central control (a management accountant for example) while making each department or section head responsible for all matters (costs and revenues) in that portion of the business under his/her control. These portions are known as 'cost centres' and the principle is called 'responsibility accounting'.
- To maintain a sensible balance between patterns of income and expenditure in order to avoid liquidity problems.
- To ensure that items of capital expenditure are necessary and affordable.
- To enable management to compare actual results with the corresponding budget figures as soon as possible after the end of the time period. This gives the corrective action the opportunity to be effective sooner rather than later, to limit any damage.

17.3 Fixing the budget

This may be conveniently explained using an example. At a meeting of the budget committee comprising managing director, management accountant, budget controller, sales director, personnel manager (responsible for labour budget), production director and a financial accountant (primarily responsible for the cash budget), the sales director forecasts sales of two million product items at a selling price of £10 each. (It is assumed that only one product is manufactured.)

The production director responds by saying that currently factory capacity can only make one million items. In order to make the extra one million items the following will be required by the production departments: additional raw materials, extra machines, additional skilled labour for production and maintenance and extra warehousing for finished products.

Each of these items will have to be costed by the financial accountants, but there could be difficulties as labour may be unavailable or take time to train, raw materials may have risen in price and the extra machines may have a delivery time of eighteen months. The budget committee will then consider ways of resolving each difficulty, for example to overcome the problems listed above, some of the extra production might be subcontracted. If subcontracting can produce an additional half million units, then the budgets for next year will be produced around a sales forecast of 1.5 million units and a sales revenue of £15 million.

When the functional budgets have been prepared the budget controller will produce a master budget for the year. In effect this is a budgeted profit and loss account and balance sheet. If the actual results for the following year are exactly the same as those shown in the functional budgets, then the trading profit or loss will match the budgeted figure.

Finally, some examples of the main functional budgets:

- sales forecast in units and pounds,
- selling marketing and distribution costs,
- production costs and overheads,
- materials purchases,
- labour costs,
- plant utilization details,
- capital expenditure requirements,
- administration costs,
- cash requirements.

17.4 The sales budget

The sales budget is the starting point for any plan because it is the principal revenue generator (other sources of income may be from disposals of fixed assets or profit from investments). The usual method of compilation is for each area sales manager to agree a figure with each sales executive under his/her command. The sales director will then carry out a similar exercise with each areas sales manager agreeing budgets for each sales area. An example is shown in Table 17.2.

It is usual to allow some flexibility at each level of the sales budget, thus the five area sales managers' total makes £14,800,000, although the

Table 17.2 *Building the sales director's budget from the line sales managers' totals*

	Budgets ('£000)	
Sales manager A	3,250	
Sales manager B	2,850	
Sales manager C	3,700	
Sales manager D	2,100	
Sales manager E	2,900	
Total of sales managers' budgets	14,800	(112 per cent of directors' budget)
Sales directors' budget	13,200	

directors' budget is £13,200,000. This is to avoid the situation where one sales area seriously under performing can disrupt the budgetary process for the entire company.

It is usual to break down the sales budget between:

- different types of product,
- different areas, territories or countries,
- between different types of sales channel (company sales executives, agents or overseas subsidiaries),
- different types of customer, the public sector may be divided between health, education, defence for example), and
- operating period (usually months or quarters).

17.5 Managing the sales budget

In the following example a company has three products; during the months of June budgeted sales are shown in Table 17.3. During the month of June the actual results were as shown in Table 17.4.

Actual sales revenue of product A was £18,900 compared to the sales budget figures of £18,000 – an increase on revenue of £900, though 2,000 fewer units were actually sold (the budget was to sell 20,000 units). These variances need to be carefully analysed and are shown in Tables 17.5 and 17.6.

Table 17.3 *Budgeted Sales for month of June*

	Product A	Product B	Product C	Total
Budgeted sales (in units)	20,000	21,000	40,000	81,000
	£	£	£	£
Budgeted sales revenue	20,000	42,000	21,000	83,000
Budgeted cost of sales	15,000	31,500	18,000	64,500
Budgeted profit	£5,000	£10,500	£3,000	£18,500

Table 17.4 *Actual sales for month of June*

	A	B	C	Total
Sales (in units)	18,000	23,000	40,000	81,000
Sales (value)	£18,900	£46,000	£17,000	£81,900

17.6 Sales expense budget

The sales expense budget is the budget allocation for all selling expenses itemized and produced in the form of a cashflow projection. A detailed example is provided in Table 17.7. (As the amount involved is more than £2.5 million this is likely to refer to a business with a sales revenue of at least £20–30 million.)

It is also important to note that this is a fictitious example compiled with only a passing appreciation for media planning, but in a level of detail that is useful for the purposes of instruction.

17.7 Area and territory management (segmental analysis)

A sales person or manager should adapt the approach to the way he/she manages his/her part of the company's business according to the

Table 17.5 *Analysis of the variances*

	Product A	Product B	Product C	Total
Budget sales revenue	£20,000	£42,000	£21,000	£83,000
Actual sales revenue	£18,000	£46,000	£17,000	£81,900

(a) Price variance: shows budgeted unit sales price against actual unit sales price

A (18,000 units @ £1 = £18,900)	– £18,900	900 (F)
B (23,000 units @ £2 = £46,000)	– £46,000	–
C (40,000 units @ 52.5p = £21,000) – £17,000		4,000 (U)
Total		£3,100 (U)

(b) Quantity variance:

Although there is no variance in overall quantity, there are, however, individual changes in quantity of products A and B. The variances are at the average standard profit per unit (£18,500 ÷ 81,000 = 22.84p):

Product A (−2,000 units @ 22.48p)	457 (U)
Product B (+2,000 units @ 22.84p)	457 (F)
	–

(c) Mixture variance (standard profit for each product minus average standard profit – budgeted sales of A are 20,000 at a budgeted profit of £5000 = 25p):

A −2,000 units @ (25p − 22.84p)	43.20 (U)
B +2,000 units @ (50p − 22.84p)	543.20 (F)
	£500.00 (F)

(d) Actual profit/loss)

	Actual sales (£)	Standard cost of actual sales (£)	(£)	Actual profit (£)	Profit rate (p)
A	18,900	18,000 units @ 75p	13,500	5,400	30
B	46,000	23,000 units @ £1.50	34,500	11,500	50
C	17,000	40,000 units @ 45p	18,000	(1,000)	(2½)
	£81,900		£66,000	£15,900	

Table 17.6   *Budget statement comparing actual with budget*

	Budgeted profit			Actual profit/(loss)			Price variance	Quantity variance	Mixture variance	Total variance
	Quantity	Profit rate (%)	Total	Quantity	Profit rate	Total				
Product	Units	p	£	Units	p	£	£	£	£	£
A	20,000	25	5,000	18,000	30	5,400	900	(457)	(43)	400
B	21,000	50	10,500	23,000	50	11,500	–	457	543	1,000
C	40,000	7½	3,000	40,000	(2½)	(1,000)	(4000)	–	–	(4,000)
			£18,500			£15,900	(£3,100)	–	£500	(2,600)

Note
Unfavourable variances above are shown in brackets.
Source   Financial Training Group, *Chartered Accountants Study Manual.*

Table 17.7   Sales expense budget

	Jan (£)	Feb (£)	Mar (£)	Apr (£)	May (£)	Jun (£)	Jul (£)	Aug (£)	Sep (£)	Oct (£)	Nov (£)	Dec (£)	Total (£)
Advertising budget													
Press	17.5	17.5	17.5	17.5	17.5	17.5			17.5	17.5	17.5	17.5	175.0
TV			125.0	125.0	125.0					125.0	125.0	125.0	750.0
Radio			10.0							10.0			20.0
Cinema	40.0	40.0	40.0	40.0	40.0	40.0	40.0	40.0	40.0	40.0	50.0	50.0	500.0
Posters	5.0	5.0	5.0	5.0	5.0	5.0	5.0	5.0	5.0	5.0	5.0	5.0	60.0
Agency fees (15 per cent)												225.8	225.8
	62.5	62.5	197.5	187.5	187.5	62.5	45.0	45.0	62.5	197.5	197.5	423.3	1703.8
Sales and Expense budget													
Staff salaries	20.0	20.0	20.0	20.0	20.0	20.0	20.0	20.0	20.0	20.0	20.0	20.0	240.0
commission/bonus	80.0			40.0			40.0			40.0			200.0
car expenses			10.0			10.0			10.0			10.0	40.0
travel	3.0	3.0	3.0	3.0	3.0	3.0	3.0	3.0	3.0	3.0	3.0	3.0	36.0
subsistence	3.0	3.0	3.0	3.0	3.0	3.0	3.0	3.0	3.0	3.0	3.0	3.0	36.0
	106.0	26.0	36.0	66.0	26.0	36.0	66.0	26.0	36.0	66.0	26.0	36.0	552.0
Promotions	30.0								30.0				60.0
Exhibitions									75.0	45.0			120.0
Brochures	20.0												20.0
Direct mail	10.0	10.0	10.0	10.0	10.0								50.0
	228.5	98.5	243.5	263.5	223.5	98.5	111.0	71.0	203.5	308.5	223.5	459.3	2522.8

Table 17.8   *Cumulative sales ABC plc January to September 1989*

(£)	Eastern	Southern	Northern	Western	Total
Product A sales					
Hotels	100,000	150,000	120,000	110,000	480,000
Colleges	90,000	80,000	90,000	100,000	360,000
Hospitals	180,000	200,000	170,000	30,000	580,000
Total	370,000	430,000	380,000	240,000	1,420,000
Product B sales					
Hotels	110,000	100,000	90,000	120,000	420,000
Colleges	40,000	60,000	50,000	70,000	220,000
Hospitals	200,000	160,000	190,000	210,000	760,000
Total	350,000	320,000	330,000	400,000	1,400,000
Product C sales					
Hotels	20,000	30,000	50,000	30,000	130,000
Colleges	70,000	50,000	80,000	60,000	260,000
Hospitals	120,000	100,000	110,000	80,000	410,000
Total	210,000	180,000	240,000	170,000	800,000
Total hotel sales	230,000	280,000	260,000	260,000	1,030,000
Total college sales	200,000	190,000	220,000	230,000	840,000
Total hospital sales	500,000	460,000	470,000	320,000	1,750,000
Total sales	930,000	930,000	950,000	810,000	3,620,000

Source   Examination paper on Financial & Management Accounting, the Chartered Institute of Marketing Certificate, November 1987.

assessment criteria. If judged on sales volume alone, then clearly this is the target.

Table 17.8 shows a useful breakdown of the sales achieved by an area sales manager's team of four sales people. The year's sales revenue is presented by sales territory and subdivided by product (A, B and C) and customer type (hotels, colleges and hospitals). There are totals for sales to each customer type by product and there are totals for the sales revenue from each sales person's territory.

Presenting the results this way provides sales management with information for analysis comparison and ultimately control. The interpretation might be as follows:

Sales territory analysis

- Sales revenue in the Western territory is only 86.7 per cent of the mean of the other three territories: £936,666 (£930,000 + £930,000 + £950,000 ÷ 3.,
- Western territory sales of product A are only 61.06 per cent of the average achieved by the other three: £393,333 (£370,000 + £430,000 + £380,000 ÷ 3).
- Western territory sales of product A to hospitals is only 16.36 per cent of the mean of the other three territories (£180,000 + £200,000 + £170,000 ÷ 3 = £183,333).

Product line analysis

- Product C sales are only 56.53 per cent of the mean (or average) of the sales revenues achieved by products A and B.
- Product C sales are very low to hotels – 16.25 per cent of the total.
- Product B sales are very low to colleges – 15.71 per cent of the total.
- Sales of product B to all three customer groups are highest in the Western sales territory.

Customer group analysis

- Hospitals are the largest customers for each product buying 40.84 per cent of product A; 54.28 per cent of product B; 51.25 per cent of product C. Overall total for hospitals 48.34 per cent of sales revenue.
- Although sales to hospitals are larger than for any customer group, the sales in the Western territory are only 67.22 per cent of the mean of the other three (£500,000 + £460,000 + £470,000 ÷ 3 = £476.666).

17.8 Meeting budget, monitoring and control of territory sales

The reason for partitioning the responsibility for the achievement of certain volumes of sales of particular product groups to specific customers is to provide senior management with an organization structure that can be exactly controlled.

Consider for example how the value to senior management of Table 17.8 would be improved if there were a percentage figure expressing the cumulative sales achieved in relation to the budget. As it stands, the question should be asked why has the western territory progressed less successfully than the other three. There are perhaps three possible explanations:

Explanation	*Remedial action*
• Inexperienced or less competent sales person.	Sales and/or product training as appropriate plus closer supervision.
• Greater competition.	Determine real reasons for competitive success and counter using marketing group.
• Smaller prospective customer base.	Consider redrafting territories on more equitable basis.

However, specifically, management would want to know:

- Why sales of product C are comparatively low – particularly to hotels.
- Why sales of product B are very low to colleges.
- This is particularly interesting as the worst performing sales person overall is performing best with product B to each customer group.

The answer may be that the western territory sales person has particular experience of this product market, which enables him/her to sell effectively, in which case perhaps he/she should become a product B specialist and be groomed for product marketing management.

The value of a relatively simple table of figures can be enormous. It provides management with a mechanism for monitoring and indirectly controlling the volume of business achieved by particular sales people of specific products to the various customer groups. The comparison of different levels of achievement indicates strength and weakness, success and failure. This information is useful for the 'fine tuning' of the human resource base so that even higher targets may be achieved.

Other quantitative measures of performance might include:

- Prospecting success ratio $= \dfrac{\text{Number of new customers}}{\text{Number of new prospect calls}}$

- Average order value $\quad = \dfrac{\text{Sales revenue per sales person}}{\text{Number of orders won}}$

- Strike rate $\quad = \dfrac{\text{Number of orders}}{\text{Number of quotations made}}$

- Orders per visit $\quad = \dfrac{\text{Number of orders won}}{\text{Number of visits made}}$

17.9 Analysis of the corporate sales achievement

Another useful application of the budgeting concept is the analysis of sales revenue to some other performance indicator especially if this is done as a comparison between divisions of the business or product market segments. In Table 17.9 the sales of three product market segments are analysed:

- Sales are compared by units and by sales revenue.
- The contribution (sales revenue less variable cost) to fixed costs is examined.
- The marketing contribution is compared.
- Net profit per market segment is also detailed.

Then the following performance measures have also been applied:

1 Net profit as a percentage of capital employed (ordinary share capital, reserves and loan capital).
2 Net profit as a percentage of sales revenue.
3 The contribution as a percentage of sales revenue.
4 Sales force costs as a percentage of sales revenue.
5 Advertising costs as a percentage of sales revenue.
6 Fixed costs as a percentage of sales revenue.
7 Sales revenue compared to capital employed. Here the higher figure is better, it means that the capital invested in the business is being turned over more times.

These indicators provide a useful way for the company board to assess the performance of various sales divisions. They are based on the methods that analysts, market makers and investors apply to overall company performance when considering the feasibility of buying shares or recommending them to clients.

Table 17.9 *Analysis of corporate sales achievement by product market segments*

	Product market segments		
	1	2	3
Sales (000 units)	1000	1250	1500
£000			
Net sales value (NSV) @ £1.5/unit	1500	1875	2250
Contribution @ £0.6/unit	600	750	900
(i.e. £1.5 NSV unit – variable cost of £0.9)			
less Sales force costs	150	100	110
less Advertising and promotion	250	200	50
Marketing/sales contribution	200	450	740
less fixed costs – production	50	50	50
marketing	15	2	2
Net profit	135	398	688
Capital employed			
Plant and machinery	200	200	200
Stocks	96	120	144
Debtors	58	72	86
Total	354	392	430
1 Profit % of capital employed	38%	102%	160%
2 Profit % of sales revenue	9%	21%	30%
3 Contribution % of sales revenue	40%	40%	40%
4 Sales force costs % of sales revenue	10%	5%	5%
5 Advertising % of sales revenue	17%	11%	2%
6 Fixed costs % of sales revenue	4%	3%	2%
7 Sales revenue: capital employed	4.2:1	4.8:1	5.2:1

Source   Bolt, G. J. (1987) *Practical Sales Management*, Pitman, London.
>≥<μνβωψχζ

17.10 Using an 'expert' computer system for budgetary resource allocation

'Expert' systems are able to process and solve reasoning problems because the knowledge base (information store) is interrogated in an intelligent way, including only relevant data in the deduction process.

One way of employing expert systems in a company is to design a sales prospect recording, evaluation and ranking system. The objective is to concentrate scarce company resources on winning feasible major tenders rather than to chase after everything. The prospect evaluation system provides a methodology for continuously focussing on the best prospects for the company and can be used to budget resource allocation.

The author worked on the design of such during 1987 and 1988 for a multi-national engineering company. The key prospect information that they required was:

- Country (some have a better record of awarding contracts and paying than others)
- Order value   client contribution
  grant aid/bank finance
- Prospect status   viable
  possible
  an opportunity
- Stage in project cycle   potential scheme
  pre-feasibility stage
  feasibility stage
  government approval
  client specification ready
  pre-qualification stage
- Work type   water treatment
  power station
  industrial
  operation and maintenance

Details of all prospective tenders were keyed into the computer system and evaluated by all the decision criteria built into the software. For example:

- Country   Iraq, Iran and some other parts of the developing world are bad risks due to despotic governments who pay only cursory attention to normal business practice.
- Order value   Grant aid can complicate the tendering process as another level of bureaucracy is introduced into the scheme.
- Prospect status   Viable is obviously of greater interest than just an opportunity.
- State in project cycle   Clearly a project that is at an advanced stage and where the company concerned is a strong candidate is of greater interest than one that is only at an early stage.

- Work type Some projects are of greater interest where the company concerned has an international reputation for excellence. Consequently water treatment might receive a higher ranking than say operation and maintenance.

Other factors would also be included, including the details of known competition and any political preference. The end result would always be a readily accessible major business ranking system for the budgetary allocation of resources and a great aid to decision making.

Part Five Selling Communication

18

Direct mail

18.1 Uses of direct mail

All businesses have a choice as to the method they select to reach prospective customers. (See Figures 18.1, 18.2 and 18.3 for some facts and figures regarding direct mail.) Direct mail is different from other media in that it facilitates contact with a very specific targeted segment rather than all viewers of a television programme or readers of a newspaper or magazine. This of course is dependent on finding the correct list of people, which is why the compilation of lists of names and addresses is big business. Companies wishing to reach a target group of consumers pay the compilers a fee to rent the list for a mailing. Repeated mailings by the company require repayment of the fee for each mailing. 'Moles' are usually hidden among the names on each list to pick up on illicit use of the list.

	%	% requested
Mail order	25.4	8
Insurance	8.1	6
Credit card	6.5	4
Retailer	7.1	18
Bank	8.3	4
Magazines	5.6	16
Travel agency	5.3	40
Estate agent	2.6	74
Manufacturers	4.7	29
Book club	4.0	16
Charity	4.0	16
Gas/Electric board	2.7	4
Building society	3.1	4
Total	100.0	14

Figure 18.1 UK senders of direct mail percentage of volume (1988–9)

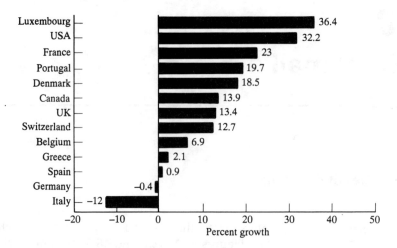

Figure 18.2   Mail growth 1983–7 inland volume

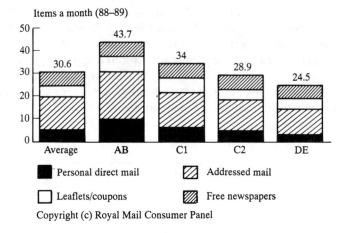

Copyright (c) Royal Mail Consumer Panel

Figure 18.3   The consumer letterbox – what comes through it?

An example of a list might be that somebody publishing a textbook on an aspect of marketing that followed a syllabus prescribed by the Chartered Institute might approach the Institute for permission to rent the list of their student members. Clearly students studying for an examination whose syllabus is covered by the textbook are a primary target market.

Direct mail is appropriate to both consumer and business to business selling. Some of the major uses are described below starting with consumer selling.

18.1.1 Selling directly to the customer

Direct mail can be an effective method of selling to people at home, eliminating the need for and cost of the retailer. Whether a letter, brochure, or even a large catalogue is sent out, there should be plenty of space to describe fully and to illustrate the products for sale. It is important to do this accurately and convincingly as the customer buys the product 'unseen'. Clearly this implies a slightly greater risk of disappointment than where a product is bought from a retailer. Therefore to achieve volume sales without volume returns by dissatisfied customers, the description, illustration, price and application of the product must be unambiguous.

A good example is the 'Next' clothing catalogue which even went as far as to include clothing samples for many of the products illustrated by photograph and line drawing. It dramatically raised the standard of this method of selling. Part of this concept of convenience shopping is to include a reply-paid order form because every obstacle placed in front of prospective buyers will reduce the number of sales.

18.1.2 Sales lead generation

Where a product cannot be sold direct because a sales executive is required to explain the features and benefits and respond to questions, then direct mail may be used for the initial contact. Direct mail can be very cost-effective in producing leads of interested prospects if it is accurately targeted to people with a need for that particular product. It is a popular medium with companies selling fitted kitchens, central heating and insurance.

18.1.3 Sales promotion

Direct mail can be effective at getting a selected group of people to a promotional meeting while still retaining control over the extent of the exposure..This approach also cuts out groups who are not expected to be buyers of the product. This has the advantage of not diluting the sales person's effort. A Mercedes dealer in the Kensington area has organized regular promotions at the Queen's and Hurlingham Clubs in the past few years, where new models can be test driven.

Another approach favoured by clothing retailers at the more exclusive end of the market is to invite account customers to 'privilege previews' before a sale is open to the general public. Hilditch and Key serve champagne and mince pies to their customers queueing on the first day of their sale.

18.1.4 Clubs

Book and record clubs have been big business for more than twenty years. Pioneered by *Readers Digest* and others, direct mail was used as a way of recruiting people to 'take advantage of a special offer' and join a 'club', thereby giving them access to products on a regular basis. Since then coins, porcelain miniatures, model cars and video cassettes have been marketed by direct mail in this way. The concept thrives on continuity, rather than one-off sales – direct mail provides the regular contact necessary to stimulate repeat ordering.

18.1.5 Dealer mailings

Where a company uses dealers to sell its products to the end user, advertising material can be designed and printed by the principal. The dealer then overprints his/her own details (name, address, telephone number) in the appropriate place and uses this medium to sell to prospects in his/her territory. This form of decentralized local advertising is popular with car and caravan distributors, package holiday companies, and suppliers of insurance and of garden equipment.

18.1.6 Follow-up to existing customers

Letters can also be used to maintain contact with consumers to advise them of new products or facilities, renew service agreements or make special offers. The idea is to encourage repeat business by stimulating loyalty to the product, brand or selling company.

Business and industrial markets are generally more tightly defined and comprise smaller numbers than their consumer counterparts. However, even the specialist trade journals will cover a broader area than a particular supplier's target as well as a selection of competitors' advertising.

Most of the uses are similar to those for selling to consumers: sales lead generation, dealers' support and follow-up mailings. Two applications are, however, particular to the industrial market: product launches and invitations to conferences.

18.1.7 Product launches

During the early stages of a new product launch, product details and the unique sales message need to be presented to a small number of people who have a major influence on certain buying decisions. Direct mail linked to an effective public relations campaign, the availability of demonstration models and professionally produced technical brochures are the key to the successful launch. The job title of these key influencers can be readily identified, a list hired and the informative brochure despatched.

18.1.8 Trade conferences

Business and trade conferences are now well established as a means of talking to your market or holding discussions with colleagues in the same industry. Direct mail is an ideal way of inviting delegates, particularly if you are looking for specific types of people who are generally difficult to meet in any other forum. Similarly, if your company uses dealers, informing and motivating them is almost as important as advertising to the market. With direct mail you can easily reach dealers, retail outlets and franchise holders, with details of your marketing plans, or invite them to take part in incentive schemes, encourage them to stock new brands, and make sure they are informed of promotional activities. It is also a way of advising them of impending public relations events and sponsorship programmes.

18.2 Mailing lists

A relevant and up-to-date mailing list is essential to a successful direct mail campaign. The names and addresses should precisely reflect the description of the target market and they should have been recently checked for accuracy. Incorrect names and wrong addresses not only waste money and resources, but dilute the ratio of positive responses to the total number of letters sent out.

18.2.1 Selecting a mailing list

There are many sources of direct mail lists but the prime distinction is between those compiled in-house and those rented elsewhere. The word 'rented' is carefully chosen, because in most instances third-party suppliers of lists levy a charge each time it is used. The payment does not usually give the purchaser unrestricted usage of the list.

In-house lists
Most businesses should be able to identify at least a portion of their target audience from existing records. These details could be compiled

from customer files, warranty cards, sales force reports, exhibition enquiries, and any responses from display advertising. All these may be used to form the basis of a mailing list. The word 'basis' is used because the details should be checked before being added to this list: this means christian names and surname, how they are spelt, any qualifications and personal title. If it is a business contact, job title and company name should be checked in addition to the address and postcode.

It is better to create the mailing list in the form a computer database. A database is recommended because this can be used to avoid duplication, facilitate cross-referencing of prospect records and to structure the address files in such a way as to qualify for mailing discounts.

A typical on-screen example might look like Figure 18.4.

Surname..	Forenames..
Personal title....................................	Qualifications..................................
Job title...	
Company name...............................	SIC code...
Address...	
....	
Postcode...	
Product purchased	(code)................ date...................
....	....

Figure 18.4

This particular example provides the user with the following sort options:

- Job title
- SIC code (industry type)
- Postcode
- Product type
- Date of purchase

Duplication of records is avoided because the computer checks each detail of the personal name and company name against those already listed in the database at the time of entry. Where this occurs a message will be flashed onto the computer screen.

There are both advantages and disadvantages of creating your own list. The main advantages are relevance of the names to the company's product, secrecy, and lack of usage restrictions. The disadvantage is the time and cost involved in creating it and maintaining it in an accurate form.

Rented lists

Specialist direct mail houses can offer an infinite variety of lists of people and businesses broken down into many classifications (sub-divisions of the SIC code, for example). One list classifies architects in the following categories:

- commerce and industry,
- education,
- hospitals and the Department of Health,
- Ministries and central government,
- local government (chief architects),
- nationalized industry.

The major sources of information about lists are:

- Direct Mail Sales Bureau, 14 Floral Street, Covent Garden, London WC2E 9RR. Telephone 071 379 7531.
- *Direct Mail Databook* (5th edition 1987), Gower Publishing Co. Ltd., Gower House, Croft Road, Aldershot, Hants GU11 3HR. Telephone 0252 331551. Contact Jonathan Norman.
- Lists & Data Sources, Ladson House Publishers, Ladson House, The Bridge, Mepal, Ely, Cambridge CB6 2AT. Telephone 0353 77714.
- Benn's Direct Marketing Services, Benn Brothers plc, Sovereign Way, Tonbridge, Kent TN9 1RW. Telephone 0732 362666.
- The British List Brokers Association, c/o Mail Marketing (Bristol) Ltd., Springfield House, Mill Avenue, Queens Square, Bristol BS1 4SA. Telephone 0272 666900.

Four titles are used to identify the people involved in the list business: list owner, list manager, list broker, list compiler.

List owner   As the name implies, this is the organization or person who owns a mailing list. It could be a magazine publisher offering current or expired subscribers' lists for use by other non-competing users, a mail order company offering its current or past buyers on the same basis, or a list compiler who has built a mailing list specifically for other people's use.

List manager   Works for a list owner. The basic function is to promote the use of a list on behalf of a list owner, to negotiate its rental, and deal with all administrative requirements including invoicing and collecting the rental charges due.

A list broker   Works for you, the list user. Responsibilities are to advise the list user on the full range of mailing lists available, and to combine experiences with that of the customer in selecting those lists most suitable for the task in hand.

List compiler   Responsible for collating information from published sources and turning it into a good mailing list format, generally as a commercial exercise through which the list can be used by others.

The cost of using such lists (generally on a one-off rental basis) depends on the degree of selectivity and how up-to-date they are. Generally, the more selective, the higher the price, ranging from, say, £60 to £125 per thousand names. It is, of course, hard to be sure just how accurate and up-to-date rented lists are. It is generally the case, however, that the more a list is used, the more accurate it is likely to be – and vice versa. Some direct mail houses will make available a sample list from any of the lists they have and you can test its accuracy either by ringing up names to confirm them or by using the sample as a test mini-mailing of your campaign.

Trade and other associations   It is quite often possible to obtain complete or part membership lists of trade associations, chambers of commerce, professional institutions etc., free of charge or at nominal cost. But there are disadvantages: for example, many qualified people remain members of an association after retirement.

Directories   For example, yellow pages, trade and town guides, local trade associations, membership lists – can be a cheap source of information for business mailings. Sifting through these will give you names and addresses, but, typically, not much more.

18.3 Renting and buying lists

Once the generic target group for the mailing has been decided, the next consideration is locating an accurate list. Accuracy is the key word, because when renting a mailing list it is important for the success of the campaign that the names and addresses are correct. So the hirer should enquire as to the source of the list when it was originally compiled, when it was last updated, and who rented it last – check up on this.

Even if the answers to these questions seem acceptable, it is still a good idea to test the list by mailing a sample. Printing the name of the sending organization on the back will assist the Post Office in returning any items that cannot be delivered. This will provide a clear indication of the organizations that have changed address. The easiest way to check that the names of the individuals on the list are correct is to telephone and enquire whether 'Mr Fred Smith is still the Company Secretary or Carole Jones the Chief Engineer?'

The next question concerns how the list is available – self-adhesive labels, Cheshire labels, magnetic tape, floppy disk, cassette, or on listing paper (in which case the telephone numbers should be included too). It is a good idea to have the information on computer media to facilitate personalization of the production with a paper back-up to monitor the response and follow up.

Another important point is the ability to make a selection from the list by business category (SIC code) or county/post code or the size of the business. With consumer lists the requirement is somewhat different: what products has that person previously bought by direct mail? What price range? Are they credit buyers? Is it possible only to have names added in the last two years?

Some list brokers impose strict conditions and will not release the names but request that they handle the mailing and they charge a high minimum job charge. Others can be very accommodating and agree not to rent to competitors for a specific period of time. It is a good idea to find out about these points before signing an agreement. Finally, confirm the price, the time and charge for delivery, the renter's policy for 'gone aways' and in writing where the user stands *vis-à-vis* the Data Protection Act 1984.

18.4 Planning a campaign

First set the objectives of the proposed campaign which might be to:

- Increase market share from x per cent to x + y per cent.
- Obtain a number of new clients.
- Increase product awareness by x per cent.

Without a relevant yardstick, measurement of the success of the campaign is impossible and it may be important at some time in the future to justify the expense involved.

Second, it is important to identify and quantify the target audience. Obtaining quotations from a list broker will help here because they will be able to provide absolute quantities of names according to the segment specification. Many list owners maintain their lists using a relational database with key fields relating to location, SIC code, and other sort criteria which might include usage frequency: (in an extreme case) 'regular user', 'occasional user' or 'first-time user' of a generic product type. The precision and selectivity of direct mail is a major advantage of the medium. Where the target market is correctly identified and up-to-date lists are used, wastage from sending unsolicited messages to the 'not interested' category is kept to a minimum.

The third decision to make is whether this proposed mail campaign is going to be implemented in isolation or as part of an on-going campaign that needs to be integrated into the total sales and marketing plan. If the latter, a considerable amount of co-ordination is required with other managers, for example timing of the mailing to coincide with TV and press advertising or an in-store promotion and making sure that any resulting incoming telephone response can be efficiently managed. The budgetary implications clearly need to be considered in detail.

The calculation below shows the actual costs involved for a typical list:

Rental of names and addresses	£60 per 1000
Supply of labels	£6 per 1000
Sticking on and stuffing of envelopes	£13 per 1000
Manilla envelopes	£19 per 1000
Postage	£180 per 1000
	£278 per 1000
100,000 direct mail letters (assuming no discount for bulk purchase)	£27,800
100,000 brochures @ 20p each	£20,000
10 per cent telephone follow-up @ £2 per call	£20,000
	£67,800

Next it is important to calculate the anticipated level of new business, which might be as follows:

Selling price per item @ £14.99
Profit margin 40 per cent = £5.996

Table 18.1 shows a range of possible responses. The figures are purely illustrative and there is no way of knowing whether they are correct without a test marketing exercise. As a result of such an exercise a number of issues could be resolved such as whether the telephone follow-up was practical or whether cheaper brochures should be used, or indeed, was the selling price the optimum one?

Table 18.1

% sale from mailing	Gross profit	Cost of mailing	Net profit/ (loss)
9	£53,964	£67,800	(£13,836)
10	£59,960	£67,800	(£7,840)
11	£65,956	£67,800	(1,844)
12	£71,952	£67,800	4,152
13	£77,948	£67,800	£10,148

The next factor to consider is the timing of the mailing. While more flexible than other media in terms of response time, it does, however, require a period of time in order to do the job. For example, there is preparation, stuffing and labelling the envelopes, the time it takes the Post Office to deliver and time for the recipient to respond. This may easily amount to a month: if that is not available, deadlines must be changed.

Another important consideration is the resources that will be required to handle the response. This must be done in an orderly manner so that the enquiries for the promised brochure or sales visit or sample are kept on file for further action or analysis.

Literature If respondents are invited to request a brochure, check to ensure stocks are adequate.

Product availability If the stocks are not available to fulfil demand, perhaps a competitor will derive the benefit.

Sales force availability and preparation If respondents are invited to request a sales visit, are the sales force aware, available and prepared for the increased volume of work likely to follow on from the mailing?

Finally, remember that if money has been requested with the order, the law requires that it be returned if the product ordered cannot be supplied in a reasonable time.

18.5 Designing the direct mail package

After researching the market, identifying the sales target, buying in or constructing the mailing list and planning the campaign comes the design of the mailing package. The four elements are the letter, the envelope, the reply device and any other inserts.

Direct mail tends to be a 'words' medium, an individual communication between advertiser and prospective customer, in which illustration and graphics are supportive of a message already expressed in words. For this reason the most widely used element in direct mail is the letter. The letter can be:

- The sole and unsupported communication between the sender and the addressee. Often it needs nothing else to go with it, except a reply device. It alone is enough to get your message across.
- Adapted and modified at will – and cheaply – to take account of changing circumstances.
- Personalized and written in such a way as to speak directly to the addressee.
- As short or as long as the sales message warrants.

A letter should be the primary consideration in any mailing. In many cases it will produce results without any supporting material. If supporting material is included in the package, it should back up the points made in the letter.

The letter is the sales person. The leaflet/folder/brochure is the equivalent of the sales person's presentation or product demonstration.

Always try to write a direct mail letter from the recipient's point of view: after all, what the recipient will be interested in is 'What's in it for me?', not 'What are these people trying to sell me?' So, like a good sales person, the letter should present the advantages and benefits the prospect will gain from buying the product or service: how it will help, what problems it will solve, why it is the most suitable product, why it is a very cost-effective option.

A successful letter should attract the recipient's attention:

- By identifying a need and offering to solve it: convince the recipient that your product is the solution to the problem or need.
- By describing how well it does what it is meant to do, how attractive it looks or how reasonably priced it is (detailed product specifications are often best left to a brochure or leaflet).

Stimulate the desire to buy/find out more about your product by using case histories or testimonials where a company's business efficiency or life-style has been enhanced by your product. This is particularly useful if they are in a similar line of business or have a similar life-style to your prospect.

Encourage the recipient to act immediately – including a reply-paid card or envelope will help, but offers or incentives can often work wonders too.

On the question of presentation, it should be remembered that there are two focal areas on the page: one at the top near the salutation (Dear Mr Brown) and one at the bottom near the signature of the sender. It is a good idea to try and use these spaces to maximum advantage.

The ideal and preferred salutation is of course the prospect's name, correctly spelt and with the correct title. With modern computers and lazer printers, there is no real excuse for not doing this. Full colour brochures can be designed with a blank space for overprinting. The office desk-top computer can print off the names and addresses file in the blank space. When hiring a list, ask the supplier to do this for you. All other forms of address ('Dear Connoisseur of fine wine', 'Dear DIY enthusiast' etc.) are a little 'naff' and increase the chances that the unsolicited communication will be filed unread in that receptable of no return – the bin!

Other points that can be used to attract attention are a good headline and perhaps a postscript in red announcing a special offer in return for a prompt response.

The body of the letter should be broken up into easy-to-read paragraphs, with sub-headings, indentations and underlinings to emphasize key points. Anything that makes the letter easier or more exciting to read will be an advantage.

Last – and very important – do not be afraid of long copy. A two-, three- or even four-page letter can often work better than a single-page 'covering note'. So, if the selling message needs three pages, then that's how long the letter should be. On the other hand, of course, it is unwise to pad out a one-page letter with unnecessary waffle that will only bore the reader.

The envelope may also be used to start attracting the prospect's attention. A well designed envelope has individuality. It can flag interest by the use of words and graphic devices, and so stand out from the rest of the mail. This gives it significance and therefore importance in the recipient's eyes. As always, however, taste and judgement have to be used. In some cases, liveliness – even flamboyance – seems appropriate; in others, discretion is the better part of showmanship. (Consumer mailings are an obvious context for envelopes of this sort. But do not automatically rule them out for business mailings. It is surprising how many business people open their own mail.)

A cheap envelope is an insult to the recipient and does no good to the status of the sender. The same is true of an envelope that is too large for its contents. It looks slapdash and ill-planned, a last-minute stationery purchase instead of a considered part of a total package. (See Figure 18.5.) Window envelopes may have an advantage over the ordinary kind in that they can cut the cost of addressing. However, it is very

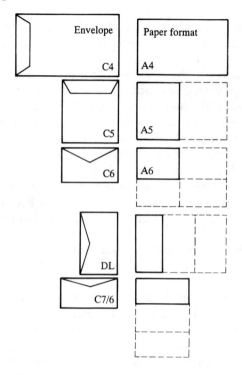

Figure 18.5   Envelope sizes

important to ensure that the whole of the address is carefully positioned so that it and the name of the addressee is clearly visible through the window.

The important role of the reply device is easily appreciated if the sender can understand that every additional task expected of the recipient will reduce the volume of the response. People are both busy and forgetful; for many individuals a stamp means a special journey to the Post Office and queueing up until a counter clerk is free (the stamp machines are frequently empty or out of order). This hurdle can be too much for many people – hence the advantage of a freepost or a first class business reply card or envelope. Also, remember that the sender only pays for those replies that are actually returned.

Other inserts may need to be included with the letter. These may be illustrations of the product or endorsements. However, it is important to make sure that these are logical extensions of the sales letter; otherwise the recipient may be confused and the impact lost altogether. Finally, remember that all this extra material has a weight and when sending this extra weight through the post there is a cost. That extra piece of padding repeated 100,000 times could amount to a much heavier postage charge.

18.6 Sample testing and analysis

Sample testing a mailing prior to the main campaign and post-mailing analysis involve the same analytical processes. The sampling of a representative group of target respondents indicates the degree of likely success. Choosing the 'representative group' is fundamental to the accuracy of the sample. Sample size is also important and with numbers much less than 5,000 the error rate can be large. Consequently it is not worth attempting this exercise with small campaigns.

The elements that can be tested are:

- *The list* for the percentage of 'return to sender/not deliverable' envelopes which indicates inaccuracy and lack of real relevance.
- *The price* – would there be more buyers at a lower price, or is the product sufficiently attractive that sales are very resilient at a higher price?
- *Offers and incentives* – are these likely to assist with the sale or merely reduce margins?
- *Choosing the right creative approach* can also be tested, for example full colour against two colour, or choice of salutation (by individual name or 'Dear Mr highly sophisticated with impeccable taste').
- *Sales conversion rate* – what proportion of enquiries will be converted into sales? Will the offer of goods 'on approval' raise the acceptance level?

Clearly, in many cases it will be necessary to test the feasibility of the exercise by mailing several samples with one acting as a control and the other representing the variable on test.

Remember to complete the analysis rather than guess the results. Accurate measurement can be useful in fine tuning the main mailing or as a reference for the next. In particular, the analysis should indicate:

- Which sectors of the market are most profitable.
- The ranking of different geographical areas.
- The range of order values or quantities.
- The cashflow pattern.
- The ratio of existing to new customers and any differences, for example in their purchase quantities or choice of products.

Finally, remember that pre-coding reply cards can make the analysis much easier!

19
Telephone selling and marketing

19.1 Telephone marketing guidelines

Because the telephone is technically so easy to use and so direct, thoughtless people have caused a great deal of trouble and inconvenience to those to whom they have attempted to sell their product. As a result of considerable complaints and controversy, the British Direct Marketing Association has produced some guidelines for the use of the telephone (see Exhibit 19.1).

Exhibit 19.1

The British Direct Marketing Association Guidelines for Telephone Marketing Practices are intended to provide organizations involved in direct telephone marketing to both consumers and businesses with principles of ethical and professional conduct.

All members of the BDMA shall comply with any relevant legislation which may supersede these guidelines. In addition, all members shall comply with the following guidelines in respect of activities not covered by specific law, or when legal requirements are less restrictive than the guidelines.

Disclosure
1 The name of the company on whose behalf a sales and marketing call is made or received should be voluntarily and promptly disclosed, and this information repeated on request at any time during the conversation.
2 The purpose of the call should be made clear at the start, and the content of the call should be restricted to matters directly relevant to its purpose.

3 The name, address and telephone number of the company responsible for the call should appear in the telephone directory, or be available through directory enquiries, or be readily available through another source. This information shall also be given on request.
4 If a telephone marketer is acting as an agent of a company, the name, address and telephone number of the agent should be disclosed upon request at any time during the conversation.
5 If a third person was recommended by a third party, the identity of the third party should be voluntarily and promptly disclosed.

Honesty
1 Telephone marketers should not evade the truth or deliberately mislead. Any questions should be answered honestly and fully to the best of the knowledge available. The Office of Fair Trading guidelines state that 'research' or 'surveys' should not be mixed in the same telephone call as selling or marketing.
2 Sales and marketing calls should not be executed in the guise of research or a survey. In cases where the words 'research' or 'survey' are used, the information obtained must not be used to form the basis of a direct sales approach either during or after the call.
3 Companies should accept responsibility for statements made by their sales staff or agents.

Reasonable hours
1 Telephone marketers should avoid making sales and marketing calls during hours which are unreasonable to the recipients of the calls, bearing in mind that the OFT recommends that calls to consumers should not be made later than 9.00pm unless expressly invited and that what is regarded as unreasonable can vary in different parts of the country and in different types of households or businesses.
2 When sales and marketing calls are initiated by a company or its representatives, telephone marketers should ask whether the timing of a call is convenient. If it is not, they should offer to ring back at a more convenient time.

Courtesy and procedures
1 Normal rules of telephone courtesy should be observed. Telephone marketers should avoid the use of high pressure tactics which could be construed as harassment.
2 Telephone marketers should always recognize the right of the other party to terminate the telephone conversation at any stage, and should accept such termination promptly and courteously.
3 If, as a result of a telephone contact, an appointment is made whereby a representative of a company is to visit a consumer at home, the consumer should be provided with a clearly identified contact point in order to facilitate possible cancellation or alteration of the appointment.
4 Confirmation of any order placed should be sent to the customer and any documents forwarded in accordance with the prevailing legislation.
5 Telephone marketers should take particular care not to seek information or to accept orders or appointments or invite any other action from a minor.

6 When consumer sales and marketing calls are made by a company or its representatives, there should be a cooling-off period of at least seven days for oral contracts resulting from such calls, and the recipients of the calls should be so informed.

Restriction of contacts
1 Sales and marketing calls should not be generated by random or sequential dialling manually or by computer.
2 Sales and marketing calls should not knowingly be made to unlisted or ex-directory numbers.
3 Unless expressly invited, consumer calls should not be made to individuals at their place of work.
4 Members should subscribe to the Telephone Preference Service (when it becomes available).
5 Members should delete from their telephone contact lists those persons who have specifically requested not to be contacted by telephone for sales or marketing purposes.
6 When sales and marketing calls are initiated by a company or its representatives and automatic message and recording equipment is used, it is necessary either

a to effect immediately an introduction on the lines of 'This is a computer call on behalf of . . .', or
b to have a 'live' operator introduce the call under those circumstances where the nature of the call is of a personal or a sensitive nature.

Definitions
1 Business calling: sales and marketing calls for an individual as a representative of his or her company.
2 Consumer calling: sales and marketing calls for an individual not as a representative of his or her employer or company.
3 Sales and marketing call: a call designed to generate a sale of a product or service, or to lead towards a sale of a product or service, to the specific company or consumer as a result of the information given during a telephone conversation.

19.2 Advantages of using the telephone

The principal advantage of using the telephone is that a large number of prospective customers can be questioned regarding their need for a company's products in a short space of time. Undertaken with skill and professionalism, a discussion can be brought to a selling close quickly and effectively. A prepared script can provide well-considered responses to any objections, leading to a smooth, controlled dialogue. If the wrong person is contacted, it is relatively straightforward to conclude the discussion; indeed, it may be possible to obtain the name of a better prospect.

On the negative side, the prospective customer can easily terminate the conversation by simply replacing the receiver. Consequently, a necessary skill is to create interest immediately. While it is frequently possible to obtain repeat orders by telephone, there is very little chance of being able to take an order from a new customer unless it is for a very well-known product or it is merely for a sample quantity.

If the product does not fall into either of these categories but it has been possible to identify a clear need, as a sales person you should make an appointment to meet. Do the selling face to face and decline to give away too much at this stage. Keep key sales messages for the meeting.

19.3 Telephone technique

Using the telephone for business purposes requires special skills which have to be learned. Unfortunately most people regard themselves as already qualified once they know how to push the buttons. The results without professional training can be disastrous. Listed below are a number of techniques that need to be absorbed and thoroughly practised before using the telephone in a sales or marketing context.

19.3.1 Always retain the initiative

If the prospect is not there, do not leave your company name or number, because you risk a negative decision without having the chance to state the benefits to be derived from your company's product or service. Promise to call back having established when your prospect is likely to be contactable in his office. If your contact will not speak to you on the telephone, try somebody else in a more senior position or another company altogether.

19.3.2 Brevity not verbosity

Once the appointment has been made or the potential qualified, bring the call to an abrupt end. The objective has been achieved. All that can happen from additional chatter is the loss of what has already been achieved. The temptation to continue talking when the contact accepts your offer is great; the release of pressure creates a delusion of tremendous achievement. Resist the temptation or the customer has time to change his/her mind. Also, you could have made two more contacts in the time wasted losing one.

Second, if too much information is imparted over the telephone, nothing is left for the sales presentation or the brochure or the invitation to an exhibition or in-house product demonstration. If the prospect is keen to talk, politely decline saying either that you would rather discuss it at whatever has been arranged, or that you have two in-coming calls holding on for you.

19.3.3 Save your message for the prospect

Don't tell the lady on the switchboard what your call is about; every additional person told weakens the chance of achieving your objective. Secretaries and PAs, however, require careful handling; these days many are graduates and professionally qualified. They can be really helpful if approached with tact and respect. It's all a question of judgement: if the person answering sounds of limited intellect, keep the message private and ask to be put through. If you are still asked what it is about, you can say that it is business, or that it is rather technical or that it involves computers or lazer technology. Always be polite but firm; offer to call back rather than argue; keep the secretary at a lower executive level than yourself. Do not leave your name or telephone number for the manager to call you back. Next time you call, it might be an idea to try 9.00am or lunchtime or 5.45pm. This only applies in the case of the private sector, because most local authorities, hospitals and public services (gas, water, electricity and telephone) close the switchboards at 5.00 or 5.30pm, as do most banks, insurance companies and retail conglomerates.

19.3.4 Do not offer to send too many brochures

Brochures cost money and letters have to be typed. If too many brochures are sent to people who are not interested, you may not have enough for the good prospects.

19.3.5 Be available for returned calls

If, after a meeting, a prospect telephones you, be available. Don't let your secretary tell him/her you are in a meeting. It sounds as though you are not interested or at least not focusing on the main event – their business. It is better, if you really cannot talk there and then, for your secretary to say that you are out of the office. Then ask if you can 'phone back and do so within twenty-four hours.

19.3.6 Do not make appointments too far ahead

The danger with scheduling meetings and events in the distant future (one month or more) is that the customer may forget why he/she wants to see you and 'go off the boil'.

19.3.7 Be careful with switch selling

On the telephone it can be dangerous to change objectives in mid-conversation because you are deviating from a carefully prepared plan. A wandering story can give the impression of a similarly unclear mind and the prospect may decide that you are just a time-waster.

19.3.8 Interest the prospect

The person at the other end of the telephone line may have had twenty or thirty calls already that day. Make a positive effort to be better, more positive, more professional and more knowledgeable about his/her needs: make it sound as though you are smiling, successful, and that this is a good opportunity for them to solve a pressing problem or to make a saving compared to the current source of supply.

19.3.9 Seek commitment

If you make a selling proposition such as 'If I could offer you a product thats. . . faster, at half the price, in a choice of colours, would you buy one?', the customer must agree to the fundamental need otherwise you have no basis for agreement and just waste the telephone sales executive's time. Once the prospect has agreed to the proposition, in his/her own mind he/she is duty bound to keep to the commitment.

19.3.10 Keep away from price on the telephone

The quickest way to terminate the possibility of obtaining a sale is to get involved in talking prices over the telephone. Price is only relevant to benefits; once the prospect has had the opportunity to see the product, price becomes value rather than just cost. Anyway, many products have more than one price depending on the actual configuration or quantity required.

19.4 Telephone marketing (selling)

The telephone has a number of excellent uses in the sales cycle. Principally it is for:

- prospecting for new business opportunities,
- making appointments,
- cycling accounts,
- re-charging dormant accounts,
- handling customer enquiries.

The main advantage is that it is cheaper and quicker in crisis communication to telephone than to get in a car and drive to see someone.

19.4.1 Prospecting

The nineteenth-century use of the word 'prospecting' was generally associated with searching for gold, diamonds and silver. In the second half of the twentieth century it has been applied to selling: it means quite simply looking for customers. But, in the same way that prospectors four and five generations ago did not start digging holes just anywhere, so today the intelligent sales executive does preliminary research or coarse screening to eliminate the less likely business prospects before the detailed examination begins.

There are probably three major sources of data that may sensibly be used for prospecting: leads from third parties as the result of advertising that are passed on to the territory sales executive; the names of visitors to an exhibition; and third, lists of names produced as the result of desk research and segmentation analysis.

Prospecting by telephone is the process of sorting the 'leads' or potential customers into categories of sales potential; these typically may be: good short-term prospect; medium-term possibility; and total waste of time. The sales person telephones the named individual and asks a short series of questions to establish whether in fact the prospect has an interest in buying that particular company's product or service. Where the interest is considerable it is likely that further action may result – for example the sending of a brochure or fixing a time to meet.

19.4.2 Making appointments

The telephone is by far the best way to make appointments in professional business circles. Clearly, before the second world war when a much smaller percentage of the business population had telephones, sales people used to call on the off-chance. In the 1990s, this would not generally be appreciated. Indeed, cellular telephones now provide the technology for sales executives to update customers on their expected time of arrival according to the density of motorway traffic.

19.4.3 Cycling accounts

Some organizations are able to use the telephone to make sales to customers that have identifiable purchase cycles. Essentially, the technique involves synchronizing selling activity to the customer's buying habits. So, for example, if a trade customer regularly buys ten cases of wine each month, a telephone call might be used to make sure of the next sale.

Account cycling, to be really effective, needs to be highly organized, with records identifying weekly, monthly and three-monthly customers and the products, the quantity and the price that make up their usual requirement. An effectively managed cycling programme can save a company a lot of time and money because the experienced sales executives are used to obtain new business rather than servicing existing accounts.

19.4.4 Recharging dormant accounts

The telephone can be a very cost-effective way to revitalize inactive customers who fail to respond to direct mail and promotional activity. Timing, a professional friendly approach and a 'good offer' can make a sale in just a few minutes. Taking the credit card number there and then even avoids difficulties arising from impulse purchasers who later change their minds.

19.4.5 Handling customer enquiries

Dealing with customer enquiries is another important role for a telephone sales department. These will be both of a pre-sale and post-sale nature and provide a valuable service and effective channel for making a sale. Where a prospective customer or an existing customer has an easy access to helpful informative selling staff, goodwill and additional business will be forthcoming.

19.4.6 Crisis communications

The late 1980s and early 1990s have seen an unprecedented number of crises in the broad sales and marketing arena: Pepperami, Union Carbide, eggs and Perrier to name but a few. If the Department of Health telephones to tell the company that its product must be recalled, it's no use saying that it could take a few days for British Telecom to install the extra telephone lines for all the calls that must be made: immediate action is required. This means one or two hours. Consequently the unfortunate company or trade association must call in specialists with the equipment already in place and the skills learned, tried and tested.

Infoplan, who handled the Perrier benzine scare, had a full-page advertisement in the national newspapers, the day after the news broke, with a hot-line. Some 25,000 telephone calls were taken. Speed is important in these situations because opinions can be formed about the products affected in one or two days which can be very hard to shift later. There is a great benefit in putting over the story of the company affected right away.

19.5 The difference between market research and telephone marketing/sales

The telephone marketing industry prefers the word marketing to 'selling', choosing not to distinguish between marketing and selling where the objective is to obtain business. Where the telephone is used to obtain information that is not to be used for sales and marketing purposes, this is telephone market research.

The principal differences are listed in Exhibit 19.2.

Exhibit 19.2

- Telemarketing that is sales-orientated
- Market research information that is gathered which is confidential
- Market research information that cannot be used for sales purposes
- Market research as an information-gathering technique

Source   British Direct Marketing Association (1990) *Survey on the UK Telephone Marketing Industry*, McGraw-Hill Book Company, Maidenhead, Berks.

Mixing the two types of telephone marketing activity is regarded as being unprincipled, unethical and totally unacceptable. It has even been given a special name: selling under the guise of a market research survey is called 'sugging'. As with most unethical activities, control is dependent on enforcement. Companies and individuals thought to be guilty of sugging are brought to the attention of the Professional Standards Committee of the Market Research Society. Members found guilty are almost certain to have their membership of the Society terminated. Members and non-members are also likely to have the matter referred to the registrar of the Data Protection Act.

19.6 The Data Protection Act (1984)

Apart from compliance with a Council of Europe convention, the rationale for the Act was to regulate the use of computer-processed information as it relates to individuals. Virtually everyone who is a 'data user' (a person who holds data and either alone or jointly or in common with other persons **controls** the contents and use of the data) falls under the scope of the Act. 'Data' refers to files of 'personal' information capable of being processed by computer. 'Personal' means information relating to a living individual which allows identification of that individual. Obviously market research and telephone marketing companies fall within these boundaries where their data are stored within a computer system.

All data users are required to register under this Act, which means they have to lodge with the Data Protection Registrar:

- Details of the organization/person who will be the data user.
- Information regarding each purpose for which they control and use automated personal data files.

A fundamental part of the registration process is the listing of the range of purposes for which a company collects, holds and processes personal data. Information classified as 'confidential survey research' is treated very differently under the Act from all other seventy or so 'purposes for registration'. In fact, the Data Protection Registrar has prescribed a unique purpose definition for confidential survey research, and agencies registering data under this purpose will keep the identities of respondents confidential and not use such data for marketing or selling to individuals. The important distinctions (as far as the Act is concerned) between survey research and all telephone selling and marketing are:

1 Research agencies will **not** disclose any data obtained at an individual level, in an identifiable way: i.e. it will remain confidential.
2 In return for point one, research agencies do not need to disclose to data subjects any data held on them when an access request is made.
3 Also in return for point one, agencies do not need to:
   a keep data up to date or correct, or
   b inform the respondent beforehand of the full nature of the enquiry if doing so would distort information supplied.

These are important concessions allowed for data used **only** for research or historical purposes, and so not to be used to influence the individual supplying it.

Telephone selling/marketing organizations involved in this type of activity have to register:

- all the current and future purposes for which they hold this personal data,
- full descriptions of all the types of personal data held, for example health records or expenditure details, both existing and future,
- a full description of the sources of the data (this may include relatives, employers, company customers etc.),
- all the types of people or organizations to which the data will be disclosed in a personally identifiable way,
- keep such records up to date and accurate, and
- provide any data subject who makes a request with a copy of all the information they hold on him/her.

This quite clearly represents an enormous volume of work. Failure to comply is an offence against the Act, which can lead to compulsory deregistration. This prevents the individual or company from trading. Under the Act, if the individual or organization registers the purpose as 'confidential survey research', however, then the data cannot be passed on in an identifiable form to a third party unless:

- the person to whom it is supplied is also constrained by the Market Research Society code of conduct and will be using the data only for survey research purposes, or
- the respondent has given specific permission.

Organizations involved in confidential survey research are exempt from these conditions and may register under a new 'Method 2' scheme. This greatly simplifies the process because they may use a free format mode to describe their activities. The final benefit for *bona fide* research companies is that they are not obliged to divulge personal details of individuals held on file to such individuals who choose to enquire.

19.7 The telephone marketing audit

The telephone marketing audit described below is a technique designed for the purpose of selling by the author and a business associate of long standing. It is not to be confused with confidential survey research. Similar practices have probably been developed by other gatherers of market intelligence.

The objective is to determine the current and immediate future business (the next six months) of a geographical area for a particular client type. The next stage is to select an information base of companies to be audited. The usual way of doing this is to select by SIC code (standard industrial classification). It is then a question of looking up the companies in a directory (Kompass) or using the equivalent on-line service, where Kompass or ICC will extract the names for you from their database and forward a print-out (for a fee).

The next stage is product application and market training for the people doing the telephoning. It is absolutely essential that they have a thorough grasp of these areas, otherwise the response rate will fall and the value of the information obtained much reduced. The particular technique being described has always been used by an experienced sales and marketing professional with several years' business experience of the product if not the markets to be audited. If decision-makers are going to be questioned, it must be assumed that they will respond fully and in useful detail only to a professional peer.

The final stage is the telephoning, which typically proceeds in this way: when the switchboard operator replies, ask for the name of the technical director or the appropriate manager. If the reply is 'It is not company policy to give out these names over the telephone', ring off and call back in ten minutes. This time, ask for the managing director's secretary, who will usually oblige with the details requested.

When contact is made with the target individual, it is absolutely essential to state your name and the company you are doing work for, and to say that you are doing this work for a client to identify the business potential of (say) CAD (computer-aided design) in a type of industry or a geographical area. Furthermore, this information may be used to make sales by the client company where opportunities are perceived to exist. Then ask 'Is your company using 2 or 2½D?' Invariably there will be a useful response: '2½D'; 'What software are you using?' When that reply has been noted you may ask 'Is the system running on micros or a mini computer?' Then, 'How long have you been using this hardware/software?' The respondent will frequently give details of company policy for hardware and software procurement; indeed, on further questioning he/she may tell you when additional purchases are likely to be made. Sometimes the respondent will ask you if your client company will send a product brochure, or perhaps arrange for a demonstration, or even ask for a sales executive to visit.

The surprising thing about this technique is that where BMDA and OFT guidelines are followed, in particular where:

- full disclosure as to the purpose of the call is given,
- honesty about the objectives for asking the questions is made very clear,
- courtesy and professionalism are exhibited regarding manner, product knowledge, and allowing the customer to terminate the call graciously, such that the respondent feels he/she is talking to a peer,

then more than 90 per cent of those contacted respond with enthusiasm and interest. Many even volunteer that they may be contacted again in the future should the need arise.

19.8 Scripting

Unfortunately, in most instances there is deemed to be insufficient time or money to train the telephone marketing team properly about product details and product market knowledge. Recourse is therefore made to a telephone script in an attempt to keep a dialogue going in the absence of adequate knowledge. In these circumstances a good script becomes essential.

The script should be written to help the caller maintain a consistent message that focuses on the major objective. However, the person receiving the call is not working to a set piece and consequently the script must provide a framework which predicts the range of possible replies to the opening statements and has prepared responses to overcome objections so that the conversation can be steered in the required direction.

Incorporated within the script should be statements of fact about the product's benefits or the situation in the marketplace (to remedy the knowledge deficit of the telesales person). The script must have a structure leading to a close in just the same way as a sales interview – indeed, many of the traditional closing techniques are appropriate.

19.9 Inbound telephone marketing

Inbound telephone marketing is thriving in the new communications-obsessed culture of the 1990s. More advertising campaigns than ever before carry freephone or subsidized telephone numbers – 0800-numbered calls are free; 0345-numbered calls are charged at the local rate irrespective of distance. These numbers are used to make a request for a brochure, order a product or to initiate a two-way discussion relating to particular needs. First Direct launched by the Midland Group in October 1989 was an attempt to do banking by telephone.

The growth of this approach is stimulated by the immediacy of today's life-styles and the demand for a speedy service. People are reluctant to wait. Indeed, there is a major link between speed of service and customer satisfaction, particularly where there is little perceived difference between products. Another reason for the use of the inbound response is to produce measurable results for clients funding expensive marketing and promotional activity.

20
Sales promotion

Sales promotion comprises a range of tactical techniques set within a strategic marketing framework designed to achieve specific sales and marketing objectives. It is generally only applicable to mass markets with a low- to moderately-priced product. The heritage is almost exclusively in the realm of fast moving consumer goods (fmcg) in the supermarket; however, recent and continued growth is more likely to come from other sectors – consumer durables, travel, financial services and business to business. For example, a current promotion: buy a Toshiba fax and receive a free cordless telephone.

Sales promotion in its widest sense can include most activities that are described as 'below the line'. The key concept is 'added value', meaning that something is added to stimulate action, this item being above and beyond the product itself which is unchanged. It always involves an element of incentive and reward. This means that a commission is not normally payable to an advertising agency as a percentage of the spend. A fee or retainer is usually paid to a consultant for this specialist service. Items which do attract this agency commission are called 'above the line' and comprise press, TV, radio, cinema and poster advertising. Consider the example in Exhibit 20.1.

20.1 Key promotion techniques

Sales promotion, as a very innovative aspect of selling and marketing, can in certain circumstances include an extremely diverse range of techniques. However, reduced to essential basics which are relevant to a wide range of products and markets there are: 'free mail-ins', reduced price offers, competitions, couponing and promotions to the trade. In

Exhibit 20.1 'Below' and 'above' the line an example

Advertising budget		
Press	£175,000	
TV	£750,000	
Radio	£20,000	
Cinema	£500,000	
Posters	£60,00	the 'line'
	£1,505,000	
Advertising agency fee 15%	£225,750	
	£1,730,750	
Material for point-of-sale promotions	£60,000	
Exhibitions budget	£120,000	
Direct mail budget	£50,000	
	£1,960,000	

order to achieve the required response, a sales promotion must progress through six degrees of awareness with the target audience:

- being seen,
- being understood,
- provoking interest,
- being relevant,
- being stimulating, and
- being persuasive.

1 Free extra value

Free   This is extra product for the standard retail price (10 per cent Heineken, 10 per cent Mars). It can also be in an extreme case 'buy one sofabed and get another sofabed free'. It is a good tactic for deflecting attention away from price when the product itself is a leading brand with an appropriate price premium. It is not a particularly effective method for attracting new users (who wants more of an unknown product?)

Free in/on/with pack   As with the 'free' approach, these offer instant gratification. 'In packs' promotions are dominated by breakfast cereals (plastic submarines) and tea packs (a picture card), for obvious reasons as, for example, a food canner would not allow a 'hairy plastic spider' to float among the minestrone soup. The 'on pack' classic example is cover mounts on magazines of all types. However, the disadvantage is that if the on-pack item is sufficiently attractive, it disappears before the purchaser has a chance to sample the free product. Both techniques give to 100 per cent of purchasers, which clearly includes a number who would have bought anyway.

Free mail-in   The free mail-in has the advantage that nowhere approaching a 100 per cent redemption will be achieved. This is more likely to be 2–5 per cent, with the proportionate savings in cost. Moreover, very many free mail-ins require multiple proof of purchase. This provides the opportunity to build repeat business.

The difficult part with this tactic is judging the level of response. Under-redemption for example of 20,000 specialist poodle curling tongs creates as big a headache as 20,000 poodle owners visiting the promoter in search of their tongs. The nature of this tactic is the delay before receiving the cherished gift – which can be a disadvantage in the here-and-now society.

2 Save

Sampling   is all about a free trial before purchase – the idea being that the first will induce the latter to become a habit-forming behaviour pattern. This 'trial mechanism' is particularly effective with new products and can also be used for lapsed users.

Reduced price packs have legal restrictions as embodied in the Trade Descriptions Act 1968 and the Price Marketing [Bargain Offers] order 1979. The first requirement is that the reduced price must be 'real'. This must be sustainable and nothing about the offer should be misleading. In the case of a retailer reduction, the product must have been demonstrably offered and sold at the higher price for at least twenty-eight days in the past six months. This could, however, be in only one store in a chain.

Where the price reduction originates from the manufacturer, it must be demonstrably different from the generally supplied product price to that area where the reduced offer is made.

Couponing   is the addition of a redeemable voucher to a packet, or part of a leaflet that is put through the letterbox, or part of a display advertisement in a magazine. The voucher is clipped and used in part payment for the product.

This sales promotional technique is generally used at the time of a new product launch to encourage consumers to try it out, or some months later to trigger a retrial and perhaps encourage a pattern of repeat purchases. Other tactics involving the use of coupons include reducing the price gap between competitive products, or extending the number of distribution outlets for the product.

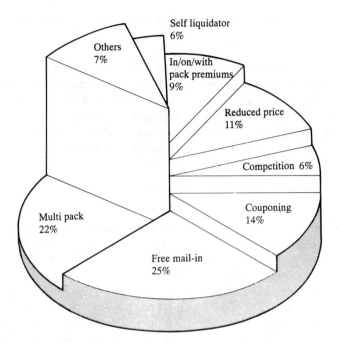

Figure 20.1 Where the money goes
Source *Marketing* (from MS Surveys and Promotional Services)

Couponing is a popular promotional tactic because it can be accurately targeted (which streets in which postal area, or which outelts have the packet with the coupons). Second, the results are infinitely measurable and indeed predictable (using the response data from past campaigns of similar products).

Couponing is frequently though not exclusively used for sampling. An immediate or next purchase cash discount is offered to customers – Persil Automatic offers 30p to purchasers of the 4.0 kg E10 size box. The producer of the product using the coupon should beware of non-redemption, whereby retailers accept coupons against items which have not been purchased.

Charities The real moral with charities is to pick one that is in harmony with your brand for the most ethical marketing reasons. Children and animals do well whereas many deserving medical charities dealing with minority afflictions will never benefit from this tactic. The experienced practitioner will set upper and lower limits to avoid the massive injection of a substantial proportion of the past few years' corporate profits to the worthy cause in the event of an unforeseen mega-success. Andrex and guide dogs for the blind, ably assisted by Barbara

Woodhouse, was one of the all-time most successful programmes of this type.

Self-liquidating premium (or promotion)   This is now distinctly out of favour with consumers because not only do they have to send proofs of purchase but money to recieve their 'gift'. The idea is that respondents cover all costs – item, postage, packing and administration. The only SLPs that might work in this cold climate of disillusionment are those which are not only unique and good value, but also unobtainable in the high street through the usual retail outlets

3 Win

Competition   The prime reason why manufacturers run competitions and prize draws is that they have the benefit of a fixed budget. No matter how many people enter, the prize fund does not change. Contrary to general belief, the ubiquitous tie-breaker is not there to obtain free advertising slogans, but for reasons of the Lotteries and Amusements Act 1976. This Act governs the way the competitors and prize draws are organized. If you require a purchase to be made in order to enter, you must select your winners by 'skill and judgement'. The promoter is not allowed to pull winners out of a hat.

Free prize draws   In a free prize draw, unlike a competition, the manufacturer **must** not demand a purchase to be made before entering. In this event no skill and judgement is necessary and no tie-breaker required. Tie-breakers are loathed by consumers who are not gifted in the creative use of the written word. Therefore entry levels for competitions are notoriously low.

4 Joint promotions

Joint promotions use all of the other eight techniques; however, rather than buying third-party merchandise which is unbranded, a linkage with a named supplier is negotiated. A classic example of this is Rowenta offering a sample of Comfort pure silk fabric conditioner with purchases of their irons. Obviously, this type of creative strategy uses the very best of in-pack promotion and sampling between major complementary promoters.

Trade promotions
Sales promotions are the key method of marketing to the trade. Some industries treat their trade distributors somewhat like brands, and using them as profit centres, invest in them or not accordingly. The various

sales promotion techniques may be combined in a certain way to achieve a particular sales objective (20 per cent of the market in Scotland, for example) by using the resource and positioning strengths of the trade outlet. Traders can be 'incentivized' as well as consumers, but the wise marketeer would never offer a gift to the local Sainsbury's manager or the head office buyer. Furthermore, to offer anything other than the smallest diary at Christmas to a local government official or civil servant carries a custodial sentence. The target market for dealer loaders is the independent trades person – from CTN (confectioner, tobacconist, newsagent) to travel agent.

6 Incentives for sales staff and other third parties

Any gift over £10 is taxable and the onus is on the employee to state this on a tax return. However, the promoter can pay the income tax on the recipient's behalf through the Incentive Valuation Unit based in Soho, London. Companies may prefer to offer a gift in preference to cash because no National Insurance contributions are payable on the former.

20.2 Developing the promotion programme

The first decision revolves around the sales objective to be achieved. This may be a percentage increase in the number of users in a region or of a certain type. This can then be divided between non-users and competitors' brand users. Second, where is the thrust to take place? Is it at retailers, company sales force or direct to the consumer?

Once these fundamentals have been decided, the sales and marketing staff can decide on:

- Which promotional technique?
- The size of the incentive – a major incentive pulls a bigger response but it costs more and there is fall-off at a certain point.
- Which consumers are required to participate? Geographical area, type of trade outlet, readers of which magazines.
- Method of distribution: packet, letter-box drop, magazine advertisement. There are known costs and predictable responses with each.
- Duration of the promotion – if the cycle is too short many people can be excluded because the campaign is over before they are ready to re-purchase. Where a product has a shelf life of a few weeks and costs £1, a 15p reduction will not encourage many people to try it before the competitive brand is used up.
- Timing of the promotion: clearly some products are seasonal: purchase profiles differ around Christmas and the New Year and during the main July/August holiday season. Production will need

time to build up capacity, while marketing will need to design and print any publicity material.

- Developing the creative element: this is frequently 90 per cent perspiration and 10 per cent inspiration. Figure 20.2 clearly shows that the final promotion is the result of detailed and painstaking analysis of all aspects of the market, corporate objectives, previous experience both within the company and outside, and the key thrust of the brand strategy.

  - What has worked previously for the brand, the market, the competition?
  - What promotions have proved successful in similar markets with similar user profiles?
  - What about promotions abroad in similar categories?
  - What media does the target read, see or hear?
  - What are the main fashions or attitudes expressed by those media?
  - What is topical in current affairs: what's new, fresh and original – and will still be around in six months' time?
  - What's happening in the marketplace?
  - What new merchandising properties are becoming available?

- Preparing the budget. This is invariably approached in one of two ways. Either experience dictates a fixed percentage of the total promotional budget (for example with a certain toothpaste, sales promotion may account for 30 per cent of the total promotional budget and with shampoo it may be 50 per cent), or the cost is calculated as follows:

Administration:

Printing_____

Mailing_____

Promoting_____

_____   _____

Incentive cost

Per unit × expected number of
redemptions   _____

                                                           _____

20.3 Field promotions

Field promotions started to become a recognized specialist area of selling in the late 1970s and early 1980s. This development arose partially as a

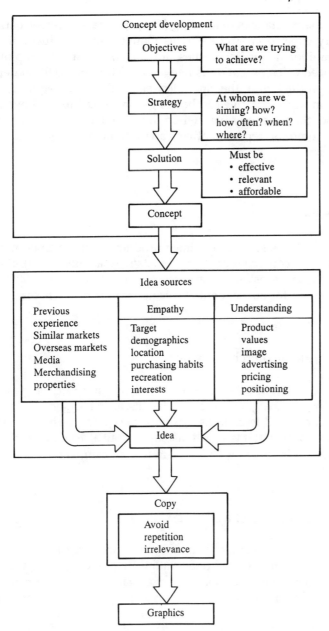

Figure 20.2 Concept development
Source Marketing

result of major changes in retailing (the supermarket, hypermarket, cash and carry expansion) and partly as manufacturers reduced the size of their traditional territory sales force. The cost of employing an experienced sales executive is between £30,000 and £60,000 depending on the product and the specialist skills that are required. A field promotion representative can be bought in for £80 to £125 per day, and of course, they are only paid when they are needed.

Field promotion representatives can undertake a range of sales-related activities:

20.3.1 Selling

Frequently this is selling new fmcg products or those 'special offers' to chemists and confectioners/tobacconists/newsagents (CTN). Stocks are maintained in an estate car and either the sale is made for cash or an order is taken for subsequent invoicing from a local wholesaler.

20.3.2 Strategic merchandising

Expensive point-of-sale material used in support of a television advertising campaign may easily be discarded if sent to the retailer through the post. Merchandising can be very effective in persuading the retailer not only that it is worth displaying, but also actually to set up the displays, and in creating enthusiasm for the campaign.

20.3.3 Contract merchandising

Merchandisers are generally employed to work up to fifteen hours a week calling on nominated retail outlets in a regular journey cycle. This may be either for one company or on a shared basis covering a range of (non-competing) products. Contract merchandising is most popular within the grocery, CTN, travel, chemist and licence trades. The merchandiser, in addition to setting up point-of-sale material, can stock-check (as a basis for re-ordering), price-mark and indeed fill up the shelves if the goods are carried in the back of the estate car. The opportunity also exists to obtain feedback about the level of sales and the relative success *vis-à-vis* competitors' products. Twenty years ago all these activities were undertaken by the company's sales force.

20.3.4 In-store selling

In-store demonstrations can be highly successful if correctly set up and fully supported by the host retailer. Clearly, where cooking and sampling of food takes place, a large area needs to be allocated with support staff to take the orders (and the cash) and to wrap the purchase. The author recalls seeing a wok demonstration in Barkers of Kensington a few years ago: twenty or thirty products were being sold every ten to fifteen minutes as the result of a highly proficient demonstration.

This type of presentation is also very successful with electrical appliances, fragrances and drinks.

20.3.5 Mystery shoppers

This technique can be used as a vehicle for selling-in to new distribution outlets or to motivate retailers to accept and maintain point-of-sale material on display for a given period. It is also a useful way of collecting market research information.

20.3.6 Field investigations

Auxiliary personnel can be very usefully employed to carry out basic research that can be used to establish details of competitors' product distribution, prices and the size and prominence of displays.

20.4 Marginal marketing

Sales promotion is particularly suited to what is called 'marginal marketing'. This is based on the idea that the market for any mature product comprises one's own and competitors' customer bases, which include three types of customer (see Figure 20.3).

- The 'immovables', who are locked into the brand of their choice. They are very brand-loyal and the only possible gain from sales promotional activity might be to increase their consumption of your product.
- The 'vulnerable loyals', who are brand-loyal but still susceptible to being 'brand-stolen' if sufficient inducement is offered. These people are a good target for sales promotion because they can be persuaded to change their choice of brand. This shift can be very significant in terms of market share.

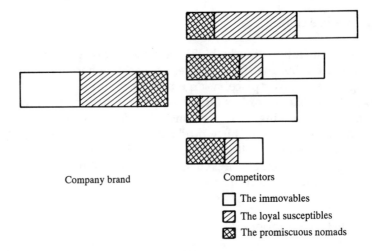

Company brand   Competitors

☐ The immovables
▨ The loyal susceptibles
▩ The promiscuous nomads

Figure 20.3   Marginal marketing – consumer susceptibilities
Source   Institute of Sales Promotion Yearbook 1988 article by Peter Holloway

- 'Brand nomads', who have no real brand loyalty, and often switch indiscriminately from one product to another. They are gained as regularly as they are lost. Although promiscuous they can be an important target in tactical promotions

Knowing these susceptible marginals can assist the sales promotion specialist in defining more realistic objectives and proposing more effective solutions. Rather than fitting into traditional demographic classifications, these groups belong to a market segment. Consequently, the marginal marketing concept offers new opportunities for effective sales promotions.

The key to effectiveness is pre-testing all the key components:

- The approach mechanism (price-off, coupon, free mail-in).
- The pitch – where, what type and what value.
- The platform – what to say and how to present the message in such a way as to initiate the relevant response.
- The communications channel (on-pack, in-pack off-pack).

Once this has been done, the campaign has a good chance of being successful.

21
Exhibitions, conferences and seminars

The common rationale of exhibitions, conferences and seminars is the creation of a favourable environment where the seller can have the complete attention of large numbers of clearly identified prospective buyers for the presentation of their sales message. In order to reinforce this message and obtain the maximum possible impact from the event a galaxy of creative talent is brought to bear when planning events. Despite the exotic locations, the sumptuous banquets and the glitter of the latest audio-visual lazer presentations, the primary objective is to sell the host's product or services. The high cost of staging such extravaganzas has been justified on the basis that the cost per decision-maker is actually quite low when the total cost is divided by the number of guests or delegates attending the event. However, irrespective of the type of event being held, sponsoring companies look very closely at the 'net new business' figures. (See Figures 21.1, 21.2 and 21.3.)

21.1 Successful exhibiting

If a company seeks the maximum return from an exhibition its role in the sales and marketing strategy should be carefully evaluated. Unlike other elements of the marketing mix, which are designed and implemented by a small team of company executives working with an agency or consultancy, organizing an exhibition involves a large number of people, both skilled and semi-skilled, from different backgrounds. They do not respond to memos and it is impossible to get them all around a table for a planning meeting.

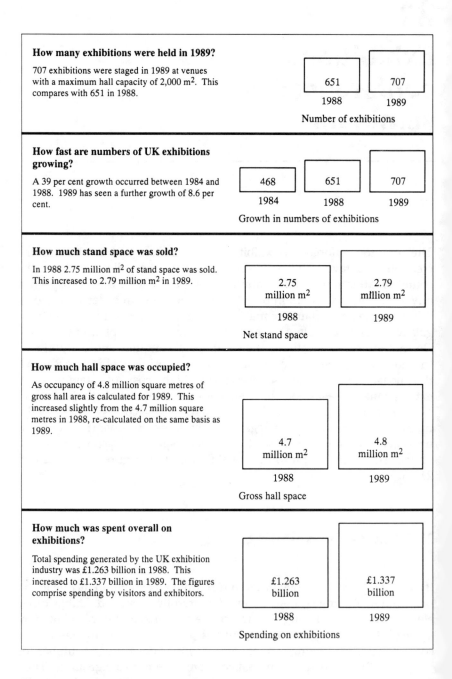

Figure 21.1　Facts about UK exhibitions
Source　Association of Exhibition Organizers

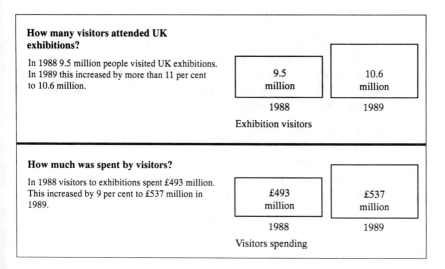

Figure 21.2   Facts about visitors to exhibitions
Source   Association of Exhibition Organizers

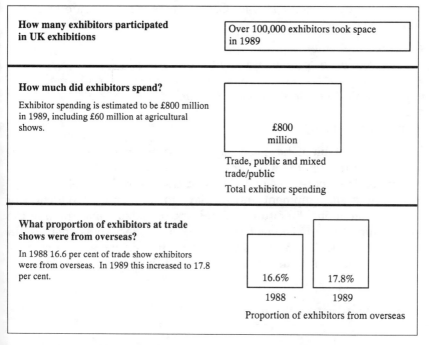

Figure 21.3   Facts about exhibitors
Source   Association of Exhibition Organizers

21.1.1 Setting the objectives

This has to be the first stage – the decision to attend an exhibition or stage a conference or a seminar will be based on which sales and marketing objectives are most important. Different types of product directed at different market groups or segments will also influence the choice of venue. Typical objectives might be:

- to create a corporate presence in the market,
- to launch a new product,
- to increase the market share of existing products or services,
- to talk to existing customers who are otherwise difficult to meet,
- to assess the quality of the competition,
- to reach new target groups of customers.

21.1.2 Planning

Once it has been decided that exhibiting fulfils the company's objectives, it is necessary to decide which exhibition should be chosen. Most markets and industries are served by two or more exhibitions, each with a slightly different profile. Comparisons may be made from the point of view of:

- exhibition theme,
- projected visitor profile and any historic analyses,
- exhibitor profile – how many are returning for a second time,
- geographical position and facilities offered,
- cost,
- the organizers.

When the exhibition has been selected, it is then a question of detailed planning – probably the most important issue is cost. This will include the hire of floor space, design and construction of the stand plus fittings, transporting all equipment and displays to the venue, production of videos, promotional literature and posters, organizing and training the stand staff plus provision of their accommodation and expenses. In addition there will be all the services essential for operating a stand – telephone, electricity, furniture, flowers and the services of a cleaner.

21.2 Exhibitions

Exhibitions are really 'public consumer shows', though in many instances the public is restricted to the trade. This is the sector of the business currently showing the better growth because those attending do so for commercial reasons rather than a 'day out'.

21.2.1 Public consumer shows

As usual it is a question of using the correct sales approach for a particular product market sector. Consequently in some industries the use of exhibitions is increasing and in others falling. The Exhibition Industry Federation, in their 1989 statistical review, quoted that 'declining product sectors are in the public consumer shows, antiques and art, electronics, furniture and furnishings'. User-chooser events, on the other hand, such as holiday and travel shows, attract large numbers. Indeed one group of exhibition organizers are providing a venue where prospective holiday-makers can not only talk to the specialists and make comparisons, but actually book holidays.

Public shows have to be carefully targeted at people with the disposable income to make the operation financially viable. For this reason ABC1-type events are the most popular, with a good theme being absolutely essential. A recent development is the promotion of the idea of 'audience participation' at the exhibitions rather than making them just spectator events. One popular way of providing this is to have a programme of lectures, seminars and workshops taking place while the exhibition is being staged. At the ski show, for example, a dry slope is constructed for use by visitors.

21.2.2 Trade shows

Trade shows are exhibitions that are not open to the general public, but restricted to members of the industry.. This usually includes employees of companies in this market segment, corporate users and buyers, agents, civil servants, consultants and associated service industries.

Other differences are that there may be fewer exhibitors but each will make a large investment in the stand in terms of space, design and range of products available for demonstration. Also, senior management from the exhibiting company will attend to take advantage of meeting and negotiating with the visiting management of prospective buyer organizations.

21.2.3 Overseas trade fairs

Exhibiting at an overseas trade fair can be valuable experience. It is also a relatively inexpensive method of testing the potential market for the product or service in question. For some markets it is virtually the only way of entry. This applies particularly to the Soviet Union and the former Comecon countries and other still centrally planned economies like China. In these countries, exhibiting, or even better an invitation to exhibit, is often a necessary prelude to doing serious business and often the only real way of testing the market, contacting distributors and beginning realistic discussions. In addition, the exhibitor will learn much about the competition and the product's sales channels as distributors for a competitor's products engage the company's stand staff in discussions. (See Figures 21.4 and 21.5.)

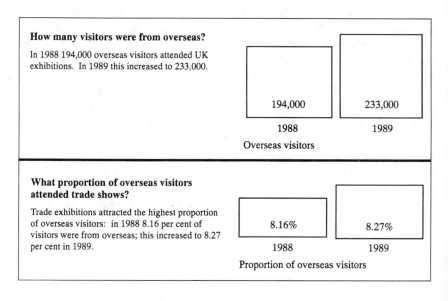

Figure 21.4   Facts about overseas visitors
Source   Association of Exhibition Organizers

Clearly, before making a positive commitment, the would-be exhibitor needs to:

- set exhibition objectives,
- analyse the expected visitors' profile,
- calculate the expected overall cost,
- commission and print necessary product and promotional material,
- retain a designer for the stand and a contractor to erect it, and
- plan for qualified staff to manage the stand for the duration of the exhibition.

In order to assist in this exercise an export market research scheme is operated by the British Overseas Trade Board. The objective is to help

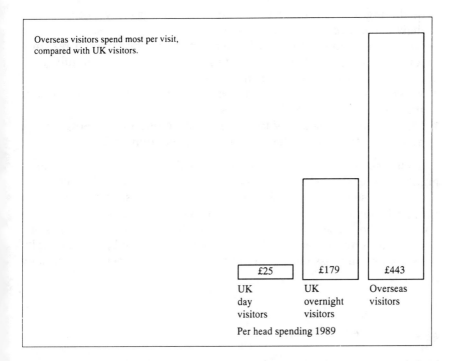

Overseas visitors spend most per visit, compared with UK visitors.

£25 — UK day visitors
£179 — UK overnight visitors
£443 — Overseas visitors

Per head spending 1989

Figure 21.5 How much did visitors spend per visit?
Source Association of Exhibition Organizers

and encourage UK firms and trade associations to evaluate overseas business opportunities properly before spending large sums of money. Participation is open to all exporters and potential exporters of goods and services produced in the UK. Grants are available for research carried out by research cconsultants, although support is also given towards the purchase of multi-client studies and for research undertaken overseas by the applicant's own UK-based market research staff. However, in the case of in-house research, the BOTB must be satisfied that the applicant's research capability is comparable to that of professional agencies.

The level of support grant varies according to the method used: the following may be used as a guide:

- Professional market research consultants: up to 50 per cent of the essential travel costs and interpreters' fees plus a daily allowance for one researcher.
- Setting up an in-house market research organization: up to one third of the salary of a qualified researcher for one year for time spent doing

qualifying research projects, one third of overseas travel costs, and a daily allowance.

- Up to one third of the cost of purchasing published market research (but not directories). Where studies are commissioned jointly with other companies, up to half the costs.
- Where trade associations commission research, up to two thirds of the cost may be covered by grants.
- Management consultancy for advising on setting up or re-organizing an export department, half the fee to a maximum of £5,000.

In all cases, except for grants to trade associations, there is a maximum grant of £20,000 per project and £40,000 per company per year. Companies seeking to qualify should prepare a research brief and a proposal, including terms of reference, research methods, timescale, and, in the case of in-house research, details of researchers' qualifications and itinerary. Where *ad hoc* research is to be carried out by consultants, submissions from three different agencies are normally required.

21.2.4 Mobile exhibitions

Mobile exhibitions in the UK have two forms, first the Rail Ambassador Exhibition Special marketed by HP:ICM, which is a BR train that can be totally redesigned for each customer, and second what are called 'road shows'. These are frequently thirty-foot trailers which when static become exhibition stands with displays in the usual way. After display in one venue the trailer is hitched up to a motorized unit and towed to the next event.

The Rail Ambassador Exhibition Special, when totally designed and the rolling-stock resprayed (at a cost of some £30,000 to £60,000), makes for an unusual and truly impressive display. Complimentary services include meals, hotel accommodation and synchronized travel arrangements. There is the advantage of a single focus on the exhibiting company that is not diluted by the rival attractions of neighbouring exhibitors.

Road-transported mobile shows are encumbered by restrictions of space and weight, though by taking the exhibition to the customer they reach people who in the normal course of events would be unable to leave their office for sufficient time to go to a static exhibition. They also have the advantage of flexibility – they can easily 'set down' in a field or the corner of a car park or industrial estate. Road shows have further advantages where an industry or market is more regionalized than national. The 'big' exhibitions are generally focused around London,

Birmingham, Manchester and Glasgow. This is by no means appropriate to the marketing strategy of all industries and their market sectors. For example, a road show vehicle can be of immense moral support to a local or regional distributor organizing a promotion in a particular area.

The road show has an interesting financial angle – once the motorized unit and trailer have been purchased and equipped for £60–£80,000 they are relatively cheap to move from location to location. With a static exhibition this sum can represent the budget for a four-day presence at a major event.

21.3 Conferences

The message is clear. The conference customer is demanding quality: purpose-built rooms, good food, effective security and a high standard of personal service. These expectations were confirmed in a survey conducted by the Queen Elizabeth II Conference Centre, Westminster, and published in *Marketing* (see Table 21.1).

The reasons given for holding the conference were interesting:

Product launch	26%
Sales force meeting	16%
Dealer/distributor meeting	8%
AGM of shareholders	8%
Training course	7%
Other	35%

The 'other' figure included conferences and seminars not falling within the specialist categories: promotions and receptions or dinners. Clearly companies believe that face-to-face communications are important both to create the necessary impact and to motivate those involved with the selling. Training managers usually prefer to hold their courses away from the delegates' usual place of work to avoid the situation where they are called back to work to resolve a crisis. The average number attending meetings was 320, but most fell into the 102–200 range. The majority of the meetings covered by the survey lasted one day or less, which suggests that companies are going for short meetings to achieve cost effectiveness and maximum impact. (See Table 21.2.)

21.3.1 Video conferences

Video conferencing is the art of being in two places at once thanks to telephone landlines and communications satellites. It is quite simply the

Table 21.1   *What factors are important*

Type of meeting	%	Minimizing travel time	Sleeping accommodation at conference venue	Top class food	High standard service	Security	Private entrance/ reception rooms	Purpose built conference room	Experienced senior person assigned to event	Availability of break out rooms	Display/exhibition area	Private conference office	Office and communication equipment	Rehearsal/slide preparation room	AV equipment and operators
Product launch	26	6	13	3	1	5	9	4	2	9	7	13	8	12	11
Sales force meeting	16	8	9	4	1	7	13	2	3	5	14	11	5	12	9
Dealer/distributor	8	5	9	5	3	8	11	2	1	4	5	10	14	11	11
AGM	8	9	13	6	1	14	8	3	2	6	5	11	9	11	3
Training	7	6	4	1	1	6	12	4	3	6	9	9	9	13	13
Other	35	5	13	3	1	6	12	4	2	8	11	7	9	14	9
All types of meeting	100	6	13	3	1	5	12	4	2	7	10	11	9	14	8
Average mark*		2.0	2.6	1.6	1.2	1.9	2.5	1.6	1.5	2.2	2.4	2.5	2.3	2.7	2.3

Key
1 = essential
2 = preferred
3 = relatively unimportant
4 = irrelevant

Source: *Marketing*, 8 June 1989 (from QEII Survey)

Table 21.2 *How many attend?*

No. of delegates	All meetings	Product launch	Sales	Dealer/distributor	AGM	Training	Other conference	Dinner	Display/promotion
10–30	9	2	–	–	–	3	3	–	1
31–50	6	3	1	1	–	1	–	–	–
51–100	16	6	3	3	1	–	2	–	1
101–200	27	8	3	1	1	3	10	1	–
201–300	12	2	3	–	1	–	6	–	–
301–500	14	3	1	1	1	–	8	–	–
501–1000	15	3	2	1	4	–	3	1	1
1001–2000	4	–	2	1	–	–	1	–	–
2000+	2	1	–	–	–	–	–	–	1

One questionnaire, no numbers given

Source: Marketing, 8 June 1989 (QEII Survey)

simultaneous transmission and reception of television pictures and sound between two or more locations. The manager or director can be present at an urgent conference without having to leave the office and spend hours in an aeroplane. Examples of how effective this medium can be are available every evening on ITV news and BBC2's 'Newsnight'. Discussions take place each evening between studio guests and people in other studios all over the world with good quality audio and visual communication.

The technology has been available for more than a decade but problems with international standards and high on-line costs have restricted its use. Progress with resolving the former and reducing the latter, as well as digital telephone switching systems, have resulted in the expansion of this medium. Video conferencing may take place either in-house or at special conference centres which can be booked on a half-hour basis at a number of locations within the UK.

The in-house alternative offered by Mercury Communications is frequently the attractive alternative, particularly where security is important. This is strengthened by the use of encryption technology to scramble outward transmissions and unscramble incoming messages. The current hardware comprises a split screen TV system mounted in a large cabinet with a hand-held pad for focus and zoom control. In addition, transparencies, 35mm slides, facsimile, white boards and graphics screens can also be linked into the transmission. Sound and vision is currently restricted to six participants, but sound only may be extended to 200.

The hardware known as a Codec unit now costs £50,000 and transmission costs £415 an hour in Europe and £725 worldwide. However, these costs quickly diminish once the out-of-pocket cost of overseas travel, and the opportunity cost of the non-productive time of many senior exeucutives while travelling, are brought into the equation. While it is possible to work on the plane and in a chauffeur-driven car, the balance of the time in transit is both fatiguing and non-productive.

21.3.2 Exhibitions and conferences

Increasingly conference organizers are seeing the holding of an attendant exhibition as a good means of bringing in more revenue. Exhibitions of this nature, usually small and specialized, can be useful if the delegates are the right target audience for your product or service. Caution must be exercised, however, when booking into an exhibition at a conference, that the event has been arranged to give the delegates the opportunity and the time to view the exhibition and hold the often necessary specialized discussions with the exhibitors. For instance, the coffee-breaks could be scheduled in the exhibition. A buffet lunch might be served in the exhibition area. If it is properly done, this form of exhibiting can be very cost-effective for the exhibitor. If it is not properly arranged then it can be an unproductive waste of time at the periphery of an important event.

21.4 Seminars

Most dictionaries describe a seminar as a discussion class of advanced students under the guidance of a tutor. The most common form of seminar is where the manufacturer or supplier of a product stages a half- or one-day event. Speakers of high standing are invited to present papers to a carefully selected small audience of prospective buyers and some existing customers. Among the 'impartial' speakers will probably be one or two of the company's resident 'experts' or prestige users who can be relied on to present a very positive corporate message. During the coffee and lunch breaks, senior executives of the host company mingle with the delegates to reinforce the product message and obtain important feedback.

Frequently, the second half of a seminar conforms more closely to the original definition of the word, with the delegates being divided into tutorial or study groups under a chairman. The brief is usually to put together a group statement about requirement enhancements to the sponsoring company's product, or a statement about the direction in which the industry is working or a comparative analysis of certain competitors' products with those of the host. A secretary is generally available to take down the findings of each group. These are later word-processed and bound together to form a short report and circulated to all participants at the seminar. A public relations specialist might extract additional mileage from the event by arranging for key participants to be interviewed for the trade press with supporting photography.

21.5 The generation of sales leads

Although there may be specific short-term reasons for a company to commit itself to the expense and time involved in organizing or participating in an exhibition or conference, the medium- and long-term objective should be to generate sales. Calculating the directly attributable business gained can, however, be difficult because of the time lags involved unless the order is signed on the stand. Consequently, many companies aim at doing a thoroughly professional job on the basis that this will optimize the results from participation. The vehicles for achieving this maximum effective impact are: stand design, using skilled and experienced staff on the stand and creating an accurate database of prospects for future contact.

21.5.1 Stand design

A well-designed exhibition stand will not only attract an above-average amount of attention, but create a favourable impression on those visitors who linger for a demonstration or discussion. The exhibition-goer presented with a large choice of stands to visit will almost certainly be attracted to the interesting and unusual ones. This usually means that they have been creatively designed.

As stands get more expensive because greater attention is paid to the design, so some companies are looking at re-usable systems that they can dismantle and use again at another venue. Of course this means that a certain amount of flexibility must be incorporated in the design as venues vary in terms of the constraints that the main structure imposes on the exhibitor (stand height or shape, type of access and indeed available transport).

21.5.2 Stand personnel

Selling at an exhibition is rather different from selling to someone in an office. For example, the sales person at an exhibition has to initiate the conversation. Asking 'How can I help you?', for example, will drive many people away just because it is so unprofessional. Furthermore, the discussion has to start without the sales person knowing anything about the visitor or the organization he/she represents. This information has to be extracted and written down for future reference or contact. Frequently the sales person has no time to write up the notes from the discussion before someone else requires attention. There is also the constant problem of deciding which person is the most important as a prospective customer or who will·be the most difficult to meet again.

Another way an exhibition differs from normal office business is that large products can be demonstrated as well as domestic household products (food processors, ovens, vacuum cleaners). Consequently, the sales person must know how to demonstrate the products effectively.

Many companies are unable to take enough sales people 'off territory' to work the stand. Consequently there will be people on the stand who know very little about selling. Extreme care has to be taken that these people in their ignorance do not lose the company business. Everyone working on the stand should attend a short internal company course so that they know their role. Secretaries and marketing assistants should be used as a screen and a funnel to direct key prospects to the sales person; everyone must have some basic product knowledge and all visitors should be logged for possible future contact. Part-time staff should not interrupt the sales person when what looks like an important discussion is going on, and wordprocessing facilities must be available to produce quotations at the show. Finally, the stand manager should ensure that everybody has seen at least once the Visual Arts film with John Cleese on 'How not to exhibit'.

21.5.3 Compiling a customer database

If the primary objective of the conference or exhibition is to create immediate additional sales, the secondary objective is to obtain names of 'good prospects'. These days most visitors to trade events wear name badges but still the problems of creating an accurate and useful database for follow-up action are considerable.

The exercise of 'logging-in' visitors is by no means straightforward in the hussle and bustle of a busy exhibition: scraps of paper get lost, and computerized information mysteriously disappears. This is before any attempt is made to rank visitors in terms of their potential as customers. This qualifying can only be done effectively by sales and marketing executives and their managers. The details then have to be logged before the next sales interview takes place.

In practice the discipline of a sales person writing up interview notes can be difficult unless the staff working the stand get essential rest periods. Two hours on, two hours off at a busy exhibition is a good policy, providing the time necessary to record details while the information is fresh. Another good idea is always to obtain the visitor's business card which provides an accurate record of much key information.

Pre-designed customer contact forms are another aid to the recording of useful information. These can even be organized as data-input documents for easy keying by secretarial or wordprocessing staff.

Non-sales and marketing specialists should be used to filter and manage the flow of customers coming into the stand. Good business prospects must be guided towards sales specialists while the casual enquiry can be politely and effectively handled by a receptionist. The reception staff must attempt to hold likely prospects in a waiting area until a sales person is available and direct the brochure-gatherers to the exit. If the volume of prospects is too large to handle efficiently, the receptionists must obtain a business card, record the key areas of customer interest, apologize for the fact that all the sales people are occupied and ask if a sales person might telephone later to make an appointment to visit the prospect at the office.

21.6 Location

The choices of location are many and various but the vast majority are short-haul European destinations for the major reason that the people attending these events are generally busy and need to minimize the amount of time they are away from their office. A mini poll was conducted of four leading firms in 'incentive travel' and their top ten venues in each case for 1988 are listed in Table 21.3.

A brief explanation of the phrase 'incentive travel' is necessary because it may not immediately seem in context, in that most of these

Table 21.3 *Worldwide top incentive destinations including UK among survey respondents by passenger numbers (1988)*

	Sheridan		CID		Travel Org		Page and May	
1	Amsterdam	1000	Cannes	240	Algarve	1996	Wembley	6000
2	Munich	800	Cyprus	200	Pinewood	1500	Harrogate	3000
3	Montreux	700	Vienna	170	Majorca	1332	Florence	850
4	Palma	500	Amsterdam	160	Monaco	1123	Montreux	800
5	Marbella	500	Innsbruck	95	Amsterdam	588	Luxembourg	620
6	Paris	450	Flims	80	Bangkok	559	Algarve	610
7	Orlando	400	Sardinia	70	Orlando	540	Monaco	460
8	Los Angeles	380	Costa del Sol	60	Paris	528	Paris	240
9	Hong Kong	360	Florida	50	Berlin	500	Amsterdam	210
10	Scotland	340	Cairo/Instanbul	40	Deauville	500	Berlin	200

Source: Upton, G. (1989) *Marketing*, 6 April.

events included in the survey were concerned with a new product launch or distributor meetings. For example, Page and Moy's Florence, Montreux and Luxembourg meetings were in fact a Fiat launch, a Volvo dealer conference and a Goodyear tyre launch. As such they are better categorized as overseas conferences.

Another dilemma to resolve is the balance between most people's wish to visit somewhere new and exotic and the cost of achieving this. Long-haul destinations incur high travel costs and these can be prohibitive if large numbers are involved.

Also to be considered is the Inland Revenue's attitude as to whether such expenses are justifiably deductible from business receipts for corporation tax purposes. Exotic locations such as the Bahamas and Barbados are more difficult to defend as being wholly necessary for the business in question. As a consequence, European locations feature with only one exception in the top ten resorts (see Table 21.4).

Table 21.4 *Overseas top ten most popular incentive destinations among survey respondents (1088)*

Country	Number of delegates
1 Algarve	2606
2 Majorca	1832
3 Monaco	1583
4 Montreux	1500
5 Paris	1218
6 Amsterdam	1058
7 Florida	990
8 Florence	850
9 Munich	800
10 Berlin	700

Although not featured in this survey, the Channel Islands are growing as a preferred location for the smaller and medium-sized events, offering a good compromise in terms of meeting facilities, the opportunity for relaxation at the end of the day and a short return flight.

22
The subtle sell

22.1 Public relations

The importance of public relations still remains largely unappreciated, and consequently under-utilized, by most sales and marketing managers. This is their loss because there are areas where PR can increase sales and indeed limit the loss of sales where other marketing disciplines have little to offer. The power and reach of PR can be compared to a powerful network of contacts and should not be confused with simply circulating press releases to copy-hungry journalists.

The potential for public relations to assist in stimulating sales is immense. The drawing together of a number of sales and marketing techniques and presenting one consistent corporate message is an important contribution to any sales campaign. This concept of the communication circle is described below (see Figure 22.1).

The Institute of Public Relations has defined the role of PR as 'the planned and sustained effort to establish and maintain good will and mutual understanding between an organization and its public'.

The main function of PR from a selling point of view is in creating a favourable climate for the company by influencing attitudes among the various 'publics' in the business environment. These groups can include politicians and shareholders as well as customers, suppliers and employees. Clear messages about a company's policy on environmental issues, not testing products on animals, nutritional values of ingredients and customer care can directly affect sales in a substantial way.

The contribution of PR to selling may be explained under five headings.

Effective communication of an image
Public relations can get a message to the marketplace when other methods of communication are restricted.

Consider, for example, the tobacco industry: for more than twenty years its advertising, particularly of cigarettes, has been severely

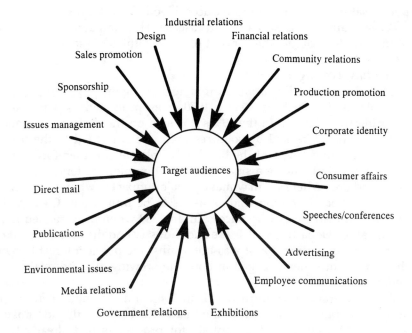

Figure 22.1 The communications circle
Source Marketing, 8 June 1989 (QE II Survey)

restricted (TV advertising banned in the UK in 1965, cinema advertising banned in 1986, health warnings imposed on all display advertising in 1971). With only magazine and billboard advertising remaining, it would have been very difficult to sell brands without 'public relations' (in the broadest sense) to plug the gap. If advertising is restricted, consumer opinion-forming is similarly restricted, which only leaves competition on price. Very few reputable companies are prepared to sell on the basis of price alone. The quality of Dunhill tobaccos (Rothmans) for example is reinforced and promoted through the image of their clothes and travel goods. The name Dunhill is marketed with strong brand identification to overcome the restrictions in tobacco advertising.

Another example concerns Flora margarine. Restrictions on advertising the health benefits of polyunsaturates persuaded the company to turn to PR. The ensuing campaign concentrated on raising awareness of the problem of heart disease and the ways of tackling it. Six major factors were identified: smoking, lack of exercise, high blood pressure, obesity, stress and diet. Information packs were prepared and made available to health and education professionals.

Flora then used advertising to promote the high polyunsaturate content of its product. PR was again used to link increased polyunsaturated fat intake to reduced blood cholesterol showing how this can reduce the chance of heart disease. The campaign was also one of the first to promote the concept of the healthier life-style.

Promoting a caring image

In other instances PR is used to promote a caring image. Toothpaste for example in the 1960s and early 1970s was promoted as a means of ensuring fresh breath. In the 1990s it is sold on the basis of a chemical formula. This is backed by solid research which has led to the use of substances which prevent the build-up of plaque and therefore reduce tooth decay, influencing a small number of opinion leaders.

A third area where PR may make a major impact is where a relatively small number of opinion leaders needs to be influenced. Clearly, the brewing industry was very successful in 1989 when it persuaded Lord Young at the Department of Trade and Industry and the Monopolies and Mergers Commission that it was not against the public interest to have the same companies engaged in both the brewing and the retailing of beers.

Another example concerned ICL in 1983 and the initial contract to supply computer equipment to the Inland Revenue for the administration of PAYE taxation. The contract for processors had already been awarded to ICL, but the company was determined to secure the additional contract to supply some 11,000 terminals or visual display units. There was a feeling in the computer industry that perhaps another company might obtain this contract worth an estimated £11 million. ICL were taking no chances: a total of 175 MPs were lobbied in an attempt (which was successful) to secure the contract in the 'national interest' (jobs for Britons).

Crisis management

A fourth area where PR can make a major contribution to sales is in 'crisis management'. This is where the trading of a company is interrupted, financial performance is threatened or the public reputation of the company is being damaged.

PR is ideally suited to co-ordinating and communicating the various messages which will limit the damage. Internally, the quality control department needs to identify what went wrong, the cause, and the potential hazard to employees, the distribution trade and the consumer. The marketing department should consider what promotional or advertising support tools might be used. The sales force, once briefed, are in a position to activate procedures (which, it is to be hoped, have already been established) for product recall.

Effective management of the disaster by assembling the facts, analysing them and presenting the details to top management for decisions is a job for PR. Once these decisions have been taken, the task is to control the communications both inside the company and to third parties.

Issue monitoring

The fifth area where PR can assist sales management is 'issue monitoring'. This means providing an early warning of opinion trends which can affect a company's sales. The advantage of the early warning is that managers can take remedial action before much harm is done to sales.

22.2 Sponsorship

Sponsorship is the relationship between a commercial organization and an activity, event or life-style interest where, in return for a financial investment, specific marketing rights are granted to the company. The Cornhill one-day cricket test series and the Embassy snooker classic are probably the best known examples.

After a company has defined its specific marketing objectives, which may include increased awareness of a particular product among a certain segment of the population or a shift in the perceived position of a product, it can use sponsorship as part of a range of tactical initiatives to achieve those objectives. Sponsorship needs to be integrated with the other methods of communication (direct mail, sales promotion, PR and advertising) to achieve its greatest impact, which is essentially low key and non-intrusive.

22.2.1 Main areas of sponsorship

The main sectors of society to receive sponsorship in return for sales and marketing privileges are sport and the arts, though there is an increasing involvement in the community and the media. Sport provides the mass market audience for sponsorship, whereas arts sponsorship is targeted predominantly at the professional classes (labelled AB on the socio-economic scale). Community and media sponsorship is usually local or interest-orientated.

Sport

Table 22.1 shows the major sports sponsorship for the period November 1989 to January 1990.

Table 22.1   *Top sports sponsorship*

Rank	Sponsor	(November to January quarter) Amount/deal's timespan	Event or sponsored body
1	Bells	£7.5m/five year ext	Scottish Golf Open
2	Scottish Provident	£2.3m/three year	Cycling League and ten city centre events
3	Courage	£2.1m/three year ext	Rugby Union Club League
4	Wilson Sports	£1.5m/three year	Backing of American Football League and equipment support
5	Pearl Assurance	£1.5m/three year	British Open Snooker
6	Henderson Unit Trust Management	£1.5m/three year	Whitaker Bros and Grand Prix series and events (equestrian)
7	Labbatt	£1m	Canon Williams Formula One Team
8	Benson and Hedges	£1m/five year ext	Irish Masters Snooker
9	Midland	£1m/three years	School leavers participation in sport
10	*Daily Telegraph*	£500,000/three year	Club Athletics and Women's League
11	NM (finance)	£400,000/1990	English Open (golf)
12	Bass	£250,000/three year	Gloucester Rugby Union Club
13	Motor Vehicle Supply	£250,000	Cycling, including Wincanton Classic Event
14	Teacher's	£250,000	New club golf Scramble contest

15	Ambre Solaire	£150,000	Freestyle ski-ing
16	Blue Circle Ind.	£150,000/three year	Kent County Cricket Club
17	Norwich Union	£120,000 (joint deal with MFS Association)	Rugby League
18	Embassy	£117,000	World Indoor Bowls Championship
19	Bass	£100,000	Derbyshire County Cricket Club
20	Bass	£100,000/three years	Carling Black Label behind Leicestershire
21	Puma	£100,000/three years	Borough of Wigan to sponsor leisure facilities
22	Top line	£100,000	Welsh Amateur Athletics Association
23	Scottish Brewers	£100,000	Scottish Lawn Tennis Association
24	Dubai Government	£100,000	Nations Cup at Hickstead (equestrian)
25	NatWest	£80,000/two year ext	Basketball Cup
26	NatWest	£75,000/three years ext	Colts County Championships (Rugby Union)
27	Nescafé	£50,000	Deal with James Wattana (snooker)
28	Telescan	£50,000	Wigan Wasps Swimming Club
29	Farrah Leisurewear	£50,000	Players pool deal for Arsenal FC

Note
Sponsor deals are ranked according to value, regardless of length of deal (which is given where available). Shortest sponsorship deals are ranked higher where values are equal.

Source: Marketing, 15 March 1990 from RSL Sportscan.

Golf, cycling, rugby league, cricket, snooker, American football, grand prix, rugby union, tennis and athletics are the major sport beneficiaries. Sports arenas are also in receipt of backing to finance ground improvements (in line with modern thinking on crowd control and safety), hence 'Fosters Oval' and 'Bass Headingley' on the cricket test circuit.

Examination of the Table shows that a wide range of industries are involved beyond the very familiar insurance companies, brewers, banks and tobacco companies. Sports goods suppliers (Puma), cement (Blue Circle), cosmetics (Ambre Solaire), newspapers (*Daily Telegraph*) and even the Dubai Government now feature among the growing list of sponsors.

The Arts

Table 22.2 lists major arts sponsorship drives, each designed for well-targeted audiences but involving much smaller numbers than the sports sponsorships. Indeed, the achievement of a balance between involvement and commercialization has traditionally been a problem in sponsorship and the arts. Unfortunately, press coverage is often limited

Table 22.2   *Top arts sponsorship*

Company	Amount/duration	Venue/function
Shell	£3m/three years	British Academy of Film and TV Arts
Lloyds Bank	£1.3m/five years	BBC Young Musicians of the Year
Scottish and Newcastle		Beck's Bier behind Bruce McLean Sculpture Tour
Parker Pen	£170,000	Philharmonia 14 concert US tour
Panasonic Europe	£110,000	European Community Baroque Orchestra
Dai-Tchi Kangyo Bank	£110,000	Royal Academy Summer Exhibition
Lilley Group	£100,000	Links in a Fine Chain – Scottish Arts and Design Through the Ages
Pirelli	£70,000	Bankside Galleries Vision of Venice Show

Note
This list is not exhaustive of all arts sponsor deals signed during the period.

Source: Marketing, 15 March 1990. (This list is not exhaustive of all arts sponsorship deals signed during the period.)

because the event is of limited news interest. The objective is clearly to create something newsworthy in its own right, but unfortunately this rarely happens.

Community
This can involve sponsorship deals that are local in focus, such as environmental concerns, events directed at recruitment and those intended to promote charities. Some football clubs have been successful at offering the club's facilities for the entertainment of business prospects in return for sponsorship.

There is a great deal of interest in ideas for environmental sponsorship, but selection standards are very strict and deter many would-be enthusiasts. Before protection of the environment gained popular support, many companies neglected to spend money keeping their 'house in order' and are consequently not eligible.

Charities are moving towards sponsorship as the primary source of finance as funds from donations are shared among an ever-increasing number of rivals. One of the most successful initiatives was the Storehouse Group sponsorship of a design competition for the National Society for Prevention of Cruelty to Children (NSPCC). The winning design subsequently appeared on a range of Habitat products.

Media
The most widely known is probably the National Powergen sponsorship of the Independent Television News for a reported £2 million. Only a national monopoly could indulge itself thus for what must be of limited commercial benefit. Sponsorship programmes are supposedly not allowed on the BBC, though some appear, usually when they have been bought from an overseas broadcaster. The IBA's code for radio sponsorship permits publicity for charities, arts reviews, places of interest and events.

22.2.2 Marketing goals from sponsorship

The traditional marketing objectives to be achieved from sponsorship are now being extended. The first new objective, advanced by the tobacco company R.J. Reynolds, has been called the principle of 'association with the event experience'. This implies that sponsorship, in reaching the consumer subliminally, is a more acceptable way of reaching a consumer than, say, direct mail or TV advertising. Since as many examples of the latter are successfully known to drive people from the room in an attempt to avoid the excruciating boredom, this concept does have a certain credibility!

The Prudential Insurance Company has recently advanced the concept of 'social permission', whereby a consumer is said to pass judgement on the moral outlook of a company before commitment to a business relationship. This interesting concept is probably going to increase in importance as environmental issues are taken more seriously, though the number of motorists that have stopped using Esso petrol as a result of the Alaska oil disaster is probably insignificant. It would be reassuring to believe that large companies appreciated this concept rather than casually shirking their environmental responsibilities.

22.3 Character merchandising

Character merchandising is the transfer of a well-known 'personality' to a product or service in order to obtain instant awareness or market positioning for the associated product. The personality may be a well-known individual (Daly Thompson as associated with Lucozade) or a cartoon character (the Pink Panther used by Jockey to launch their boxer shorts line). Other examples include company logos (Guinness and Coca Cola have been used on collections of casual clothes) and theatrical products (CATS t-shirts and sweat shirts). (See Figure 22.2.)

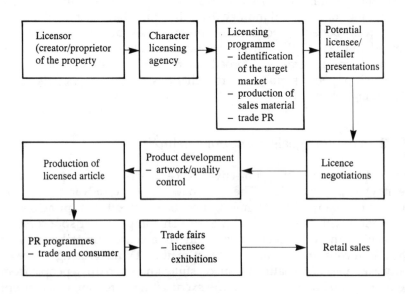

Figure 22.2   Character licensing programme chain

Character merchandising combines the elements of advertising and sales promotion and is used to define an individual brand image within a competitive marketplace. The character that has been borrowed adds 'value' or popularity to the manufacturer's product by association. This association is particularly successful when aimed at the child and teen market segments.

The key elements of character merchandising are:

- The licensor – who is the creator or proprietor of the property.
- The property – the image on which the licensing programme is based.
- The licensee – the company or individual taking up the licence to develop the merchandise.
- The licensing agent – the individual or company authorized by the licensor to develop the licensing programme with the licensee.

22.3.1 Selling character life-styles

The identification of the target market at which the product and the licensed character are to be directed calls for an understanding of their interests, life-styles, feelings, values, purchasing attitudes and activities. The city executive in taking a golfing umbrella to the office is expressing personality: this is amplified by any character or logo on the fabric. Thus an Abbey National symbol suggests someone saving to buy a property, while somebody with the Pimms or Pol Roget lettering is indicating a stylish party-goer.

22.3.2 Brand extension licensing

This is a recent development in character merchandising and requires a direct synergy between the character that is licensed and the product to be developed. As the costs of new product development increase, this concept has become more popular because it can substantially reduce the risk of a failure. Thus the Robinson foods character 'Spikey' appears on their new products, because he is a much loved character of whom there is a high awareness among mothers of young babies.

22.3.3 Design licensing

This is the co-ordination of a targeted merchandising programme following the success of a well-known design concept at retail level in a specific product area. Designs from the popular *A Country Diary of an Edwardian Lady* have been successfully translated into a range of stationery products: calendars, diaries, ceramics and home furnishings.

22.4 Corporate identity

An organization's identity is how it presents itself to the world as well as how it is seen by its employees and customers. Thus corporate identity is derived from the products and services it supplies, the environment or buildings where it makes them, and the communications media used (brochures, TV advertising) to get the message to the buying public. There is a fourth element, corporate behaviour, expressed by how the organization goes about its business. Thus some of the companies involved in large hostile takeovers have gained one type of image while other more benign giants are perceived as having a more customer-orientated image.

Where the organization chooses to put the emphasis can affect how it is viewed by the general public. Companies like IBM, Porsche and BP have one name and one visual image across everything that they do. It is impossible to separate the idea of the corporation from its products. IBM is computers, Porsche is cars and BP is petrochemicals. On the other hand, companies like Unilever and Proctor and Gamble operate through a series of apparently unrelated brands. There seems to be no attempt to make a link between the brands and the corporation as a whole. Indeed, as far as the consumer is concerned, the corporation does not exist.

22.4.1 Identity matters

An organization's uniqueness and potentially the source of its greatest advantage lies in its approach to business. This uniqueness or identity is expressed in everything the organization does – the products and services that are offered for sale, the offices and buildings that people see, the promotional material they read, and the executives that are interviewed on the television news. This identity can inspire loyalty, assist recognition and attract customers, or it can work negatively and thwart the best marketing strategy.

An effective corporate identity depends on two things: credibility and consistency. The image must be seen to emerge from the organization's very roots, reinforced by the values of the products and the behaviour of the staff both individually and collectively. The expression of image used by Michelin since 1898 has been Bibendum – supposedly inspired by a pile of tyres. The strength of this image is that it is both friendly and memorable, which is unusual for a symbol of an industrial company (see Exhibit 22.1).

Exhibit 22.1 Michelin's Bibendum

2.4.2 Visual style

When companies use identity as expressed through design, their objective is to 'add value' to what they sell by creating an image of quality or uniqueness. This is very much what happened when the Apple micro-computer was launched in 1980–81. The company was called after a fruit and the product sold like other electrical goods from high-street shops. This was in stark contrast to the other sombre

Exhibit 22.2 Kellogg's well-known image

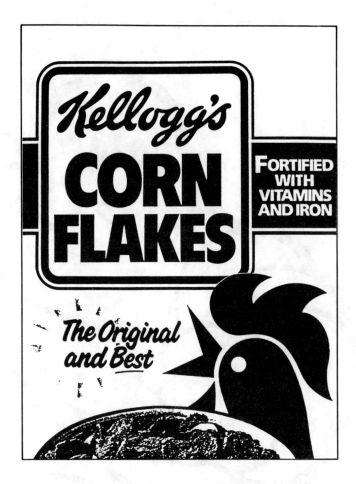

computer companies like IBM, NCR, Honeywell, DEC and ICL wh
only sold their computers to offices and factories. The Apple revolutio
in style created a new level of orthodoxy; others followed – Peach Tre
Apricot and Acorn.

22.4.3 Branded identity

The idea of branding emerged in the middle of the nineteenth centur
when developments in technology combined with an increase in th

level of literacy to form the first mass market. The logic was to take any household product (that was no different from any other), then endow it with special characteristics through the imaginative use of a distinguished name, stylish packaging and bold advertising.

Branding is still one of the most powerful ways of promoting a product. The strength lies in the fact that the brand is created carefully and deliberately to appeal to a particular group of people. The concept is then reinforced by a strong visual image such as on the Kellogg's Corn Flakes packet (see Exhibit 22.2). Even if the words 'Corn Flakes' were to be written in Russian, the name 'Kellogg's' and the chicken's head design would be enough to identify the product.

Bibliography

Aaker, David A. and Day, George S. (1978) *Consumerism – Search for Consumer Interest*, 3rd edn, Free Press.

Assaell, Henry (1987) *Consumer Behaviour & Marketing Action*, Kent Publishing Co.

Association of Exhibition Organizers — statistics 1989–90.

Baker, Alan (1990) *Which Exhibition 1989–90*, Conference & Travel Publications Ltd,

Bates, Anton (1986) *Get to Know Franchising*, British Franchise Association,

Bolt, Gordon J. (1987) *Practical Sales Management*, Pitman, London.

Bolt, Gordon J. (1983) *Market Research & Sales Forecasting – A Total Approach*, Kogan Page, 2nd edn.

British Direct Marketing Association *Guidelines* (for telephone selling and marketing),

CACI (1984) *Acorn User's Guide,*

Carnegie, Dale (1973) *How to Win Friends and Influence People*, Cedar,

Cowling, Anthony (1990) *Guidelines for Registering under the Data Protection Act For the Purposes of Carrying Out Survey Research – Update March 1990*, report for the market research society.

Crouch, S. (1984) *Marketing Research for Managers*, Pan, London.

Fenton, John (1984) *How to Sell Against Competition*, Pan, London.

Financial Training Group, Chartered Accountants Study Manual.

Gillam, Alan (1982) *The Principles and Practice of Selling*, Heinemann Oxford.

Goldmann, Heinz (1973) *How to Win Customers*, Granada Publishing,

Jamieson, David (1989) *Customer Satisfaction*, Industrial Market Research Ltd.,

Journal of Marketing Research, February 1973 and May 1975.

Keith Steward Associates Ltd., reported produced for Communica Ltd. (unpublished).

Keith Steward Associates Ltd., report produced for Real Time Business Systems Ltd. (unpublished).

Key Postal Advertising, catalogue of direct mail lists.

Kompass Directory, 1988.

Kossen, Stan (1982) *Creative Selling Today*, Harper & Row, London.

Kotler, Philip (1984) *Marketing Management, Analysis Planning and Control*, 5th edn, Prentice Hall, Englewood Cliffs, NJ.

Lancaster, G. and Jobber, D. (1990) *Sales Technique and Management*, 2nd edn, Pitman, London.

Lund, P. (1979) *Compelling Selling*, MacMillan Press, London.

Marketing, various articles and supplements published 1988–1990.

Mendlesohn, J. (1986) *Franchising and the Law*, British Franchise Association,

Mintel, report on pub entertainment 1987–8.

Olins, Wally (1989) *Corporate Identity, Making Business Strategy Visible Through Design*, Thames & Hudson,

Palmer, R. E. and Taylor, A. H. (1969) *Financial Planning and Control*, Pan, London.

Strafford, J. and Grant, C. (1986) *Effective Sales Management*, Butterworth-Heinemann, Oxford.

Smith, R. and Dick, G. (1981) *Getting Sales*, Kogan Page,

Taylor, A. H. and Steward, K. J. (1990) *A Financial Handbook for Sales and Marketing Managers*, Cassell, London.

Walsh, L. (1987) *International Marketing*, 2nd edn, Pitman, London.

Watts, David (ed) (1987) *Thirty Years of Which*, Consumers Association, London.

Whitehead, Paul and Whitehead, Geoffrey (1984) *Statistics for Business*, Pitman, London.

Index